SAVE YOUR STOMACH

OTHER BOOKS BY THE SAME AUTHOR

The Laboratory of the Body

The Family Book of Preventive Medicine
with Benjamin F. Miller, M.D.

Freedom from Heart Attacks
with Benjamin F. Miller, M.D.

Your Heart: Complete Information for the Family
with William Likoff, M.D., *and* Bernard Segal, M.D.

Adult Physical Fitness Manual, President's Council on Physical Fitness

How Long Will I Live?

The Silent Disease: Hypertension

The Disguised Disease: Anemia

Don't Give Up on an Aging Parent

The Truth About Fiber in Your Food

SAVE YOUR STOMACH

The answers to every question
about the stomach; how it works,
how to keep it healthy,
how to overcome any of its problems

LAWRENCE GALTON

Introduction by William S. Rosenthal, M.D.

Professor of Medicine
Director, Sarah C. Upham
  Section of Gastroenterology
New York Medical College

Crown Publishers, Inc./New York

Inquiries should be addressed to
Crown Publishers, Inc., One Park Avenue, New York, N.Y. 10016

Printed in the United States of America
Published simultaneously in Canada by
General Publishing Company Limited

Library of Congress Cataloging in Publication Data

Galton, Lawrence
Save your stomach

Bibliography: p. 00
Includes index
1. Stomach.   I. Title. [DNLM: 1. Stomach—
Popular works.   2. Stomach diseases—Therapy—
Popular works. WI300 G181s]
QP151.G34 1977   616.3′3   76-26882
ISBN 0-517-52672-X

Second Printing, May, 1977

Contents

Introduction

DISORDERS OF the gastrointestinal tract and its attendant organs, the liver and pancreas, have an enormous impact on the well-being and survival of people in this country. It is generally accepted that 60 percent of adult patients who seek assistance from primary care physicians have complaints involving the digestive system. These complaints stem from diseases that range in severity from fatal to trivial.

At the serious end of this spectrum, malignancy affecting the gastrointestinal tract has become the most common cause of death from cancer. Similarly, cirrhosis of the liver is of increasing concern. This leading cause of death has a peak incidence in middle life, when its victims bear heavy family responsibilities.

Other major digestive diseases, while they do not provide such a heavy contribution to mortality statistics, are responsible for prolonged periods of discomfort and suffering. Outstanding among these is peptic ulcer, various types of which affect as many as 20 percent of the population at some time during their lifetime. One can only speculate on the effects of this disease on work efficiency and life-style. As a disease common during the productive years of life, peptic ulcer undoubtedly affects national economic data adversely. Gallstones and gall bladder disease are extraordinarily common, affecting to some extent over one half of the aged population. Indeed, in certain ethnic groups such as the Pima Indians, gallstones are present in the majority of women as early as the fifth decade of life.

Less spectacular problems such as indigestion, heartburn, gas, diarrhea, and constipation are considered aspects of normal living by many individuals who believe themselves to be in good health. One of the few quantitative measures of the magnitude of these so-called minor complaints is the hundreds of millions of dollars spent annually in sales of over-the-counter and prescription medications designed to alleviate these problems.

The lay public has only fragmentary medical information, usually derived from personal experience. Nevertheless, there is a high level of interest in gaining and maintaining good health. The media usually respond to this interest with presentations focused on current topics of limited scope. Contradictory information abounds. An overview is difficult to attain.

It has become politically expedient in this atmosphere to legislate crash programs of research or medical care directed at specific medical problems or population groups. Crash programs have worked, the most notable perhaps being the Manhattan Project, which developed the atom bomb. However, this was merely the exploitation of prior discoveries of such men as Einstein, Bohr, and Fermi. Crash programs do not produce great discoveries as a rule. Truly revolutionary findings in science are more likely to result from less restricted research support. Time and again a new finding in a seemingly unrelated area of investigation provides a dramatic change in direction leading to brilliant new answers. A recent example of this was the chance finding of a new protein in the blood of an Australian aborigine in the course of an investigation of genetic differences in blood proteins in different population groups. Benefiting my own specialty area, this research project in basic genetics led to the discovery of a major hepatitis virus. The torrent of hepatitis research stemming from that finding has dramatically increased our knowledge of hepatitis and cirrhosis and probably will result in vaccines to sharply decrease the incidence of viral hepatitis. No crash program likely to be undertaken prior to Blumberg's discovery of the Australia antigen would have had any real chance of success.

A medically naive public is easily persuaded by politicians or others with something to gain (including scientists) that a crash program or a war on one disease or another is the appropriate way to improve health care. Instead we need careful nurturing of basic and clinical science with sustained support. This will attract the best minds. Such researchers must be assured that political changes will not affect their research support or their academic position. We should also avoid crash programs in healthy care delivery that help that segment of the population suffering from a designated disease but leave untouched those unfortunates with equally unpleasant illnesses outside any such program. An example of this is our heavily funded colon cancer research—at the expense of the overall digestive disease programs. Improved health care delivery is more likely to result from carefully considered general measures for the entire population.

I've said that an overview is difficult to attain. Lawrence Galton has provided a balanced and extremely readable overview. He has avoided trendy pitfalls. In an informal but comprehensive manner, he explains how the digestive tract works, what can go wrong with it, how a diagnosis may be reached, and what can be expected from treatment. The material is almost completely free of medical jargon, but accurate and current. For those interested in good health, this book will raise their consciousness with respect to digestive disorders. *Save Your Stomach* not only can help those common heartburn-gas-upset-stomach-type sufferers but it answers the many questions that usually trouble patients and their families, including important questions they frequently don't know to ask. This book will help the reader to better understand the GI medical care he needs and thereby reinforce the value of treatment.

—William S. Rosenthal, M.D.
Professor of Medicine
Director, Sarah C. Upham Section of
Gastroenterology
New York Medical College

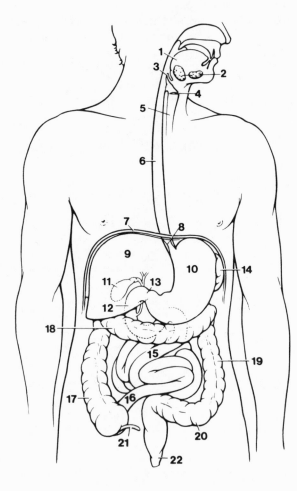

1. Tongue
2. Salivary glands
3. Epiglottis
4. Larynx
5. Trachea
6. Esophagus
7. Diaphragm
8. Cardiac sphincter
9. Liver
10. Stomach
11. Gall bladder
12. Duodenum
13. Pylorus
14. Spleen
15. Jejunum
16. Ileum
17. Ascending colon
18. Transverse colon
19. Descending colon
20. Sigmoid colon
21. Appendix
22. Rectum

PART ONE

The Wonderful World of the Gut

1 Overview: The wonderful... needlessly mysterious... too often needlessly troublesome world

THE MOST mysterious part of the universe for many of us is not some distant planet, the ocean floor, or anything else removed from us. It is a long, circuitous, churning world within us.

Call it the gut, belly, stomach, middle—all terms commonly used for the gastrointestinal tract. If discovered on some adventuresome voyage, it would be a source of wonder, even awe.

In a year more than half a ton of food is minced, solubilized, extracted, and converted in the stomach. A tube open to the outer world at both ends, the gastrointestinal tract is within the body and yet, strictly speaking, materials in it are not within the body, not until all the mincing, solubilizing, extracting, and converting is done and absorption takes place.

Is your digestive system like everyone else's?

Not in every way.

Stomachs, for example, can differ in size, shape, even location, with some perching high, never falling below rib level, others dipping almost to the groin. If our faces varied as much as our gastric juices, some of us would have noses no larger than navy beans while others would sport noses the size of twenty-pound watermelons.

Some people are ready burpers, others not—the difference lying in the angle at which the esophagus, or gullet, joins with the stomach.

(Though, happily, if they have to, nonburpers can learn to burp with some facility.)

The gut sustains us. But it also disturbs and perplexes.

We feed it, and more and more we worry over what we feed it.

We spend over $218 million a year for laxatives, $127 million for antacids, and even more for calmatives, antispasmodics, and so on.

One-sixth of all major illnesses involve the gut. Five million people are hospitalized annually—more than for any other disease category.

One-half the population of the United States complains about something wrong with the digestive system.

Yet, the gut, traditionally short on glamour, has had almost no press.

Except in commercials, the growl of a stomach can hardly compete for prime TV time with the thump of a heart. Digestive disorders are generally consigned to the uncomfortable and unattractive rather than to the life-threatening category. Relatively little has been done to help the public understand the functioning and malfunctioning of the system.

Only two thousand physicians in the United States devote themselves exclusively to digestive problems. And only in very recent years has a new breed of physician-scientist applied special talent and training to researching the gut and obtaining significant new insights about it.

Complex though it may seem, the digestive system is scarcely beyond understanding.

It is the purpose of this book to help you discover that this understanding can be fascinating as well as useful. It will take you on an informal tour of the gut, pointing out the landmarks along the way, as you follow the traffic.

You will be able to take a close look at some of the major phenomena: from the churning of the stomach and the rumbling of the gut to the activities of gut fauna and the anatomical maneuvers involved in everything from swallowing to defecation.

You will be able to delve into many other gut matters:

● What is in intestinal gas, where it really comes from, and what is best for it when it is troublesome;

● How long it takes various foods to empty out of the stomach and what that has to do with hunger, satiety, and appetite control;

● Why some things you eat, and even some you apply to the skin, can be smelled on the breath;

- What the tongue may show;

- The mechanisms now believed to exert basic control of hunger;

- What causes thirst and which drinks quench it best;

- What is normal transit time in the gut—from swallowing to final disposition—and why what is normal for Americans is three times as long as for native Africans, and how this may explain why Africans are virtually immune while we are commonly prone to appendicitis, hiatus hernia, diverticular disease, cancer of the colon, hemorrhoids, varicose veins, and possibly even diabetes and coronary heart disease. And how transit time may be speeded.

Also you may consider the following:

- The varied gut effects of emotions;

- The truth—and if so to what extent—of what they say about cholesterol, sugar, coffee, salt, and, most recently, milk;

- Queer cravings and the reasons for them;

- Some very marked changes in therapeutic diets;

- Three fundamental new approaches to weight control;

- Vitamins, big minerals, trace minerals, the undiscovered micronutrients, and the emerging concept of supernutrition;

- And a suggested "nutritional insurance" formulation.

A major section of this book deals with the two dozen most common gastrointestinal problems—from everyday complaints to the most serious. About each: the nature, symptoms, causes, methods of diagnosis, methods of prevention, and treatment, including home treatment where possible.

And for those problems for which surgery may be needed: when surgery may be essential and when not, the surgical procedures available, how long they take, how much hospitalization is required, how long for recovery, what to expect immediately after surgery and during recuperation, and chances for success.

Another section offers information on gut medicines and medicines that may affect the gut—both prescription and over-the-counter: when and for what they can be useful, how they work, what side effects they may sometimes produce and how such effects can be countered.

If this book does well what it is intended to do, it possibly will entertain you a little and perhaps inform you of much that you may not have known before so that you gain power to use your digestive system more effectively, to control its functioning and prevent its misfunctioning, and thus improve your health and well-being.

 A journey through

THE MOUTH, of course, is the beginning.

The food comes in, the teeth chew it, the tongue gathers it and tosses it backward, and down it goes through the gullet into the stomach.

But there is much more to the story even at this start of the journey.

Consider the digestive system as a series of way stations: the mouth; the pharynx, or throat; the esophagus, or gullet; the stomach; the small bowel with its three distinctive areas—duodenum, jejunum, and ileum; and, finally, the large bowel: the ascending, transverse, and descending colon, sigmoid, and rectum.

Vital as it is for speech, the mouth's primary job is the reception of food.

As soon as food enters, impulses that are set up in tactile nerve endings as well as in taste buds and olfactory areas indicate whether the food is to your liking or not. If acceptable, a whole series of events follows.

You chew—a voluntary act and a reflex one, too. You close your teeth voluntarily on a piece of food but the pressure on teeth and gum causes the jaws to open reflexly. (A dog's teeth may build up to a pressure of 300 pounds. Human teeth exert not much less powerful forces; when you bear down on your molars for grinding, the force can reach 270 pounds.) The jaws again close and the process goes on as long as anything is left to chew.

In chewing, the jaw drops, lifts, protrudes, retracts, swings from side to side. Chewing involves a lot of motion, and the lips are also in motion, returning the food to where the teeth can keep getting at it.

At last, a moist mouthful reaches the top of the tongue, and with further mastication unnecessary, the bolus, its new name, meaning a soft mass of chewed food, enters the gullet at one swallow.

Ordinarily, by the time food is ready to be swallowed, most of this mass of fine particles has been chewed to less than two millimeters (eight one-hundredths of an inch) in diameter, the largest not exceeding twelve millimeters. Nerve endings in the mouth sense particle size in the bolus and determine when swallowing is in order. The efficacy of the system is such that rarely does a bolus get stuck in the normal esophagus.

But something else has accompanied the chewing.

Even as food is broken into particles, it is mixed with saliva and turned into a mushy mixture. It is chewing that stimulates the salivary glands—in the parotids below and in front of each ear; the submaxillaries inside the lower jaw; and the sublingual beneath the tongue.

To be sure, the salivary glands are secreting saliva to some extent all the time, turning out one to one and a half quarts a day. Saliva has a cleansing action useful for oral hygiene. The salivary glands have another important job—as a regulatory factor for body-water balance. The glands stop secreting whenever body fluid content falls to a low level and this leads to dryness of the mouth, which arouses the sensation of thirst.

But when you start chewing, saliva flow mounts. If you are chewing something inedible—sand, for example—the saliva will be watery. But if it is an edible substance, the saliva will contain not only mucin, which makes it viscous, but also an enzyme, ptyalin, which converts cooked starch into sugar. To that extent digestion actually starts in the mouth.

If you want to determine this for yourself, take a bite of unseasoned raw potato and chew it until you begin to taste a little sweetness, as the starch, with the help of ptyalin, turns into sugar.

THE DELICATE ART OF SWALLOWING

It seems routine and, of course, it is. Yet swallowing is no simple matter.

The bolus of food is on the tongue and now the tongue flips it backward into the pharynx, and now, too, fortunately, everything becomes automatic.

The pharynx—from the Greek for throat—is where the nasal passage joins the foodway, and it is this joining that makes it possible to breathe through the mouth.

But the joining makes for a treacherous situation: Air should take one route—down the trachea, or windpipe; and food should take the other—down the gullet; and the food certainly should not get into and block the windpipe, nor should it slip back into the mouth or find its way up into the nose.

Nature has done the engineering well. As you swallow, a number of things happen automatically.

The opening of the airway, called the glottis (Greek for tongue), lies just behind and below the tongue. And right above the glottis is a flap of tissue called the epiglottis (Greek for on the tongue) attached to the root of the tongue.

With swallowing, the glottis instantly moves under the epiglottis so this flap of tissue can seal it off. That leaves open only the foodway and the bolus moves into it. So nicely is the airway sealed off, in fact, that if you ever make the experiment of stopping halfway in the act of swallowing, you will find yourself unable to breathe until you complete the act.

Of course, accidents happen. On occasion, you swallow the wrong way, which is to say that the epiglottis did not function effectively for some reason or other and a bolus or a swallow of liquid moved into the glottis. But that is provided for, too: The very entrance of anything other than air into the glottis sets up a cough, an explosive phenomenon that blows the material out.

With swallowing, too, the uvula and soft palate go into action. The uvula is the flap of tissue that hangs down in the center at the back of the mouth. As you swallow, the uvula° and palate close the nasal passages. And, with the tongue blocking return of food into the mouth, the bolus moves into the esophagus, or gullet.

Swallowing, to be technical, is called deglutition, and, from birth, an infant carries out deglutition with as much finesse as an adult who has been rehearsing the procedure for half a century.

THROUGH THE GULLET

The esophagus is a hollow muscular tube extending from the pharynx to the stomach, generally ten to twelve inches long in an adult. As it passes from the pharynx downward, it goes through the chest, or thorax, and then through the diaphragm, the partition that separates chest from abdomen.

As the bolus of food you have just chewed, wetted down, and swal-

---

°It is the uvula that gets the blame for producing snoring as it flutters in the air currents passing it by.

lowed enters the esophagus, it distends the tube. That is a signal for a series of circular muscles in the wall to go into action. First, circular muscles immediately above the bolus contract, then others along the whole route do, pushing the bolus along—so effectively that you could swallow while standing on your head and the muscle contractions would take care of the bolus.

The wavelike progression of alternate contraction and relaxation of the circular muscles in the esophagus is called peristalsis and it takes place in the stomach and intestines as well. Although the normal peristaltic wave is downward, it rarely may be reversed as the result of mild digestive upsets or more serious disorders such as obstruction in the stomach or intestines.

A bit different from the others, the last circular muscle in the esophagus, at a level just below the diaphragm, at the lower end of the tube, remains contracted much of the time instead of alternately contracting and relaxing. It thus serves as a sphincter, which is any muscle that closes any body opening. Since it happens to be near the heart, although it has nothing to do with the heart, this one is called the cardiac sphincter.

Now your bolus of food, having been pushed along by the peristaltic waves that travel at a rate of about two inches per second, arrives at the cardiac sphincter, and the alerted sphincter relaxes so the bolus can enter the stomach.

THE CHURNING VAT

The stomach is waiting expectantly, alerted by your chewing, its juices already flowing, when the bolus drops into what generally looks like a J-shaped vat about ten inches long.

One misconception about the stomach is its location. Many people think of it as being on a level with the navel, the belly button. Commonly, however, it is at rib level with its upper end just below the heart.

Another misconception is that all stomachs are much alike in configuration. Not so. If you were to draw a line through the stomach, a lengthwise central line or axis, much of the line would run vertically in some people but in others would be transverse. Where, in some people, the stomach is held up high, no part of it falling below the level of the ribs, in others part of it dips a little or a lot below, even in some cases coming close to the groin area.

It is the widest portion of the gastrointestinal tract and the most muscular. Its upper section is called the fundus and often holds some gas even when the stomach is empty. The lower portion, the pylorus (from the Greek for gatekeeper), ends in a sphincter muscle that is, in fact, a gate, remaining closed until the right time. And in between fundus and pylorus is the corpus, the body of the stomach.

The human stomach can comfortably hold about a quart and a half, and that is capacity enough though it is not much in comparison to the huge stomach in cattle with 300-quart capacity, but then cattle have four compartments and loads of bacteria to convert cellulose into simpler, absorbable materials, and the cellulose has to be held there to give the bacteria opportunity to do their job. Man depends very little if at all on cellulose for nutrients and has no bacteria in the stomach, although there are bacteria, quite useful kinds, further along in the gastrointestinal, or GI, tract.

For centuries, of course, nothing was known about digestion. Not until the eighteenth century did a Frenchman, Réaumur, manage to obtain some stomach juice from a pet kite and, placing it along with food in a glass jar, see the juice dissolve the food.

When, not long afterward, Lazaro Spallanzani, an Italian abbé, came to the conclusion that human stomach juice could melt food away, controversy quickly followed. William Hunter, one of the great Englishmen of medicine in the late eighteenth century, soon was declaring with great emphasis: "Some Physiologists will have it that the stomach is a Mill; others that it is a fermenting Vat; others again that it is a Stew Pan; but in my view of the matter it is neither a Mill, a fermenting Vat, nor a Stew Pan— but a Stomach, gentlemen, a Stomach." No one knew what Hunter meant, which may have been why his reputation vastly increased.

The truth would await a shotgun accident in a trader's store in Canada in June 1822, in which the blast tore off the skin and muscles of the upper part of the abdomen of Alexis St. Martin and, in addition, the outer layer of the wall of his stomach. On being called to help, the best that Dr. William Beaumont, a young United States army surgeon, could do was to stitch the stomach edges to the skin.

Happily, for himself and for science, St. Martin lived with a hole in his stomach. Beaumont, with St. Martin cooperating, could look in and see the stomach move. He could also see digestive juice oozing onto the stomach lining. He could lower into the stomach a piece of meat on a string, pull it out half an hour later and see a bit of fraying at the meat edges; insert it again for another half hour and pull it out to find half the meat gone; reinsert it for another hour whereupon it was gone, completely dissolved.

St. Martin's stomach peephole also enabled Beaumont to discover that gastric juice appeared only when food was being chewed or when it entered the stomach. And when he sucked up some pure juice through a rubber tube, it proved to be hydrochloric acid.

About a century later, Dr. Anton Carlson, often called the "grand old man" of American physiology, made some other discoveries with the aid of a man who, because of a severe burn of the esophagus, had to be fed through a surgical opening in his stomach. Measuring the amount of gastric juice flowing under varying circumstances, Carlson found that it was copious when the man smelled something he liked to eat but dried up when he saw or smelled something unappetizing. Which could be why the culinary art is so valued: Everything else being equal, you are likely to digest better a dish you like than one you do not.

Millions of tiny glands in the mucous membrane lining of the stomach produce gastric juice—highly acidic, containing as much as 0.5 percent hydrochloric acid, which can help break down proteins and carbohydrates.

And gastric juice also contains enzymes to help, the principal one being pepsin. Pepsin breaks down proteins by breaking down the linkages containing many of the amino acids, the protein building blocks. Pepsin also helps to clot milk, which improves the use of this food by keeping it from moving too rapidly through the GI tract.

So the bolus of food is now in the stomach, the juices flowing—and the stomach in motion, which is important. After the cardiac sphincter has opened to admit the bolus, it closes again. At the other end, the pyloric sphincter is closed. And the peristaltic waves start up. They move the bolus about. The waves advance toward the pyloric portion of the stomach, the bolus with them, but the pyloric sphincter does not open—not yet—and much of the bolus is forced back into the fundus.

And this goes on until the bolus has been thoroughly knocked about, with plenty of opportunity for acid and enzyme action.

Then having become semifluid and gruellike—and now known as chyme (from the Greek for juice)—it is ready, its consistency right, to go into the duodenum. Obligingly, the pyloric sphincter opens smoothly, and into the duodenum goes the chyme.

All the while, a bit of gurgling and rumbling of the stomach has been going on. This is because there is always a bit of trapped air in the stomach and you take in a bit more with the bolus; the air gets churned around with the bolus and some noise is to be expected.

AND SO INTO THE SMALL BOWEL

Digestion, of course, means breaking down food into simpler substances so that they can be absorbed into the blood and utilized by the body tissues.

There has been a bit of this in the mouth, more in the stomach, but it is in the small bowel that the main business is carried out. In fact, if necessary, you can live without a stomach (thousands of people do so) because the small intestine will do the stomach's work as well as its own. And that work includes not only digestive activities but absorption as well, which is the prime point of eating, however pleasurable the taste of good cooking on the palate.

It is a long bowel, the small one, the longest section of the GI tract, twisting and coiling for more than twenty feet.

The first portion, however, into which your bolus-now-chyme enters upon exiting from the stomach, is not long—only about ten or eleven inches and some one and a half to two inches wide. It is called the duodenum—from the medieval Latin for twelve because its length was originally measured by finger widths, which came to twelve.

Chyme entering from the stomach is, of course, acid. And in the duodenum, which is shaped like a horseshoe, the acidity is nicely neutralized even as enzymes work on the chyme to facilitate digestion.

Vital to all this activity are secretions pouring into the duodenum from two glands, the liver and the pancreas, as well as from the gallbladder, which is a storehouse for some of the liver's essential output.

INTO THE DUODENUM—FROM LIVER
AND PANCREAS AND GALLBLADDER

The liver is a remarkable gland, largest in the body, and the most versatile of all body organs. In an infant it occupies close to half the abdominal cavity, accounting for the abdominal pudginess. In an adult it weighs three to four pounds. It lies on your right side, close up against the diaphragm.

Often called the chemical factory, it has innumerable roles—some five hundred or more known to date. Among other things, it filters out old red cells from the body; it acts as a detoxifier, taking any poisonous sting out of chemicals and drugs; it builds up sugar into glycogen (a compact form for storage in small space) and, when the body needs more sugar, reconverts the glycogen to glucose and releases it bit by bit into the bloodstream; it synthesizes lipids or fatty materials; it rearranges amino acids from proteins into building blocks for regenerating cells (a service needed by all parts of the body and especially the lining of the GI tract, which is renewed every three days); and it produces complex chemicals needed by the body, such as blood proteins and cholesterol.

Evidently, Nature realized the overwhelming importance of the liver and, for one thing, provided liver tissue in surplus; we can, if necessary, get along with as little as one-fourth of normal liver tissue. Also, the liver can regenerate itself. Cut away part of it, even a major part, because of disease, and a new section grows.

Not the least of the liver's jobs is to produce bile. Bile contains many things—antacids to neutralize acid from the stomach (it is present in chyme); salts that emulsify or break fat in the chyme into small globules for digestive action. (Without the salts much of the fat in the diet could not be digested.) Bile also contains some waste materials, notably those remnants of old, worn-out red blood cells broken down in the liver. These are not needed to form new red cells and form a pigment that gives bile a yellow green color that is also imparted to chyme. (As the chyme moves further through the GI tract, the color turns reddish brown.) Additionally, bile contains cholesterol, which, unhappily, sometimes drops out of the solution to form gallstones.

The liver makes a pint or more of bile a day. It is always producing it and when the bile is not immediately needed in the duodenum, when there is no chyme there, the material is stored in very concentrated form (water from it largely withdrawn) in the gallbladder. The gallbladder is a two- to three-inch-long organ that hangs, like an eggplant, under the liver, and holds an ounce or so of concentrated bile.

As soon as chyme moves from your stomach into the duodenum, the gallbladder contracts and pushes bile into a duct, the cystic, which joins up with another, the hepatic duct, coming from the liver, to form the common bile duct. And a mix of bile from the liver itself and concentrated bile from the gallbladder moves into the duodenum to surround the chyme.

Actually, just before the entrance into the duodenum, the common bile duct joins a duct from the pancreas, and along with the bile the chyme is treated to pancreatic juices.

Named after the Greek for "all meat," because it is free of bones and fat—also known as sweetbread—the pancreas is the next largest gland (after the liver) in the body, usually about six inches long and weighing about three ounces, and located at the back of the abdomen behind the lower part of the stomach.

It is famed, of course, for producing insulin. But it also produces pancreatic juice, better than half a pint a day, and the juice is loaded with an array of enzymes. There is pancreatic amylase to split the starch in chyme, while pancreatic lipase is a fat-splitter. Also, the juice has trypsin and chymotrypsin for protein-splitting—and much more, including lipase, nuclease, phosphatase, and lecithinase to get the chyme thoroughly digested.

Nor is it all a matter of juices from the pancreas. The mucous membrane lining of the duodenum—and of the whole gut, throughout its entire length—is full of millions of glands supplying special juices, each with its special enzymes, for each food. Total production of digestive juices per day can run to two gallons, a quantity greater than the total amount of blood in the body.

THE MIXING OF THE CHYME

Your chyme does not just sit there being bathed with bile and juices. If a lot of movement went on in the stomach, a great deal more goes on in the small bowel including the duodenum.

First, there is segmentation, a regular series of constrictions that make a stretch, or loop, of intestine look multilobed, much like pearls on a string. Then the lobes constrict and the previously constricted portions relax; in effect, each pearl becomes string while sections of string become pearls. This goes on as often as ten times a minute, not pushing your chyme along, but mixing it thoroughly with bile and juices.

Next, there is pushing, produced here, as in the esophagus and stomach, by peristaltic waves, with a circular muscle behind the chyme contracting as the muscle ahead relaxes. The waves progress at a rate of as little as about four-fifths of an inch a minute to as much as ten inches per second.

In addition, the two movements—segmentation and peristaltic—produce enough energy to lead to a third, pendular. The intestinal loop begins to swing, and that, too, helps in mixing the chyme with the bile and juices.

TO THE NEXT STOP

As long as chyme is in the space encompassed by the wall of the digestive tube, it is, fundamentally speaking, in the outside world.

It has to get out of that space, through the wall, and pass into the circulation to do any good, and this is absorption.

To be sure, you can absorb some drugs (nitroglycerin, used by many heart patients, is one) through the mucous membrane of the mouth. You can absorb small amounts of water, simple salts, simple sugar, and, very definitely, alcohol through the mucous membrane lining of the stomach. But absorption of most materials is a function of the small intestine, particularly the next two sections of it after the duodenum, the jejunum and the ileum.

All told, the entire intestinal tube is twenty-eight feet long on the average. After the ten- to eleven-inch duodenum comes the eight- or nine-foot jejunum, the slightly longer length of ileum, and, beyond that, the large intestine.

Actually, there is no distinct dividing line between jejunum and ileum; they run into each other imperceptibly, with a gradual change in diameter, the average for the jejunum being 3 to 3.5 centimeters (there are 2.54 centimeters to the inch), while that of the ileum is 2.5 or less.

And now, that bit of chyme, in both jejunum and ileum, encounters what looks like a velvet lining because of about 4 million tiny projections called villi, each 0.5 to 1.5 millimeters long and just visible to the naked eye. In the jejunum they are somewhat longer and broader than in the ileum.

The villi greatly increase the absorptive surface of the gut. Almost incredibly, thanks in no small part to them, the actual absorptive layer has an area of over a hundred square feet, five times the skin area of the body as a whole. Moreover, the villi are always moving, tossing materials about, which aids absorption.

Each villus has, at its base, cells that serve as intestinal glands, pouring out more enzymes. Among them are enzymes to break down any remaining protein fragments in chyme into basic amino acids; lipase to supplement that in the pancreatic juice in breaking down fat molecules into glycerol and fatty acids; sucrase to turn ordinary table sugar (sucrose) into glucose and fructose; lactase to break sugar molecules (lactose) in milk into glucose and galactose. These relatively simple basic molecules—amino acids, glycerol, fatty acids, glucose, galactose, and fructose—are what the body needs as working materials from which it can build up protein, carbohydrate, and fat of its own kind, which differs from the kind in plants and animals.

And it is only these simple molecules that usually can be absorbed in the jejunum and ileum. Of course, in some people under special circumstances, in some way as yet unknown, intact protein molecules can get through the intestinal lining into the circulation. Such large intact protein molecules are known to be antigenic, capable of arousing body defenses against foreign invaders, leading to the production of antibodies as defense. Unfortunately, with repeated absorption of small amounts of intact protein, there may be an allergic reaction, a reaction between antibodies and the antigenic protein molecules, leading to asthma or skin rash.

ABSORPTION

How does absorption take place?

Within each villus is a collection of fine, hairlike blood vessels—

capillaries—into which can go the amino acids (from proteins) and the glucose, galactose, and fructose (from carbohydrates). There are separate lymph capillaries for glycerol and fatty acids from fats.

The blood capillaries connect to tiny veins that in turn connect to the portal vein that goes to the liver, where the nutrient cargo is removed. Fructose and galactose are turned into glucose which, along with the original glucose, is turned from sugar to a starch, glycogen. Actually, glycogen is a large chain molecule and the links in it are glucose molecules so that when glucose is needed, the proper number of links can be released by the liver into the blood.

A well-fed adult may have as much as four ounces of glycogen in the liver and, as further reserve, as much as eight ounces stored in muscle; all told, fuel enough for a day. For it is glucose which is the major fuel, supplying about two-thirds of body energy, with fatty acids from fats providing much of the rest.

As blood exits from the liver via the hepatic vein (hepatic from the Greek for liver) and then moves into the inferior vena cava—a large vein that goes directly to the heart—and from the heart through arteries to be carried to all body tissues, it has in it a supply of glucose and a supply of protein molecules that the liver has built up from the amino acids coming to it; the cells of all tissues can pick up both from the blood to carry on their work.

What happens to the glycerol and fatty acids from fat? Everybody knows about the blood circulation system. But the body has another circulatory system—the lymphatic. While chemicals and other components of the blood float within blood vessels in plasma (a straw-colored liquid), a similar fluid fills the spaces between the cells in body tissues, and nutrients can be carried to the cells by this tissue fluid, the lymph. In this way, from the lymph capillaries in the intestinal villi, glycerol and fatty acids move in the lymphatic system to the cells.

The cells need fat. It is in every one of the thousand trillion body cells. It is fuel, too, burnable to form carbon dioxide and water, and releasing heat and energy. In fact, it yields more than twice the energy of an equivalent amount of glucose.

Fat is readily storable. About half the stores are under the skin. There is also a considerable amount in the omentum, a great "apron" hanging down over the stomach, abdominal wall, and intestine, providing insulation, but producing "pot belly" when present in excessive amounts. Cushions of fat protect joints from jarring and also make beds in which the kidneys rest.

Actually, because there is only limited space for glycogen storage, any excess will be converted to fat for storage in adipose tissue (adipose, from the Latin word for fat). After a day or so of fasting, when there is no glycogen left, it is the fat stores in adipose tissue that are used to provide glucose for the blood. In fact, with adipose tissue accounting for roughly 15 percent of body weight on the average (as much as 50 percent in some of the obese), even a non-obese individual could, if necessary, survive on adipose tissue calories for up to a month.

Unfortunately, not everything there is to be known about absorption is known as of now. And the particularly mysterious area is vitamin absorption.

Some evidence suggests that vitamin A is turned into a protein complex to get into the blood via the villi, but other evidence indicates it may be converted into a compound that travels through the lymphatic system.

About the absorption of vitamins D, E, and K, little is known except that it requires the presence of bile and pancreatic juice.

And the mechanisms for absorption of the other vitamins—including thiamine, riboflavin, nicotinic acid, pyridoxine, pantothenic acid, ascorbic acid (C), and B_{12}—are not known except for the one fact that a special material, called intrinsic factor, has to be secreted in the stomach if B_{12} is to be absorbed in the small bowel.

ON WITH THE JOURNEY

Your mouthful-become-chyme has, in the three hours or so it has been in the small bowel, given its all, that is, nutrients. But it has hardly disappeared. There are remnants that move on to the colon, the large intestine; much may seem odd about that five-foot length of tube.

The last of the small bowel, the ileum, joins with the large bowel, but it is a queer, not very accurate kind of joining.

It is somewhat reminiscent of a T-junction on a road. The left part of the T is a dead end, a small sac called the cecum (from the Latin for blind), sometimes also called the blind sac and the blind gut. It has no known function but because in herbivorous animals, such as the rabbit, the cecum is large, making up half the colon (and serving as a kind of fermentation vat), there is some thought that it may be a leftover from the times when our forefathers were herbivorous.

Attached to the cecum is another appendage of no known present use, the vermiform appendix, about four inches long (sometimes a little more or less). It is called vermiform because it is wormlike.

Chyme will take the right-hand turn at the T-junction and move into the true colon, which after six feet leads into the rectum and anus.

It is near the groin, on the right side of the body, that the colon starts and, viewed as a whole, its various parts describe the shape of a horseshoe.

At the start, the part known as the ascending colon works up to a point near the bottom of the rib cage, still on the right side of the body. But then the transverse section of the big bowel makes a ninety-degree turn and carries over—under liver, stomach, and pancreas—to the left-hand side of the body. And now the next part, the descending colon, moves down along the left side. Then, finally, between the descending colon and the rectum, comes the sigmoid colon—and there is much variation here. In some people it is short, in which case it runs virtually straight down into the pelvis and toward the rectum. In other people it is long and loops over far to the right before reaching the rectum. In some extreme cases it is so long that it has to loop high into the abdomen before turning down again to reach the rectum. Its length can vary all the way from forty centimeters to eighty-four and even more.

In contrast to the small bowel, the lining of the colon has no villi; instead it has deep, tubular pits. Like the small bowel, the colon has various movements, including pendular, or swinging, as well as propulsive peristaltic.

What is happening to that bit of chyme now?

It is moving slowly, much more slowly now, and it may take twenty-four hours for it to get through the five-foot length of the colon. Also, it is shriveling increasingly as it moves.

All through its journey to now, a lot of juice has been poured onto it—from the pancreas and liver and intestinal glands. There is no more digestion to be done here and a minimal amount of absorption, except for the fluid. The body needs the water, and what has not been absorbed in the small intestine is absorbed here. Throughout the length of the colon the water is sopped up and returned to the bloodstream.

What is left of the chyme is becoming less bulky. It loses two-thirds of its mass as the water is drawn out. In an average day you may introduce some twelve ounces of chyme into the colon but only about four ounces pass out.

The fluid absorption starts in the ascending colon and can also go on all along the tract down to the rectum—which is what makes it possible, when necessary, to introduce fluids into the body by way of the rectum, including glucose, minerals, and various drugs.

The large bowel secretes no enzymes. It does, however, secrete a juice, thick and rich in mucus, to serve as a protective covering for the lining and to lubricate movement of the drying-out chyme.

Something else is happening to the chyme. Bacteria are working on it.

At birth an infant has a sterile gut. Even within hours, however, bacteria appear in the feces, having probably entered the GI tract by way of the mouth. But these are not the kind that take up permanent residence. Within the first week other bacteria appear but then they change again in type after the nursing period as a general diet comes into use.

At all ages, the stomach is usually almost free of bacteria; its acidity destroys most of them. But the large intestine swarms with them. They are normal inhabitants, and *they* secrete enzymes that break down any remaining small amounts of starch, fat, proteins, and other materials that escaped digestion in the jejunum and ileum.

As the bacteria ferment the remaining carbohydrates, hydrogen, carbon dioxide, and methane gas are released and compose some of the gas found in the colon. Most of the gas, however, is derived from air swallowed with food.

As the bacteria act on any remaining protein and amino acids, indole and skatole are formed; these substances help to give feces its characteristic odor. And the color of the feces derives chiefly from stercobilin, a product that bacteria produce from bile pigment.

The bacteria are hard workers, and it is through their efforts that a substantial portion of the daily needs for vitamin K and several of the B vitamins—riboflavin, nicotinic acid, biotin, and folic acid—are synthesized in the colon.

LAST OF THE CHYME

The chyme, its bulk down and acted upon and changed by bacteria, is now feces, also known as stool. Now it is a mix not only of food residue and bacterial products but also of bacteria. In fact, as much as one-third of the bulk of the stool may consist of bacteria, many of the friendly type but some capable on occasion of contaminating water supplies and food and producing varied diseases, including cholera, typhoid fever, and dysentery.

Normally, the stool is soft, formed, brownish in color. An abnormality in color, consistency, or even odor may be linked to a disorder of the gastrointestinal tract or of the accessory glands of the tract. Black tarry stools may indicate intestinal bleeding, likely high up in the tract. Some drugs, notably those containing iron or bismuth, can produce tarry stools. Bright red blood in the stool may indicate disorders ranging from hemorrhoids to malignancy. Clay-colored stools stem from deficiency of bile, suggesting either decreased liver production of bile or some obstruction in bile flow. Bulky, fatty stools with foul odor are characteristic of cystic fibrosis. Other causes of fatty stools include gallbladder disease, pancreas disorders, intestinal malabsorption, and excessive fat in the diet. Stools with large amounts of mucus often occur in colitis and other intestinal tract irritations.

END OF THE JOURNEY

The chyme-become-feces is now ready to move on and out, and the remainder of the journey is short.

The rectum is a six- to eight-inch continuation of the sigmoid colon, the last inch of it being the anal canal, which is the rectum's opening on the body surface. The anus is kept closed by muscular rings, the anal sphincters, except during evacuation.

Several times in a twenty-four-hour period, a strong wave of contraction starts up in the transverse colon and moves toward the descending colon, and pushes all the contents of the colon, among them that bit of chyme-feces, toward the sigmoid colon. And here it stays until evacuation occurs.

The rectum is supplied with nerve endings and can transmit the sensation of fullness to the brain, signaling the call to stool. And that is most likely to occur after breakfast because overnight the feces mass has accumulated in the sigmoid and the first meal of the day starts up a gentle peristalsis throughout the intestinal tract; upon reaching the sigmoid the contractions move the fecal mass into the rectum.

Now, as the rectum fills, there is a strong wave of peristaltic contraction there, which causes the internal anal sphincter to relax automatically.

But the external sphincter stays closed until it is voluntarily commanded to open, while simultaneously the diaphragm and abdominal muscles contract, building up pressure—as much as 280 millimeters' worth of mercury (twice the pressure in the arteries). The force of the pressure exerted downward empties the rectum.

With normal motility—spontaneous movement—of the colon, there may be one or more bowel movements a day. If chyme in the colon moves through too slowly, there is exaggerated time for water absorption, which becomes excessive, and the chyme becomes hard and dry so that evacuation becomes more difficult and less frequent—constipation. On the other hand, if motility is excessive, with chyme moving through too rapidly, less water is absorbed and the material arrives at the rectum in a more fluid state so that evacuations are loose and more frequent—diarrhea.

Which means that if you want to judge whether all is right with your colonic motility, the best criterion is not the number of movements but the consistency of the stool.

3 Special points of interest

IT MAY all seem very simple: the hollow tube of the digestive tract receives food, churns it about and prepares it for absorption, absorbs the absorbable and rejects the rest, and in due course gets rid of the rest.

However, there still are some riddles about it. And there are complexities—but they are understandable and even fascinating.

CHEWING—AND AN EXTRA SERVICE

Early in this century, a food faddist group made food chomping a ritual. Each mouthful was to be chewed no less than 50 times, the more the better, even 150 times; good for the health, it was said.

Thorough chewing—but certainly not anything like a ritualistic 50 to 150 times—has its virtues. It does more than just produce small particles that facilitate swallowing.

For one thing, the small particles have other values. The smaller they are within reason, the more surface they present for the action of digestive juices and enzymes.

There is also the additional aid to digestion. Thorough chewing, with prolonged contact of tasty food with the tissues in the mouth, increases secretion of stomach juices, preparing the stomach for more efficient action on the material it is to receive.

Moreover, thorough chewing stimulates more salivary secretion. And the saliva, in addition to its lubricating effects, has a solvent action that improves the taste of the food, which also enhances secretion of the stomach.

Failure to chew effectively leads to indigestion in some people who have lost their teeth and try to eat food that requires effective chewing; also for those with ill-fitting dentures, or with facial nerve paralysis that interferes with the action of chewing muscles.

THE COATED TONGUE

Does the tongue mirror general health or lack of it?

Not entirely, but some disorders can be suspected from the tongue's appearance.

The mobile mass of muscle, which is what the tongue really is, is kept clean and normally colored by the cleansing action of saliva, the mechanical action of chewing, the presence in the mouth of its usual colonies of microorganisms, and adequate nutrition.

So if not enough saliva is secreted, or the diet is such that little or no chewing is required, or the bacterial colonies change, or vitamins needed to maintain the normal tongue covering are deficient, the tongue may change in appearance.

It may become coated, which means that food particles, sloughed-off surface cells, inflammatory excretions, or fungus growths may be deposited on its surface. This often happens in people whose saliva flow is diminished because they breathe through the mouth, or who suffer from dry mouth because of some drugs, or who have mouth or throat infections, and even in those who are treated with antibiotics that may destroy the normal bacteria and allow fungi to multiply in their place. And with fungi overgrowth, especially in smokers, the tongue may have a "black" or hairy appearance.

Sometimes, too, an allergic reaction in the mouth, because of sensitivity to some food, may cause the tongue to swell and lose some of its outer cells, which then coat the surface.

ON THE BREATH

At some time or other, just about everybody has an unpleasant breath odor—halitosis.

Among possible causes are infection of nose or mouth structures; poor oral hygiene; a lung abscess or other lung disorder; cirrhosis of the liver; diabetes; and excessive air swallowing and belching.

But there are many other possible causes and quirks—in foods and in individual GI systems. Garlic odor can be counted on to remain on the breath for hours because garlic is absorbed; it passes through the liver into the general blood circulation, and, since it is volatile, is excreted via the lungs. Similarly, some volatile oils applied to the skin and absorbed from there are recognizable on the breath.

There is a suspicion among physiologists that in some people enzyme activity in the intestine may falter a bit, allowing incompletely digested but absorbable substances of offensive odor to be liberated.

And because experiments have demonstrated that material not normally found in the stomach can be introduced rectally and then recovered from the stomach, some odoriferous substances on occasion may pass back upward from the intestine and even reach the mouth.

There is also some thought that in some people substances like fats, fatty acids, or some abnormal product of faulty digestion of fats may cause unpleasant breath and that trial of a low fat diet may be warranted to see if the halitosis clears.

THE BURP

There is an old story, supposedly true, about a parson who had no small problem. Every time he blew out the altar candles, his breath caught fire. It seems that no one told him to pinch out the candles to solve the problem but a bit of medical investigation indicated an ulcer, which was constricting the opening at the far end of his stomach into the duodenum and some explosive gases were being released in the stomach and not getting through, backing up instead.

Belches are not unusual; belching out—eructating is the technical word—explosive gases would be.

And bubbling can be a very curious business.

All of us, of course, swallow some air during a meal. There are air bubbles in saliva and they get down into the stomach. Infants swallow a lot of air during feeding, enough to distend their stomachs and make them stop feeding, but after a change of position to help them bring up the air, they happily go back to the feeding.

Some of us swallow large amounts of air. Chewing on gum, sucking on candy, or smoking excessively can lead to excessive secretion of saliva, which carries air with it. Food bolters often gulp large amounts of air in their rush.

A prime signal to the brain to initiate belching is considerable distention of the stomach with air, which produces pressure on the nerve endings in the gut wall. And the burp then may come involuntarily. But, with lesser distention—enough for some feeling of discomfort—the burp can be initiated voluntarily.

Curiously, however, some people are misled. Their brain somehow has come to interpret some inflammation or even contraction in the gut as distention. They feel as if they do have gas pains and distention, which would be relieved if they belched. But they have nothing to burp up so they swallow air in order to have something to belch. It is common, for example, for a heartburn sufferer to try to get relief by burping, but there is no success because the source of discomfort is not gas but an inflammation or contraction of the esophagus.

In belching, the glottis, or opening of the airway, is closed and both the chest and diaphragm muscles contract to build up pressure within the abdomen. The pressure is transmitted from the abdomen to the stomach, and when there is enough pressure to overcome the resistance of the cardiac sphincter at the entrance to the stomach, up comes swallowed air.

If you eat a meal large enough to make you feel full, at some point you may even burp or bubble at the instant the cardiac sphincter opens to receive the next bolus.

Some people have extreme difficulty in belching because the stomach is so shaped and positioned that the esophagus enters it at an angle that interferes. Happily, there is a solution: By changing body position the angle can be changed and a burp results. The proper position, however, has to be found by trial and error.

Sodium bicarbonate or an effervescent drink may induce burping and provide some relief from swallowed-air distention of the stomach.

There is another possible "fooler" about what seems to be excessive swallowed air in the stomach. Stomach fullness and distention sensations sometimes can arise not from air in the stomach but from gas formed in the intestine. Often there are abdominal cramps as well, and relief comes not from belching but from eliminating the gas the other way. But it is not uncommon for people with intestinal gas to try to belch their problem away and in the process of belching they swallow more air, which only increases their discomfort.

HICCUP

A hiccup, or hiccough—singultus, in medical jargon—is an involuntary spasmodic contraction of the diaphragm, along with a sudden closure of the glottis. The diaphragm contraction—actually many contractions—causes uncontrolled breathing in of air but the airway is closed so the air inflow is checked. And the peculiar noise of hiccups is produced by the attempt to inhale while the air passages are closed.

Almost anything that can irritate or stimulate nerves or brain centers controlling the action of the diaphragm and other muscles of breathing can trigger hiccups—and that encompasses a long list. It can be a matter, of course, of too much alcohol, and also of gulping food or swallowing hot or irritating substances. It can be a matter of emotions. Or of disease or disorder—of stomach or esophagus or elsewhere in the bowel; of pregnancy; of bladder irritation, liver inflammation (hepatitis); of tumor; and even of surgery, after which hiccup is sometimes a complication.

Most hiccups are at worst annoying or embarrassing and soon stop or can be made to stop. You can employ the method that works best for you. Standard home remedies include a series of deep, regular respirations or, alternatively, holding the breath; holding the tongue and pulling it forward; sipping water slowly or, alternatively, drinking it rapidly; swallowing dry bread or crushed ice (according to one recent medical report, swallowing dry a teaspoonful of ordinary sugar is often effective); applying a little pressure to the eyeballs; applying cold to the back of the neck; and breathing into a paper bag and rebreathing from it. The paper bag device has the effect of stopping the normal exchange of air with the environment and after a few breaths the air in the bag will have an increasingly high carbon dioxide content, and so will the air in the lungs and finally in the blood; as a result, the automatic breathing centers in the brain will call for deeper, stronger breathing, and this often makes the diaphragm contract more regularly and stops the hiccups.

In extreme cases of prolonged hiccups, sedative drugs and tranquilizers may be used. But even in such cases, one simple method that is almost always successful involves introducing a plastic or rubber suction tube through the nose to a distance of three or four inches to stimulate the pharynx by a jerky to-and-fro movement.

NAUSEA AND VOMITING

It goes without saying that they are unpleasant and nausea even verges on being almost indescribable.

They usually have a function but sometimes they may last beyond any known purpose; the gut—and the body—can become overzealous.

Nausea is described in many ways—perhaps most commonly as a sick feeling, a tightness in the throat, a sinking sensation or, as some put it, a disagreeable feeling of impending vomiting. And it generally does come in advance of vomiting, although it may occur without it, in waves or continuously; and with nausea, there may be pallor, racing pulse, faintness, weakness, and dizziness.

Apparently, nausea is designed to stop food intake, and vomiting to forcibly, quickly expel food or anything else already ingested but likely to be harmful in some way. Nor does the ingested material itself have to be bad. When, for example, you experience motion sickness in a plane, bus, ship, car, or elsewhere, whether you know it or not, you lose gut peristalsis. The GI tract becomes static, incapable of handling food properly. In that condition you are better off without food.

Many things can trigger nausea and vomiting. Unpleasant odors can do so; also, emotional disturbances, intense pain anywhere in the body, some toxins produced by bacteria or other organisms, drugs (especially opiates), and motion sickness.

Motion sickness is caused by stimulating effects in the inner ear produced by movements of the head, neck, and eye muscles and also by "pulls" on the organs in the abdomen. For example, some people become sick simply from being rotated or from riding backward, some from up and down motion. When there is a rapid movement downward, a sudden stop, then an upward motion, organs in the abdomen sag and pull on their attachments, producing a sinking feeling, and sometimes nausea.

Impulses from the inner ear—and from all other sources such as pain, unpleasant odors, toxins, and emotional upsets—go to the central nervous system and then the brain.

In the brain there is a vomiting center and a center called the chemoreceptor trigger zone. To the vomiting center go the impulses from the gut and other structures. To the chemoreceptor trigger zone go impulses from poisonous agents.

What follows is a neatly integrated series of activities.

Impulses travel up higher in the brain to produce the sensation of nausea. As the impulses become stronger, they reach the vomiting threshold.

Now a message flashes to the salivary glands and saliva flows in quantity. Another set of messages goes to the chest and diaphragm muscles and you breathe in sharply. This, along with the sudden contraction of the abdominal muscles that also have been alerted, pushes pressure up in the abdomen. Almost at the same time, the glottis is being closed off so when the vomitus comes up you will not suck any into the air passages.

Meanwhile, too, the stomach is in the act. At its far end it starts to contract and, as the body of the stomach, the cardiac sphincter, and the esophagus get signals to relax, the stomach contents are forced out— through the mouth and sometimes the nose as well.

Nausea and vomiting have their uses, but if they are protracted they can be harmful. Not only can they interfere with nutrition; they can cause losses of important substances—electrolytes—needed for normal cellular function. Medical treatment can be effective and is certainly called for.

STOMACH ACID

Of all the phenomena associated with the gut, perhaps the one that causes most puzzlement and even disbelief along with alarm and hypochondriasis is stomach acid.

Stomach acid? In no small part thanks to Madison Avenue techniques, you have undoubtedly heard another term—acid stomach—which implies that acid in the stomach is a disease, something to be treated, neutralized, constantly monitored. And it is—usually needlessly—with antacids at a rate of about $100 million worth a year in the United States alone.

It may seem incomprehensible that the stomach can secrete acid— hydrochloric acid—strong enough to dissolve even iron, and yet not itself be dissolved by it, but it is normal to have a quota of acid in the stomach, and it is not really incomprehensible at all.

Hydrochloric acid is in the gastric juice along with enzymes, the principal one being pepsin, and pepsin, which is needed to break down proteins, needs the acid in order to work.

Once it was thought that digestive juice with its acid flowed only when food was in the stomach. It is now known that there is even a bit of intermittent, on-off flow at other times when the stomach is empty. And that is normal.

And there have been some reports that there is an "emotogenic" secretion that occurs in emotional states such as anger, resentment, and hostility.

But it is when food is in the stomach—or even in sight or on the way —that the main flow occurs.

And how much flow occurs depends on several things. One is the size of the meal; the larger, the more flow, thanks to the mechanical stimulation of secretion by food mass.

In addition, there is chemical stimulation caused by some substances, called secretagogues, which are naturally present in many foods or are released while they are being digested. The chemical action of the secretagogues and the mechanical action of the food mass itself cause the release of a hormone, gastrin, which acts on the secreting cells of the stomach to up their production. Some foods in particular—meat, especially liver, and fish, and extracts of them such as bouillon—have potent secretagogues.

Along with the mechanisms for turning on appropriate juice flow for digestion, there are mechanisms for turning it off. For one thing, by the time the acidity in the stomach reaches a certain level—technically, pH° 1.5 or so—the hormone, gastrin, is no longer being released. And some investigators believe that a special hormone, secreto-inhibitory, to stop juice flow may be released by the stomach lining. Moreover, as chyme begins to move into the small bowel, a hormone, enterogastrone, is released there and it has an inhibiting effect on stomach activity.

But how does the stomach resist the strong acid—and also the tissue-dissolving effect of the enzyme pepsin? There are two protective factors. One is the mucus secreted by the stomach's mucus glands; it has an acid-buffering effect. The other is the presence of materials—antienzymes—in the lining cells, which protect them from digestion by pepsin.

The protection does sometimes fail. Excessive secretion of acid stomach juice is an important factor in producing duodenal ulcers.

On the other hand, in some people, stomach secretions contain almost no acid. The condition—achlorhydria—is not of grave importance since the GI tract is flexible enough so that the rest of it can carry on with digestion.

STOMACH EMPTYING

With a full stomach you are no longer hungry, of course. And how long it stays relatively full helps to determine when you will next be hungry. And if you have overindulged and your stomach is full to the point of discomfort, how long it stays that way is of some concern.

Many things determine stomach-emptying time.

On average, food tends to remain in the stomach three to four hours. But it will stay there longer if the meal is high in fat. Fat stimulates much less acid secretion than does a meal predominantly of protein, and to make up for that the stomach holds onto a fatty meal for an additional period of

°The pH of a solution is measured on a scale of 14. A truly neutral solution, neither acid nor alkaline, such as water, would be 7. A pH of less than 7 indicates acidity; more than 7, alkalinity

time, even up to as much as six hours. On the other hand, a meal mainly of starch tends to empty more rapidly out of the stomach.

Thus, you can expect to become hungry again sooner after a breakfast of juice, cereal, toast, and tea than after one of bacon, eggs, and milk.

Food consistency counts too. Liquids, whether you take them alone or with solid foods, leave the stomach rapidly. There are some exceptions. One is milk, out of which, on contact with the stomach juice, solid material is precipitated. And while most liquids are weak stimulants of stomach secretion, the broth of meat or fish is one exception because it has high secretagogue content; coffee also contains secretagogues, formed during roasting.

Alcohol makes a fast escape. Moreover, some of it is absorbed into the blood right from the stomach without waiting to go further in the GI tract. Alcohol in the blood can be detected within five minutes after it is swallowed. Diluted with water, it is absorbed even faster. On the other hand, taken with fats such as milk or olive oil, its absorption is slowed. (Olive oil reportedly is used by vodka-toasting Russians to enable them to keep toasting.)

Hunger counts, too. If you are ravenous, anything you eat is likely to move on from the stomach faster. With intense hunger, the whole tone of the stomach is keyed for activity.

Exercise too has an influence. But while mild exercise just after eating will shorten the emptying time of a meal—which may be a help in relieving discomfort from too much indulgence—strenuous exercise has a different effect, at first. It temporarily stops stomach contractions, but then it makes up for that by increasing them. There does not appear to be any effect on stomach secretions; and the end result is that stomach emptying is not significantly slowed down.

Position can also count. In some people stomach emptying is facilitated when they lie on the right side, which causes the pyloric end of the stomach and the duodenum to hang down a bit. In the supine position, the main body of the stomach hangs down, food tends to pool there, and emptying is slowed.

Pain—severe or prolonged—anywhere in the body through nervous system ramifications slows down stomach movements and stomach emptying.

EMOTIONS AND THE GUT

For centuries it has been observed that fear can produce a dry mouth and an empty sensation at the pit of the stomach, indicating some association between emotions and the digestive system. Dr. Beaumont, the army surgeon who looked into Alexis St. Martin's stomach, noted changes in appearance with excitement and anger.

Other studies suggested that emotional states could have only a slow-down effect on stomach motility and secretion. But more recent evidence indicates that emotions can work two ways, inhibiting when they are depressive in nature (sorrow, fear) and actually augmenting when they are aggressive (hostility, resentment).

The evidence was obtained under very special circumstances, involving a man named Tom who as a child had swallowed steaming-hot clam chowder. It burned and blocked his esophagus, making it useless, requiring surgery to provide an artificial opening, from outside, into his stomach.

From the age of nine, Tom learned to chew his food, then remove it from his mouth, and introduce it into a funnel attached to a rubber tube leading to his stomach. Later, he married. Only his family and close friends knew about his injury; he never ate with others.

Then one day in New York while doing physical labor, he began to bleed from the opening, which apparently had been irritated by his movements at work. The bleeding was severe and hospitalization was necessary. And while he was in the hospital, two distinguished medical investigators, Drs. Steward Wolf and Harold Wolff, who were doing research on the effects of emotions on the body, persuaded him to become a subject for study.

The two investigators noted many things in the course of their study. When Tom became resentful or angry, they could see his stomach change, much as if it were about to receive a meal, its pink color becoming red, juices flowing freely.

On the other hand, when he was sad, fearful, or depressed, the stomach lining became pale, secretions decreased and, when the depression was severe enough, even introduction of food made no difference: The stomach remained pale and juice flow was restricted.

When food was introduced while he was angry or anxious, it would be out of the stomach in less than usual time because of excessive flow of gastric juices. When it was introduced while he was depressed, it might remain in the stomach undigested for many hours.

Emotionally induced excessive acidity could, of course, have consequences: aggravation or possibly induction of a peptic ulcer and, if some of the excess is carried with a gas bubble back up into the esophagus, heartburn.

Disturbances elsewhere in the gut may be caused or accentuated by emotional disturbances. Anger, resentment, guilt, anxiety, humiliation, conflict, and feelings of being in overwhelming situations are capable of increasing mucus and other secretions in the intestines and of increasing contractions and other activities there, producing diarrhea and other discomfort. Depression, fear, dejection, feelings of futility or defeat decrease secretions and other activities and often produce constipation.

THE MARVELS OF METABOLISM

First digestion, then absorption, and then last, but hardly last in importance but rather the point of it all, metabolism.

It stands for the sum total of all the processes that have to do with disposing of the nutrients you absorb, with the chemical reactions that go on within body cells to make use of these nutrients.

You can divide metabolic activity into two basic types: the catabolic which, in a way, you might consider destructive; and the anabolic and constructive.

In the catabolic, absorbed materials—glucose, amino acids, and fats—are broken down further into simpler materials. The end products include carbon dioxide, water, and nitrogen-containing wastes. But there is also, in the process, the release of energy that the body cells need to function. Catabolic reactions are also called exothermic because they liberate the energy as heat.

In the anabolic and constructive phase of metabolism, the cells use absorbed nutrients to synthesize or manufacture more complex materials—tissue proteins, tissue carbohydrates, and secretions such as enzymes and hormones. These building-up reactions are endothermic; they require heat and depend for it on the catabolic phase.

And a lot of remarkable mechanisms and controls go into seeing that, once you have absorbed nutrients, they are stored efficiently and circulated so they are available to supply cell metabolic needs.

Carbohydrate metabolism.   You absorb carbohydrates—starches and sugars—in your diet after they are broken down into simple sugars—glucose, fructose, and galactose. The glucose is of prime importance; galactose and fructose are changed by the liver into glucose.

Immediately after you have eaten and there has been a chance for absorption, the blood sugar (glucose) level goes up and each 100 milliliters of blood may contain as much as 120 to 130 milligrams of glucose. After a few hours, the glucose level drops off to between 70 and 100. And it stays this way between meals.

The liver helps significantly to keep the level constant, releasing more glucose into the blood as body cells take up what is already there. The kidneys help, too, by taking any excess of glucose (usually anything more than 170 to 180 milligrams per 100 milliliters) out of the blood and excreting it in the urine.

The pancreas, too, is very much a factor in control through the hormone insulin, which a portion of the gland—the islets of Langerhans—secretes. It is insulin that ushers glucose from the blood to the cells and stimulates oxidation of it in the cells. Insulin also can stimulate the liver to convert glucose to glycogen and even to fat.

All of which is why a lack of insulin resulting from disease of the pancreas can produce hyperglycemia—excess sugar in the blood—which is diabetes.

On the other hand, an excess of insulin can produce hypoglycemia—too little sugar in the blood—with such symptoms as nervousness and muscular weakness.

Fat metabolism. Fat is absorbed in several forms known as neutral fat, fatty acids, phospholipids, and cholesterol.

After you eat a meal containing fat, the blood fat content increases markedly; the plasma, the liquid portion of the blood, has a milky appearance for up to six or seven hours, after which the fat level drops off. Total blood fat concentration can vary greatly in healthy people, all the way from 600 to as much as 1,200 milligrams per 100 milliliters of blood.

Fat, like carbohydrates and proteins, is oxidized by body cells and also incorporated in cell structures. Some of it is excreted in breast milk and also in sebaceous gland secretions of the skin. And some is stored in the body as adipose tissue in areas called fat depots.

Just about half your stored fat is in the subcutaneous tissues, beneath the layers of skin. As much as 8 percent of it is in depots between muscles; 12 percent in the kidneys; 10 to 15 percent in tissues in the abdomen; and 20 percent in genital tissue.

The stored fat, incidentally, while it comes mostly from fats in the diet, may also include some converted from carbohydrates and even some converted from protein.

That stored fat is not by any means inert fat. It does not just stay in the depots but is continuously being called up for use and replaced by new fat coming in. When reserves of fat are required for energy, large amounts are brought to the liver for distribution.

Protein metabolism. Proteins from foods are broken down in the GI tract into amino acids, which are the basic building blocks of proteins.

Proteins are remarkably varied and vital, and it is by combinations of various amino acids—differing chains of them—that the body builds up those proteins it needs.

Many body structures—cell walls, membranes, muscles, connective tissues among them—are mainly protein. No cell of the body can survive without adequate protein. Hormones are proteins; so are enzymes. So are vital blood elements; including the immunoglobulins that make the antibodies that rush to the defense when the body is invaded by disease microorganisms.

More than twenty different amino acids are commonly found in proteins. Some can be produced within the body but there are eight that cannot be. These—isoleucine, leucine, lysine, methionine, phenylalanine, threonine, tryptophan, and valine—must be provided by protein foods.

After you absorb them, amino acids—unlike carbohydrates and fats—may be stored only temporarily in the tissues, notably liver and muscle. They are used to form specific needed proteins.

The metabolic rate. The rate at which all the processes of metabolism—catabolic and anabolic—are carried on in the body varies.

There is what is called a basal metabolic rate that is the lowest rate when you are at complete physical and mental rest. In effect, the body's metabolic fires are then burning low to suit reduced need. (And, because the metabolic rate can vary so much at other times, this basal rate is often used as a test for diagnosing metabolic problems, especially any malfunctioning of the thyroid gland in the neck—whose hormones act as governors of the metabolic rate.)

When you exercise, the metabolic rate goes up. So, too, when the body temperature is elevated; a high fever can more than double the rate. And the rate goes up, too, after eating.

4 Hunger, appetite, thirst, taste, smell: phenomena, controls, curiosa

UP FROM the spinal cord comes the brain stem. And near the top of the brain stem, deep in the brain, lies a small bundle of cells, no larger than a lump of sugar—the hypothalamus.

It is the body's emotional brain. It controls anger, joy, sex, fear, and other drives. It directs the body's many rhythms, including those of activity and rest.

And it is there, in the little bundle, that the appestat lies, the control mechanism that tells you to eat when your tissues need nourishment and to stop when your needs are satisfied.

You are not trapped by it—not at all. You can eat when your body is not urgently in need of food and you can stop eating when the need is still there. You can go on a hunger strike if you like.

But the appestat is remarkable: It is able to maintain a memory of what food intake has been, to keep tabs on the nutritional state of the tissues and, usually, to regulate with precision your overall food consumption.

Just how precisely can be seen when you consider that many people do not count calories, do not even weigh themselves periodically, yet in the course of, say, twenty years during which they may consume better than twelve tons of food, their weight may stay at the same level or vary just a few pounds. If the weight gain or loss in that time is within a five-pound range, it means a matching up of food intake and food burnup with an error of about one-fiftieth of 1 percent. If the mechanism were to err even by just 1 percent, the gain or loss would be about 250 pounds.

Even among the vast majority of the mildly and moderately over-weight—all but the grossly obese—if the mechanism is faulty, it is not by much. Usually in, say, a decade, weight gain, even among those who make no great effort to "get hold of themselves," will be less than a hundred pounds, which means that the mechanism, if it is off, is off by less than 1 percent.

HUNGER AND APPETITE—
NOT QUITE THE SAME

You can define hunger in many ways, and, of course, that has been done. According to one definition, it is an uneasy sensation occasioned by the want of food; according to another, it is a complex of sensations evoked by depletion of body nutrient stores.

Most common of the sensations is a discomfort centered in the area around the stomach, variously called emptiness, gnawing, tension, and pangs.

Hunger, of course, leads to a desire for food, which is appetite. And yet appetite can be present without real hunger as it may be when you have a pleasurable desire for some particular delicacy. However much your hunger may be assuaged by your regular meals, you may have an appetite, a keen longing, for, say, lobster or apple strudel.

You are familiar with another sensation, too—satiety, the feeling of having had enough; it is time to stop eating even though more food may be available.

THE WORKINGS

It used to be thought that an indispensable element in hunger was something that went on in the stomach—hunger contractions.

The stomach, once it is emptied of food, does begin to contract. At first, there are mild, rhythmic contraction waves, three per minute. After a variable period the contractions become stronger and may last longer. As the activity of the empty stomach becomes more vigorous, the contraction waves succeed each other with increasing rapidity until they overlap each other.

The contractions stop when food is ingested. Even in advance of the

first swallow, the stomach begins to relax, more and more with each suc-
ceeding swallow, so it can enlarge to a volume sufficient to hold a full
meal.

But because people whose stomachs have been removed still get
hungry, the stomach's hunger contractions cannot be an essential in the
hunger phenomenon.

Stomach contractions are supposed to send impulses to the brain,
evoking the sensation of hunger. Of course, they do reach the brain, and
you are aware of them, but the knowledge of the appestat center has
opened up a new picture of appetite regulation.

It is a double-acting center, as experiments with animals have very
clearly established. When one area of the small bundle of cells in the
hypothalamus is experimentally damaged in animals—cats, dogs, rats,
mice, and monkeys—all become obese. They eat more or less continuously.
With experimental damage to another area of the bundle, exactly the opposite happens. The animals do not take food when it is available nor seek
it even when they are starving.

The first of these double-acting centers is the appetite center; the second, the satiety center. If both are working properly, one inducing food
consumption and the other braking it, food intake should be exactly what
is needed, no more and no less.

In a sense, the appestat would seem to work much as a thermostat—
instrumented to sense when a room is cold, turning on a furnace and shut-
ting it off when a desired temperature is reached.

In fact, it has been proposed that the appestat is made to work by impulses it receives based on temperature variation of the blood—a drop
below normal stimulating the appetite center and food intake, and an
increase in temperature stimulating the satiety center.

It has also been proposed that rather than temperature variation, variations involving amino acids in the blood regulate the appestat.

Another theory, which has the most adherents, is the glucostatic-lipos-
tatic theory—two mechanisms presumed to jointly influence hunger and
appetite via the appestat. The theory holds that meal-to-meal regulation of
food intake is concerned with one's immediate energy requirements and
depends upon variations in the concentration of glucose in the blood; appetite is stimulated when the concentration drops and hunger is satisfied
when with food intake the concentration rises. The mechanism is glucosta-
tic, tending to keep the blood glucose level reasonably static. According to
the theory, long-term regulation of food intake, directed at keeping body
weight stable, is achieved by a lipostatic mechanism—a fat-in-the-body

stabilizing device. It controls the daily mustering-up of a quantity of fat the body needs, which is proportional to the body's total fat content. The lipostatic mechanism may regulate body weight by correcting errors in short-term intake, acting to cut down food intake whenever enough energy can be derived from the mobilization of surplus body fat.

It would account for two phenomena. The first is the voluntary fasting that normal animals undertake after they have been made obese by forced feeding in the laboratory. The second is the tendency for experimental animals whose appetite centers have been surgically damaged to at first increase food intake and gain weight rapidly but then to reach a plateau where intake levels off and the animals maintain themselves at a higher weight. The appetite center obviously has been set awry so that normal weight is not maintained, and if an animal made obese by damage to the center is fasted for a time to bring weight down to the nonobese level, it will, when allowed free access to food, build its weight back up to the obese level attained at the previous plateau, but not beyond. The lipostatic mechanism could be limiting the weight gains by forcing the use of the accumulated fat as at least a partial replacement for food.

At present, although the theory remains acceptable, and seems to help explain many facts about appetite and hunger, it must await further evidence before it can be regarded as the definitive explanation.

But whatever it may be in the blood or tissues that determines the activity of the appestat, other areas of the brain are involved. The appestat cluster of cells in the hypothalamus receives nerve projections from the cerebral cortex, the convoluted sheet of gray matter on the surface of the brain from which comes most of our thinking, planning, imagination, language, creativity, and capacity for abstraction.

So the appestat may be consciously controlled. And, other factors, especially the emotions, stimulate the center. The appestat appears to be notably responsive to worry, tension, and other emotional stresses. Many people overeat because of boredom, frustration, or discontent with family, job, or social relationships.

THIRST

The most abundant material in the human body and the most abundant in the diet is a simple chemical—two parts hydrogen and one oxygen. But water is absolutely vital. Lack of it in the diet will produce quicker death than lack of all other dietary requirements combined. You start getting thirsty—a signal for replenishment—when you lose just 1 to 2 percent of your body's water.

Water makes up about half the adult body—54 percent for men, 48 percent for women. It comprises 77 percent of the body of a newborn infant.

Two main sources are liquids and solid foods; and the daily intake from liquids is about 1,200 milliliters (1.2 quarts) and from solid food° 1,000 milliliters (1 quart). Some water—about 300 milliliters a day—is produced in the body when carbohydrates, fats, and proteins are oxidized during metabolism. Thus, the total availability of water per day is about 2½ quarts.

But about the same amount is lost per day—on the average, about 1,300 milliliters in urine, 650 in perspiration, 450 through the lungs as water vapor in exhaled air, and 100 in the feces. (Diarrhea can increase greatly the fecal loss of water and the loss had better be compensated for.)

Water loss can vary considerably. The 2½-quart loss is for a sedentary person. But someone doing hard physical labor can lose five times that or more. On occasion sweat loss in hot weather can run to more than a quart an hour, which is not a serious consequence if the water is promptly replaced.

If you should happen to get into negative water balance—dehydration —the extracellular fluid (the fluid outside and in the spaces between cells) will become concentrated. To compensate, water will then shift out of the cells themselves into the spaces. The kidneys too will attempt to compensate for the water deprivation—by concentrating urine and excreting a smaller volume.

If the negative balance becomes more severe, you will experience nausea, vomiting, and loss of coordination. As water loss gets beyond about 5 percent of body weight, you may collapse. And if the loss exceeds 10 percent, death may occur. Entirely without food but given water, you can survive for two months or more, even as you lose half your body weight. Without water, you will lose your life, quite likely, before you have lost twenty-five pounds. But such negative imbalance is hardly likely to occur unless water and food containing water are totally lacking.

Almost as soon as you start to need water, you know it. Thirst, of course, is unmistakable. Unlike hunger, which may fade after a time, thirst

°Some vegetation can be 80 percent or even more water; fresh meat, 70 percent; bread, 30 percent or more.

is continuously present until it is quenched. And the very first symptom of intracellular dehydration—loss of water from *within* cells to compensate for the loss in the extracellular fluid—is severe thirst.

The thirst develops because the salivary glands in the mouth stop secreting saliva whenever the body fluid content falls and this produces a dryness in the mouth that arouses the sensation of thirst.

As you have probably discovered, just wetting the mouth and throat relieves thirst only very briefly. The whole body is calling for fluid and it has to be swallowed. Once it is, water gets to the intestines very quickly (it is in the stomach only briefly) and is rapidly absorbed; thirst usually disappears almost immediately after drinking.

Different beverages have different thirst-quenching abilities. The primary requirement for quenchability is high water content. Taste also may be important; so, too, sugar content.

Sweet drinks or sweet-tasting drinks do not quench thirst as well as nonsweet drinks. Generally, low calorie or diet drinks, containing more water and less sugar than sugar-sweetened drinks, have more quenchability. Curiously, many people find a tart lemonade to be a better thirst quencher than a sweet soda even though both have the same amount of sugar (12 percent) and water (88 percent).

Different drinks contain varying amounts of water. Beer, for example, has more water (92 percent) than milk (90.5 percent for skim or buttermilk, 87 percent for whole milk). It also has more than lemonade (88 percent) and regular colas (90 percent) but less than diet cola (99 percent), tea (99 percent), and coffee (99 percent). Beer is on a par with ginger ale (92 percent), ahead of root beer (90 percent), and far ahead of both a martini (80 percent) and wine (76.6 percent).

Alcoholic beverages are not particularly good thirst quenchers; people drinking them often find that they still are thirsty. That is because they contain not only less water but also the alcohol itself has a dehydrating effect.

But, in terms of quenching thirst, beer, with its alcohol content of about 3.6 percent, is a better choice than wine with 18 percent, a martini with about 18.5 percent or more, and 100-proof whiskeys with about 50 percent alcohol.

Water remains the best thirst quencher—but not, of course, all water. Seabirds can drink salt water freely, but not humans. The human system is such that the salt in salt water cannot be excreted except by use of even greater quantities of water, and the body has only a very limited capacity for salt. Seabirds have the advantage—in the form of glands, above the eyes, that secrete a fluid very rich in salt. The birds can shake off the secretion and, without problems, use the seawater that the glands then desalt.

TASTE AND SMELL

Both are obviously important. Some tastes and smells can arouse the appetite; some, nausea. And foods that taste good—aided, as we have seen, by saliva that dissolves them and makes them taste even better—stimulate the flow of stomach juices and aid digestion.

We have about three thousand taste buds—pale, oval bodies visible only under a microscope. They are mainly on the tongue, although a few are on the palate, tonsils, and pharynx. The four basic taste sensations are sweet, bitter, sour or acid, and salt. We cannot taste all flavors on all parts of the tongue; sweet register near the tip, sour on the sides, bitter on the back, and salty all over.

Before we can taste anything, the substance must be moistened. (The salivary glands supply the moisture.)

Thresholds for the various tastes differ. It takes relatively very little of something bitter—just one part in 2 million—to taste it. But to taste sourness, the dilution must be far less, one part in 130,000; and even much less for saltiness (1 in 400) and sweetness (1 in 200).

Our sense of smell is far more acute than that of taste, but not nearly as acute as a dog's, which is a million times more so. For example, a cubic meter of air could contain only 200,000 molecules of acetic acid (the characteristic component of vinegar), which a dog could smell; there would have to be 500 billion before man could. However, our receptors are still sensitive enough to allow us to detect a substance diluted to as much as one part in 30 billion.

The sense of smell is located in odor receptors in the upper passage of the nasal cavity. The size of the receptor area in man is only about one-fourth of a square inch; it is forty times that in a dog. The organ of smell, which can detect scents at a distance, is obviously more important as a danger-warning system in animals than in man.

The odor receptors are cells with long hairlike cilia attached to them. The cilia are embedded in a mucus layer that rests on the cells, and all odors must be soluble in the mucus before they can be detected. Somehow —nobody knows exactly how—the submerged cilia manage to send varying impulses to the brain so you can recognize instantly the odor of brewing coffee, frying bacon, moldy cheese, and so on.

TASTE AND SMELL DISTORTIONS

Until very recently—the early seventies—those who complained of diminished taste or smell or of distorted tastes and smells were often considered neurotics. Nothing physically wrong could be found to explain their complaints.

No longer are they classed—and should not be classed—as neurotics. And no longer is a physical explanation—and a corrective for it—lacking.

It is now called hypogeusia when it is a matter of diminished taste acuity; dysgeusia when taste perception is distorted; hyposmia when smell acuity is decreased; and dysosmia when the problem is distorted smell perception.

At the National Institutes of Health, investigators as of now have had experience with four thousand such people. They include men and women of all ages and, before they were seen, they had had their problem from seven months to as long as forty-nine years.

In some, it had developed during or soon after a cold or other acute respiratory infection; in some it followed a variety of illnesses; but in many its onset was not marked by an illness or anything else. In some, it appeared gradually; in many it developed abruptly.

The investigators finally found that, as compared with normal people, those with any of the complaints tended to have distinctly lower blood levels of the metal zinc.

Remarkably, in many cases, feeding extra zinc supplements eliminated diminished acuities and distorted taste and smell perceptions. Exactly how and why is something to be investigated further.

5 Can a pound of peanuts add more than a pound of weight? Some matters of food as fuel, calories, energy potentials, and the body machine

IT IS a favorite ploy of some nutritionists to pose a two-part question: Is it possible to gain more weight than the actual weight of food eaten? Can a pound of peanuts add more than a pound of body weight?—and then to note that people baffled by this teaser have not learned to think of food as fuel.

It is not, they like to point out, the weight of a food but rather its energy potential, or calories, that is the deciding factor. Put either a pound of peanuts or a pound of tomatoes in the stomach and, temporarily, body weight goes up by a pound. But the pound of peanuts, when metabolized, produces 2,600 calories; the pound of tomatoes, about 95.

Now, they note further, since a pound of fat as laid down for body storage is equivalent to about 3,500 calories when mustered to supply energy, a pound of peanuts cannot add a pound of weight or fat. Nor can 1 1/3 pounds of peanuts with 3,500 caloric value form a pound of body fat unless the peanut calories exceeded, in toto, the number required to replace the calories burned up that day.

Certainly, a temporary weight gain occurs from weight of food consumed, but it is canceled by excretion, respiration, and other bodily functions. Can a pound of food have greater calorie potential than a pound of body fat? Yes, a pound of pure fat or oil supplies more than 4,000 calories.

All of which brings us to some important matters of foods, their energy potential, and the body and its energy needs.

THE MEANING OF A CALORIE

Webster's Seventh New Collegiate Dictionary defines it thus: *"Cal-o-rie*—the amount of heat required . . . to raise the temperature of one gram of water one degree centigrade . . . called also *large calorie."*

Dictionary definitions will explain further that it is a unit expressing the heat- or energy-producing value in food when the food is oxidized in the body.

That is all it is—a convenient unit of measurement, not a food element that can be extracted or modified but rather a measure of energy produced after food is digested.

Once it had nothing to do with food. Originally, it was a unit of heat employed by physicists. With it, they could compare, for example, the amount of heat generated by burning a pound of coal—3 million calories—as against burning a cubic foot of gas—125,000 calories.

Then late in the last century an American agricultural chemist, Wilbur O. Atwater, applied calorie measurements to food, with the idea of trying to make nutrition an exact science. Overenthusiastically, Atwater suggested that only calories counted, and he even advised housewives—who, fortunately, did not take the advice—that in 1895, when a quarter could buy 2,020 calories of milk, or 2,850 of cheese, or 9,095 of sugar, it was silly to spend it on only the 645 calories of eggs it would buy.

HOW IT IS MEASURED

Determining caloric value of various foods is a relatively simple matter of measuring the amount of heat they produce when burned in a bomb calorimeter.

The equipment consists of three vessels, one inside the other. The outermost, of heavy metal, is designed to resist internal pressure. The middle one is insulated with cork to resist heat loss. The inner one is filled with water. And into the inner one goes a bomb containing a weighted amount of foodstuff and oxygen. The foodstuff is ignited electrically and the amount of heat produced is measured by determining the rise in the temperature of the water surrounding the bomb, converting it to calories—one for each degree centigrade rise in temperature of one kilogram (2.2 pounds) of water.

Calculations can be carried out to several decimal places, but for practical purposes they come down to this: Carbohydrates yield 4 calories per gram, or 128 calories per ounce; fat 9 calories per gram, or 288 calories per ounce; and protein 4 calories per gram, or 128 calories per ounce.

From these figures, and knowing the carbohydrate-fat-protein composition of any food, it is a simple matter to calculate the caloric value of any given amount of that food.

For example, an egg contains, along with fluid, about 13 percent protein and 10 percent fat, and no carbohydrate. So an egg weighing 50 grams would have 6.5 grams of protein and 5 of fat. As we have seen above, the protein will yield about 4 calories per gram and the fat 9. The egg, therefore, will provide a total of 71 calories—45 from fat and 26 from protein.

A lump of sugar weighing half an ounce, approximately 15 grams, contains only carbohydrate and so provides 60 calories from the 4 calories per gram carbohydrate yield.

MEASURING BODY ENERGY OUTPUT

There are also relatively simple methods for measuring the energy output of the body. It can be determined in a calorimeter or, alternatively, by measuring the amount of oxygen consumed or carbon dioxide given off and, since these depend upon the burning of food in the body, their values can be converted into calories.

The total energy output divides into two parts. One is the portion you need simply to maintain normal body functions—the beating of the heart, the movement of the lungs in breathing, circulation, muscular tone, and the secretions of the glands. The second is the portion that depends upon your muscular activity, changes in environmental temperature, and emotional states.

The first portion is relatively constant for people of the same age and sex. It is called the basal metabolic rate, or BMR.

For a BMR measurement, as you may know from personal experience or the experience of friends, you must have had nothing to eat for at least twelve hours and ideally should be relaxed mentally, physically, and emotionally; to help ensure relaxation, you spend half an hour in bed rest before any measurements are made. Then, while you are awake, but recumbent, your oxygen consumption is measured.

The BMR rate is usually expressed as a plus or minus percentage of a standard normal value, 100 percent, arrived at by BMR measurements of many people of the same age and sex. A special reason for measuring it is to get an idea of thyroid gland functioning since that functioning helps to determine metabolic rate. In hyperthyroidism—excessive thyroid functioning—the rate may go as much as 50 to 70 percent above 100 percent. In hypothyroidism—reduced gland functioning—it may fall 30 to 60 percent below. Variations of plus or minus 15 percent are considered within normal limits.

The caloric requirements for maintaining the BMR vary a bit with sex —more calories for men than women. They vary, too, with age. At one year of age, for example, 44 calories a day are needed per pound of body weight; at age 30 to 40, about 15 to 18 calories; at age 80, about 11 calories. Overall, an average adult of 150 pounds may require about 1,600 calories a day, something on the order of 70 per hour.

The much more variable second portion of energy expenditure—and therefore of caloric requirements—depends not only upon the performance of muscular work but also on the daily routine of getting dressed, moving about, going to and from the job, and sports activity.

Curiously, only thinking consumes so little mechanical energy that for practical purposes it can be ignored in considering the calories of the diet. In one study, total energy output in a group of volunteer subjects was compared during intense mental effort with output during complete muscular and mental relaxation. To be sure, the sustained mental activity noticeably accelerated the heart rate; it made breathing movements irregular; and it caused almost overpowering fatigue of mind and body. Yet, the increase in oxygen consumption was very small and indicated a rise of only 3 to 4 percent in heat production, the equivalent of only about ten calories of additional energy for a period of three hours of concentrated study.

But something else needs to be added. Despite the very small energy requirement increase involved in mental effort, there can be a large increase in muscular activity as the result of nervous stimulation. Such secondary muscular activity may account for the different heat output noted when a similar mental task is performed by two people, one high-strung and emotional, the other calm and relaxed. It could be this difference that helps to explain why one girl is underweight while her sister is obese. Energy is consumed by such things as nerve-induced fluttering motions of the hands, toying with pencils or beads, and startle reactions to noises, which are commonly unnoticed.

EXCRETED ENERGY

Not all the energy in food consumed is utilized by the body. A portion is excreted as chemical energy of feces, material that has approximately the same energy content per unit mass of dry weight as the food had to begin with. One indication of the considerable energy content of excreted material is the fact that in some parts of the world dry animal dung is used as fuel.

If it seems inefficient that an appreciable amount of energy input is excreted, the phenomenon nevertheless is universal.

And it is worth noting that since the amount of fecal material excreted is variable—there is no fixed amount that must be excreted over any period of time—it sometimes happens that a small reduction in average food intake does not lead to any weight loss but only to a reduction of excreted matter.

HOW MANY CALORIES ARE NEEDED?

The answer, of course, has to be variable.

Ideally, the net caloric energy—the total intake in food minus what is lost by excretion—should equal the energy required for body maintenance plus what is needed for work. If it is less, weight loss results. If it is more, then the body gains extra energy and since this energy is in the form of chemical potential of molecules, the body gains mass.

But what could be a caloric intake ideal for one person is not necessarily for another. Depending upon individual needs, the range can be all the way from well under 2,000 calories a day to well over 4,000.

Strictly from the standpoint of calories only—and, as you well know, there is much more involved, which we will consider later—an intake (whatever it may be) that keeps an individual at proper weight, feeling able to accomplish all he or she wants to accomplish, can be looked upon as ideal.

What that ideal is can be found in some general guidelines.

When the Food and Nutrition Board (FNB) of the National Research Council some years ago drew up tables of Recommended Dietary Allowances, it set caloric intake levels at 2,900 for men and 2,100 for women. But with further experience, it had to make modifications.

In 1963 the FNB advocated a bit lower intake. Basing its figures on a "reference" man and woman, each 22 years of age, the man weighing 154 pounds and the woman 127, both living in a mean temperature of 68 degrees Fahrenheit and engaging in light physical activity, the FNB recommended 2,800 calories for men and 2,000 for women.

But in 1968, it made further modifications. It recommended that since weight gain after the age of twenty-two no longer involves gain associated with growth but is all a matter of fatty tissue, desirable weight—defined as the average weight of individuals of a given sex and height at age twenty-two—should be maintained throughout the rest of life.

And, it went on to point out, that meant adjusting caloric needs according to age. For it had been established that the resting metabolic rate declines approximately 2 percent a decade of adult life—and physical activity, too, is likely to decrease after early adulthood.

So the FNB proposed these reductions in caloric allowances: 5 percent between ages 22 and 35; 3 percent for each decade between ages 35 and 55; 5 percent for each decade between 55 and 75; and 7 percent for age 75 and beyond.

And that would mean 1,900 calories a day for a woman of 30; 1,843 at age 40; 1,788 at age 50; 1,697 at age 60; 1,602 at age 70; and 1,490 at age 80.

And for men, it would mean 2,660 calories at age 30; 2,580 at age 40; 2,503 at age 50; 2,378 at age 60; 2,160 at age 70; and 2,009 at age 80.

6 Balanced, unbalanced, and supernutrition

WHAT WE put into the gut each day does more than stoke the body furnace.

World-famed biochemist-nutritionist Dr. Roger J. Williams recently reported to the National Academy of Sciences that what we eat or fail to eat may ultimately provide the key to the prevention of cancer and other diseases.

By applying the principles of supernutrition, he is convinced we can learn to live longer and healthier lives.

What is supernutrition? It is not counting calories. And it is not "good" nutrition as we know it today—the four basic food groups (meat, milk, fruits and vegetables, breads and cereals) and similar concerns.

Rather, supernutrition revolves about the presence of what some experts suspect are significant unknown nutrients to be found in food, nutrients scientists have not even succeeded in isolating yet, much less manufactured in a test tube and added to synthetic vitamin tablets. The only way to get these nutrients is in the natural foods where they reside.

And supernutrition could involve individualized nutrition to meet any specialized individual needs.

One example cited by Williams: an experiment in which a group of mice received what by conventional standards was a nutritious diet with adequate amounts of all established nutrients.

When, however, a daily extra supply of just 0.3 milligram of one of the B vitamins—pantothenic acid—was added to the drinking water of half the mice, there was a significant difference in longevity. The mice receiving the extra pantothenic acid lived an average of 653 days compared to an average of 550 for the others. If 550 days of living for a mouse is considered equivalent to 75 years for a human, the 653 days would be equivalent to 89 years.

Williams's interpretation of the results is not that pantothenic acid served as a miracle nutrient but rather that some animals had cells and tissues with higher requirements for the vitamin and that their lives were considerably prolonged by the supplement—increasing the average lifespan of the group as a whole by nearly 19 percent.

Williams foresees the day when many of our major diseases might be avoided by introducing vulnerable individuals to supernutrition at an early age.

UP FROM THE "ALL-ONE" NOTION

An idea that all food consisted of some single universal principle, however varied in form, was held for millennia—until the early nineteenth century when a French physiologist, Magendie, first clearly defined the differences in the values of the three foodstuffs: protein, fat, and carbohydrate.

Even late in the nineteenth century, when there was much talk of a "balanced ration," it was all concerned with what might be a desirable proportion of protein, fat, and carbohydrate.

A look for and into the "little things" of nutrition began after 1906 when a study at Cambridge University in England showed that there must be something more to it all when young animals, fed a diet of pure protein, fat, and carbohydrate, failed to grow. That search even now goes on.

PROTEIN

Protein is a basic need. Muscles, heart, liver, kidneys, brain tissue, hair, fingernails—all are chiefly made of proteins. No cell of the body can survive without an adequate protein supply. The very wall of a cell is protein, and protein constitutes 20 percent of the total cell mass.

What is in a protein? Carbon, hydrogen, oxygen, nitrogen, and usually sulfur and phosphorus, with the characteristic element being nitrogen.

Actually, protein substances are the most complex compounds in nature. They are always built up of small constituent units called amino acids (also often referred to as building blocks), which contain the nitrogen, carbon, and other elements.

And what determines the nature of any particular kind of protein is the number and arrangement of the blocks. Albumen (egg white), for example, consists of 418 amino acids strung together in a particular way to form each albumen molecule.

Proteins are complex but it is not their complexity that counts in the diet but their amino acids. Digestion quickly breaks down the complex arrangements in foods into the amino acids and the body then builds up from them its own requisite proteins: its enzymes, disease-fighting antibodies, hormones, blood and other cells. (We have seen that there are more than twenty different amino acids commonly found in proteins, some produced within the body, with eight the human system cannot manufacture—isoleucine, leucine, lysine, methionine, phenylalanine, threonine, tryptophan, and valine—the essential amino acids that have to come from protein foods. Two others—histidine and arginine—which may be manufactured in the body to some extent, are also sometimes considered essential. The remaining amino acids are glycine, alanine, serine, cystine, aspartic acid, glutamic acid, hydroxyglutamic acid, tyrosine, proline, and hydroxyproline.)

Many foods contain protein. All flesh—fish, fowl, and mammal—is rich in it. Cow's milk is—with three times as much as human milk. Cheeses often have even more. Cereals contain some, about 5 to 10 percent by weight. Fruits contain a little, about 1 percent by weight. Vegetables have a greater proportion than fruit, particularly peas and beans.

The protein foods that contain large amounts of essential amino acids are known as complete proteins and include those from animal sources, such as meat, eggs, fish, and milk. The vegetable proteins are incomplete. But it is possible with a mix of vegetables, no one of which provides complete proteins, to get a full amino acid content.

How much protein is necessary?

Studies years ago indicated that half a gram of mixed protein for every kilogram (2.2 pounds) of body weight should be adequate for normal maintenance in an adult and certainly would provide a good margin of safety. For growing children and adolescents, the studies suggested a protein intake of two to three grams per kilogram.

These are essentially the Recommended Dietary Allowances set by the Food and Nutrition Board of the National Research Council.

That means about 58 grams, or 2 ounces, of protein a day for a 127-

pound woman, for example; and 70 grams, or 2 ½ ounces, for a 154-pound man. Pregnant women and breast-feeding mothers, however, may be advised to take more, and so may people suffering from severe infections and severe burns.

How much food does it take to provide 70 grams, or 2 ½ ounces, of protein? You certainly would not want to get it from a single source—not only from the standpoint of boredom but also because variety would count heavily in terms of other nutrients. Here is an idea of the amounts in pounds (or fractions of pounds) of various foods that would be needed:

nonfat dry milk	.39
Cheddar cheese	.57
tuna fish	.63
dried beans	.70
hamburger	.73
veal cutlet	.79
haddock fillet	.84
chuck roast	.89
chicken	.95
lamb chops	1.08
sliced ham	1.10
cottage cheese	1.14
frankfurter	1.24
eggs	1.33
white bread	1.78
bacon	1.84
rice	2.29
frozen peas	2.77
canned lima beans	3.75

CARBOHYDRATES

Traditionally, carbohydrates, which include all sugars and starches, are the great sources of calories. For many in the world, 60 to 75 percent of food calories are in this form, although in the United States and other Western countries now we get less than 50 percent of calories from carbohydrates.

Carbon, hydrogen, and oxygen—just the three—make them up. And there are two hydrogen atoms for each atom of oxygen, just as in water, and carbohydrates get their name because in effect they are hydrated (watered) carbons.

Carbohydrates are an important and immediate source of energy for the body and they are relatively cheap.

There are the many sugars—among them the sweetest, fructose (also known as levulose and fruit sugar), occurring in honey, ripe fruits, and many vegetables; lactose, a sugar in milk; maltose, a sugar from malt or digested starch; and sucrose, the table sugar from sugarcane and beets and maple trees and sorghum.

The starches, which are made up of complex sugars, are not sweet like the other sugars. They are in tubers such as potatoes; in seeds such as peas, beans, peanuts, and almonds; and in roots such as carrots and beets. But our biggest source are cereal grains—wheat, rye, rice, barley, corn, millet, oats, in which better than two-thirds of the world's crop lands are planted.

Estimates for the total weight of carbohydrate in an average man is about thirteen ounces. It is steadily used, can be stored to only a very limited degree, and most of any surplus is turned into something else—fat —for storage.

The body's method of dealing with carbohydrates, no matter the form they arrive in, in food, is to try to convert them all to glucose—blood sugar.

Because starches cannot be absorbed from the gut, enzymes there work on and convert them to glucose. The enzyme sucrase turns the sucrose of cane or beet sugar into both glucose and fructose; the liver takes care of the fructose, converting it to glucose. Lactose, or milk sugar, is treated by the enzyme lactase so that it becomes both glucose and galactose; the liver converts the galactose to glucose.

The energy from carbohydrates is quickly available and quickly used. Generally, within a dozen hours or so, the last of the carbohydrates in the last meal is burned up. Unless more comes in, the fat stores will be ransacked for energy.

Alcohol, which is a form of carbohydrate, gets into the blood, detectably, within five minutes after arriving in the stomach. That is because about 20 percent of it is absorbed, unaltered, right through the stomach wall, without waiting to get into the small intestine. Some simple sugars, such as sucrose, also arrive very rapidly in the blood to provide a quick burst of energy.

So-called raw sugar has no known nutritional advantage over refined.

Brown sugar provides a small amount of minerals and vitamins.

Like sugar, pure starches, such as cornstarch, provide only "empty" calories. But the starchy foods we eat are by no means only calories. Potatoes, for example, provide significant amounts of vitamin C and the B vitamin nicotinic acid, and whole-grain cereals provide proteins as well as many vitamins.

FATS

Fats account for about 15 percent of the body weight of an average person, which does not represent overweight or obesity. It is perfectly normal and useful.

Fats serve several purposes in the body. They are essential in every cell, required for many cell-operating mechanisms; the fats in the cells account for about 1 percent of the body's total weight and they largely remain there, not consumed even during starvation.

Consumption for energy does occur, but that is from the fats stored as reserve, mostly in layers under the skin. And such fat layers serve another valuable purpose, insulating the body against cold.

Fats provide a highly efficient way to store energy. An ounce or pound or any other weight of stored or depot fat will yield about 2¼ times as much energy as an equivalent weight of either protein or carbohydrate.

That is because of the nature of typical fat molecules. Like carbohydrates, they contain carbon, hydrogen, and oxygen. But there is less oxygen, and the arrangement is such that the carbon atoms in a long string are tied to hydrogen atoms—except for some oxygen atoms at the end, which are tied to the carbon atoms. That way, without a lot of hydrogen-oxygen links, there is no water held in the molecule. In effect, it is a "dry," or at least a relatively water-free, molecule and burns better.

However much any "spare tire" around the middle—the bulge is produced because large accumulations of fat are stored not only in tissues under the skin but also in the mesentery, or membrane, that supports abdominal structures—seems persistent, the fat stores are constantly being used up and replaced.

Fats taken in the diet and not immediately used are stored in the depots; so too fats derived from the body's conversion of any carbohydrates not immediately needed. And when fats are mustered from the depots for use, they are converted to carbohydrates, whatever their origin.

A little less than half the fat calories in the American diet come from obvious, or visible, sources such as butter and margarine (80 percent fat);

oils and shortenings (100 percent fat); and bacon (50 percent fat). The larger portion comes from so-called invisible sources, including nuts (as much as 50 percent fat) and doughnuts (50 percent); whole milk cheeses and fat cuts of meat (30 percent and more fat); frankfurters and luncheon meats (as much as 30 percent fat); and cakes, pies, and ice cream (as much as 13 percent fat). Even lean pork still provides about as much fat as the cakes, pies, and ice cream. With lean lamb and most fish, the fat content is down to 8 percent or less; milk and shellfish, 2 to 4 percent; fruits, vegetables, and most bread, less than 1 percent.

If there is any such thing as an ideal amount of fat in the diet, nobody knows exactly what it is. Nevertheless, without a certain amount of dietary calories that come from fat—perhaps as much as 15 percent—there may be some difficulties in absorbing the fat soluble vitamins A, D, E, and K.

With too much fat—to the virtual exclusion of carbohydrates—a condition called ketosis can develop; lacking sufficient carbohydrates to burn, the body has to burn or oxidize fats. And large quantities of fats have to be handled—beyond the capacity of body cells to oxidize fully. As a result of the incomplete oxidation, substances called ketones are formed and accumulate in the blood and tissues. Whereupon, the kidneys try to get rid of them, but in so doing excrete important minerals as well, including large quantities of sodium. As a result, the alkaline part of the body's buffer system is depleted and the balance is upset in favor of acidosis. If uncorrected and long persistent, this condition is capable sometimes of producing disorientation, coma, and death.

The healthiest diets, based on animal studies, provide somewhere between 20 and 40 percent fat. In the United States and in many Western countries the diet, overall, has for some decades hovered around a fat content of 40 percent.

Too much? So some authorities believe—in terms of the possible role of fats, particularly certain types, in provoking heart disease.

The arrangements of carbon, hydrogen, and oxygen atoms in fats go to make up glycerol, which is a form of alcohol, combined with fatty acids.

The fatty acids—and the fats they form—can be classified as saturated or unsaturated. The molecules of saturated fatty acids are constructed with single bonds between the carbon and hydrogen atoms so that these molecules contain all the hydrogen possible—they are saturated with hydrogen.

On the other hand, unsaturated fatty acids have double bonds so that they can take on more hydrogen under certain conditions. All the common unsaturated fatty acids are liquid at room temperature but through a process called hydrogenation, hydrogen can be added to unsaturated fatty acids, and they become saturated and are converted into solid fats. Margarine is an example of hydrogenation of unsaturated fatty acids into a solid material.

Research has indicated that unsaturated fats (also called polyunsaturates) are less likely than saturated to be used in injurious ways by the body. The theory is that the normal blood concentration of cholesterol is increased by saturated fats, which are found mainly in animal fats, such as in meat, butter, and eggs. Alternately, the unsaturated fats, found in large amounts in vegetable oils such as corn oil and safflower oil, are supposed to help reduce the amount of cholesterol in the blood.

Some investigators believe that eating foods rich in cholesterol itself, such as egg yolks, also increases cholesterol in the blood.

Cholesterol is believed to be a major factor in atherosclerosis, in which fatty deposits form in arteries and can impede blood flow, leading to heart attack.

Although many physicians now consider it prudent to moderate the intake of cholesterol and fat, especially animal fat, the case, as we will see, is not by any means considered closed.

VITAMINS—A CONTINUING STORY

Casimir Funk, a Polish biochemist working in London in 1912 at the Lister Institute, originated the term *vitamine*, later to be modified to *vitamin*, and conceptualized the whole idea of certain vital nutrient accessory factors *in the absence of which disease could result*. No longer could the causes of diseases be confined to foreign, noxious agents; they included deficiencies of desirable substances.

It was not really without precedent, the idea that there are unknown vital substances in foodstuffs. Hippocrates, when he was prescribing liver for night blindness, was, although unknowingly, recommending vitamin A. Quebec Indians, giving the scurvy-ridden men of Jacques Cartier a leafy brew, were really dosing them with vitamin C. When, in eighteenth-century England, cod-liver oil was considered a prized cure-all, it was because of its rich content of vitamins A and D that made up for dietary deficiencies.

VITAMIN A

When Funk coined the word *vitamine*, no vitamin had yet been isolated. But only months later, a young biochemist at the University of Wisconsin, Elmer V. McCollum, upon finding that rats grew better and were healthier when their diet included butterfat, succeeded in extracting from butter the responsible substance, now known as vitamin A.

At one time or other, A has been called the "growth" vitamin, the "skin" vitamin, and the "eye" vitamin. Vitamin A does help to maintain the skin and the mucous membranes lining the respiratory and digestive tracts. It is also essential for the proper growth of bone and soft tissues and is necessary for the light-sensitive pigments in the eye that make night vision possible.

Among the commonest symptoms of A deficiency is night blindness. The skin may also be affected, becoming dry and pimply like a toad's skin. In children, growth retardation may occur.

With deficiency, too, there may be increased susceptibility to infection. Even now, investigators are looking into the role of vitamin A in the immune system, the body defense mechanism against infection and against cancer.

Vitamin A is obtained in two ways: directly from animal products such as liver, eggs, whole milk, cream, and cheese; and from carotenes—substances in green leafy and yellow vegetables, including kale, broccoli, spinach, carrots, squash, and sweet potatoes—which the body converts to the vitamin.

Vitamin A deficiency can occur for more than one reason.

Obviously, a diet poor in the vitamin can lead to deficiency. And even in the United States, such deficiency, if not necessarily extreme, may be far more common than usually supposed. Some recent studies indicate that, with Americans tending to drink less milk and to eat fewer dairy products, eggs, vegetables, and fruit, as many as one-fourth of all households are using diets providing less than the Recommended Dietary Allowance of vitamin A—5,000 International Units per day.

Vitamin A deficiency can occur with chronic infection that is long continued. Any infection tends to deplete A stores in the body, but chronic infection can deplete them at a rate faster than input from the diet.

Liver disease can interfere with storage of the vitamin. And absorption of the vitamin from the gut may be impaired when there are not enough fats in a restricted diet or there is a problem of malabsorption of fats since fats are needed to get vitamin A into the system. Regular use of mineral oil for constipation also can block the absorption of vitamin A and of the other fat-soluble vitamins, D, E, and K.

Indiscriminate heavy dosing with vitamin A can be dangerous. In excessive amounts, A can be poisonous. The symptoms of poisoning can be variable—restlessness, appetite loss, weight loss, hair loss, muscle pains, swellings over long bones, headache, generalized weakness and death.

VITAMIN D

If you have ever watched a cat or dog licking itself with its tongue, you have seen it doing something more than cleansing itself. It is licking up body fat from the surface of the fur where it has been irradiated by the sun, making it a source of vitamin D.

Eight years after McCollum had discovered the fat-soluble vitamin A, another fat-soluble vitamin was separated from it and given the name D by Dr. Harry Steenbock, another Wisconsin biochemist.

Few foods contain vitamin D. The only rich natural sources are fish-liver oil and the livers of animals feeding on fish, though the vitamin often is added now to milk and other foods.

But the body, given sunlight, can make its own D. Just as carotene is a vitamin A provitamin—a substance that can be turned into A in the GI tract—so there are provitamins for D, but these require sunlight rather than gastrointestinal action to convert them.

There are several effective forms of D. The most important are D_2, or ergocalciferol, produced by the action of the sun's ultraviolet rays on ergosterol; and D_3, or cholecalciferol, produced in the same way from 7-dehydrocholesterol. Both forms are stored to some extent in the skin and also in the bones, brain, and lungs, but mostly in the liver.

D is essentially a bone vitamin. It is needed for the utilization of the minerals calcium and phosphorus, both of which in turn are required for the growth and maintenance of bone. Without the vitamin, calcium and phosphorus cannot be absorbed effectively from the intestine.

In a child, deficiency of vitamin D can lead to rickets. For lack of adequate calcium and phosphorus, the bones become malformed. The legs are bent; the head may be somewhat misshapen (sometimes appearing squarish); the wrists may be enlarged; the breastbone may protrude. Weight-bearing bends the abnormally soft bones and may cause bowlegs and knock-knees.

Rickets sometimes can occur, not for lack of adequate vitamin D in the diet but because of malabsorption such as in celiac disease, requiring treatment for the malabsorption problem.

There are also cases of refractory or vitamin D resistant rickets because of poor utilization of the vitamin, and in such cases massive doses of

D may be needed. Where uncomplicated rickets can be cured by a daily intake of 400 units a day, in refractory rickets 50,000 or more units a day may be needed.

With close medical supervision, such doses can be used effectively and adjusted as necessary to avoid toxic effects. Indiscriminate dosing with large amounts of D can be dangerous. In excess, D can lead at first to such symptoms as loss of appetite, nausea, and vomiting, followed by weakness, nervousness, itching, excessive thirst, and excessive urination. With continued use of excessive amounts of the vitamin, kidney function can be impaired.

In adults, vitamin D deficiency can produce a form of rickets called osteomalacia in which bones, especially those of the spine, pelvis, and legs, lose their calcium, soften, and become bent, flattened, or otherwise deformed.

As with uncomplicated rickets in a child, osteomalacia can be cured by 400 units of D a day and adequate intake of calcium and phosphorus. Milk is a reliable source of both minerals.

VITAMIN K

Vitamin K, one of the two remaining fat-soluble vitamins, was discovered in 1929 by Henrik Dam in Copenhagen. Dam, along with Edward A. Doisy of Saint Louis University, who helped to elucidate the facts about the vitamin, received a Nobel prize for his work in 1943.

K is the coagulation vitamin. Guarding against hemorrhage, it allows blood to clot. Clotting is a complex mechanism without which we could easily bleed to death from minor cuts and without which wounds could not heal.

For clotting, a material called prothrombin is required. The liver produces it and vitamin K promotes the liver production.

The body does not have to depend entirely on food for its K—the richest sources are green leafy vegetables, pork liver, cow's milk, and vegetable oils. But bacteria in the intestine also produce it no matter what is in the diet.

Deficiencies can occur, and when they do an early sign may be black-and-blue marks (purpura) after even a mild blow. The marks are actually bleeding areas in the skin. A far more serious effect is hemorrhage. The possibility of hemorrhage is especially threatening in the newborn, most of all in premature babies. A newborn infant needs several days in order to develop the facility to produce its own vitamin K in the intestine. To guard against the threat to a newborn, women about to deliver commonly receive an injection of vitamin K; and their babies also usually receive it.

There are other situations in which K deficiency can occur. Oral antibiotics or sulfa drugs sometimes may decimate the populations of bacteria in the intestine that produce the vitamin. And extended diarrhea may interfere with bacterial production.

Sometimes deficiency may arise because of impaired absorption of the vitamin. This may occur when gallbladder or other disease cuts the flow of bile salts into the intestine (the salts are needed for K absorption); or when there is malabsorption as the result of a condition such as celiac disease, which particularly cuts down on absorption of fats and fat-soluble vitamins.

VITAMIN E

Ever since 1935 when it was isolated from wheat-germ oil by Herbert McLean Evans and a team at the University of California at Berkeley, vitamin E has been controversial because of claims that make it seem a panacea for most ills.

Because early studies had shown that it could ensure fertility in animals—without question, rats have reproductive failure when they are deficient in vitamin E—it was considered by some to be a human antisterility factor and even an aphrodisiac.

At various times and by various people, including some physicians, E has been hailed as a means of increasing male potency and assuring orgasm in women; of improving sperm quality and chances of conception; of preventing miscarriage and reducing the likelihood of birth deformities. Beyond all that, it has also been reputed to be a way of treating and preventing high blood pressure, gangrene, the kidney disease nephritis, angina pectoris, atherosclerosis, coronary thrombosis, and varicose veins.

In 1974, at a Western Hemisphere Nutrition Conference in Miami Beach, Dr. John G. Bieri, chief of the Nutritional Biochemistry Section, National Institute of Arthritis, Metabolism, and Digestive Diseases, remarked that "while 95 percent of the world's population could not care less about vitamin E's nutritional importance, 5 percent of the world population in the United States spends millions annually on vitamin E for reasons that most nutritionists and physicians would label as psychosomatic."

Not that vitamin E is not vital; it clearly is.

E is virtually ubiquitous in the human body. Much of it is stored in the liver but it is also found in most organs, including kidneys, lungs, pancreas, heart, spleen, and muscles, with high concentrations too in the adrenal glands, the pituitary gland, and the testes.

It is very definitely an antioxidant. An antioxidant protects other substances against oxidation. Food processors often use vitamin E to prevent oxygen from turning fats and oils rancid and to prevent loss of essential fatty acids and vitamin C in foods.

And it appears that in the body vitamin E could well minimize oxidation of vitamin A and retard oxidation of polyunsaturated fatty acids. It has also been reported to have a protective effect against the damage pollution may inflict on the respiratory system.

The possibility that vitamin E could have a role in retarding aging is under active study by scientists. It is based on the free radical theory of aging. Free radicals are fragments of molecules in the body that have come unstuck and seek to recombine with anything nearby. Such recombinations are oxidative reactions, the very same ones responsible for the rancidification of some foods and for which E is used as a countering antioxidant.

Vitamin E deficiency definitely can cause anemia. It does so in some infants, especially those fed formulas high in unsaturated oils. The infants respond to E supplementation. In adults red blood cell life may be abnormally shortened by a deficiency of E.

For many years Dr. Alton Ochsner, world-famed surgeon of Tulane University and the Ochsner Clinic in New Orleans, has used vitamin E as a means of reducing the danger of phlebothrombosis after accidents and surgery. In phlebothrombosis, a clot forms in a vein. It can get loose in the bloodstream and travel up to block a pulmonary or lung blood vessel. Alpha-tocopherol, which is one of the components of vitamin E, acts as an anticlotting agent and its use, Dr. Ochsner reports, has significantly decreased the incidence of venous thrombosis (clot formation in a vein) and pulmonary embolism (obstruction by the clot of a lung vessel).

There have been reports that many people suffering from intermittent claudication benefit from vitamin E. This condition results from impaired blood supply to the leg muscles so that cramping pain occurs after walking only short distances.

Recently, too, Dr. Samuel Ayres, Jr., Emeritus Professor of Medicine at the University of California at Los Angeles, has reported that vitamin E is effective for night leg cramps, a complaint for which there has been no really effective method of prevention or treatment.

The National Research Council's recommended daily allowance of vitamin E for adults is thirty milligrams.

Vitamin E found in abundance in whole grains is almost nonexistent in refined white flour and in fruits, vegetables, and meats that have been frozen or stored. Also "enrichment" of white flour and cereals with iron still further reduces the vitamin E content since inorganic iron combines with and inactivates some of the E. At the same time, the increased use of polyunsaturated fats in the modern diet increases the need for already depleted E.

Foods rich in vitamin E are fresh beef liver, wheat germ, fruits and green leafy vegetables, margarine, mayonnaise, nuts, vegetable oils, including corn, peanut, and soya oils. But vitamin E is really a group of substances, tocopherols, of which alpha-tocopherol is believed to be the most potent and important. And there could be some question as to whether the foods supposed to be rich in vitamin E—or, at least, the parts of those foods we eat—are high in alpha-tocopherol or contain other tocopherols of relatively little value.

VITAMIN C

It started life as the antiscorbutic—antiscurvy—vitamin and that was no small distinction. Today its importance is known to go far beyond that.

Scurvy was considered infectious, and an old story has it that in 1734 an English seaman aboard a brig headed for Greenland became so sick with scurvy that, to protect the rest of the crew, he was put ashore on an island and left to die. Instead of dying, however, he completely regained his health when he ate what green shoots and shellfish he could find. And when a passing vessel picked him up and he returned to England, his recovery inspired a Royal Navy physician, James Lind, to forget the infectious disease theory and look for a nutritional solution to the scurvy problem.

Lind found it in citrus fruits, although it was no easy matter for him to convince the medical world and he wrote in 1753: "Some persons cannot be brought to believe that a disease so fatal and dreadful can be prevented or cured by such easy means. They would have more faith in some elaborate composition dignified by the title of an antiscorbutic golden elixir, or the like."

And in 1928 Albert Szent-Gyorgyi, a Hungarian scientist working at Cambridge University in England, crystallized out of red peppers ascorbic acid, which he named vitamin C; it won him a Nobel prize in 1937.

Ever since, there has been no letup in studies of all the multitudinous roles of vitamin C.

Vitamin C is considered to be essential for healing of injured tissues, repair of wounds, and combating infections.

It is necessary for the growth and development of blood vessels, teeth, bones, and other body tissues. It is also vital for the body's production of collagen, a cement substance that holds cells together. (It is for lack of collagen that wounds fail to heal, old scars open, rotting gums and other signs of scurvy appear.) Vitamin C is also required if many vital reactions within cells are to proceed.

Vitamin C appears to be necessary for the normal functioning of the adrenal glands, atop the kidneys, which, along with the pituitary gland at the base of the brain, are involved in the control of reproduction and the regulation of the activities of many other glands.

Need for vitamin C is increased under many stress conditions, including pregnancy, inflammation, infection, burns, surgery, and exposure to cold. Some studies indicate that emotional stress may double or even triple the need for the vitamin.

Although not considered definitive, some work suggests that vitamin C may be of value in reducing the high blood levels of cholesterol associated with atherosclerosis, hardening of the arteries. In some studies as early as 1956 and 1961, 500 milligrams of C or more a day were found to produce decreases in blood cholesterol of as much as 30 and 40 percent. A study in England in 1973 also suggests value for C in lowering cholesterol and in preventing clotting within veins (venous thrombosis) in patients undergoing surgery.

There is also its use for the common cold. The controversy about the possible value of vitamin C here still continues. Beginning in the 1950s, when some claims were made in a popular book, drugstores regularly thereafter stocked the vitamin in large quantities during the cold season.

Nevertheless, use of C for colds was considered just a fad until 1970, when Dr. Linus Pauling published his book *Vitamin C and the Common Cold*. The Nobel Laureate brought the whole subject to the fore again with his claim that large doses—as much as 1 to 4 grams a day—could help ward off colds.

Pauling's advocacy spurred research. Some investigators conducted trials which, they reported, failed to support Pauling. But others suggest that there may be something to his claim.

One of those who has been most active in investigating C is Dr. Terence W. Anderson of the University of Toronto. In 1974 Dr. Anderson told a Western Hemisphere Nutrition Congress that, despite the limited number of adequately controlled trials, he believes there is evidence that a regular daily supplement of vitamin C may reduce the severity of winter illness, but that the dose need not be so high.

Undoubtedly, this is far from the last word.

Because man is the only mammal who cannot synthesize his own vitamin C—he may have lost the ability in the course of evolution—ours must come from the diet. Certainly there are many foods naturally rich in it: citrus fruits such as oranges, lemons, and limes; liver; many vegetables such as kale, broccoli, Brussels sprouts, cauliflower, spinach, collards, turnip greens, asparagus, and tomatoes.

But vitamin C is the most volatile of vitamins. It disappears quickly in response to heat, air, and water. And there are often substantial differences in the vitamin C content of cooked as against raw vegetables. While 100 grams of raw cauliflower contains 70 milligrams of C, cooked cauliflower contains 30. There are similar decreases in the C content of cooked broccoli versus raw (from 120 to 75); spinach (60 to 30); kale (110 to 50).

Canning cuts the vitamin C content of foods, and much is destroyed when prepared foods are held on a steam table, as in ready-to-eat restaurants. Excessive soaking, overcooking beyond tenderness, and allowing cooked vegetables and fruits to stand for a time before serving, all cut C content.

Alkali, too, can destroy vitamin C. And the old custom of adding a pinch of baking soda while cooking green or yellow vegetables as a means of helping them stay green or yellow served all too well to eliminate C.

THE B COMPLEX VITAMINS

It all began in 1896 when a Dutch army doctor Christiaan Eijkman in a study with rice-fed chickens found that something removed with bran during the polishing of the rice led to beriberi.

Years later that something came to be known as vitamin B. But then came another discovery: When the B vitamin was heated, its antiberiberi potency was lost. So something destroyed by heat had to be the antiberiberi factor, and that turned out to be thiamine—vitamin B_1.

And because what remained even after heating proved to be good for another disease, pellagra, the thought was that the B vitamin was really a complex of two vitamins, B_1 and B_2, and B_2 was the antipellagra factor.

But that was not so because the B vitamin was really a complex of many vitamins, and it was not B_2 that was good for pellagra; B_3 was good for that.

There followed the breaking down of the complex into a long list of vitamins given B numbers from 1 all the way to 15, but some of these turned out not to be vitamins.

And the list of known vitamins of the B complex today consists of five with B numbers—B_1, or thiamine; B_2, or riboflavin; B_3, or niacin; B_6, or pyridoxine; B_{12}, or cyanocobalamin; and three others without numbers—folic acid, pantothenic acid, and biotin.

Unlike the fat-soluble vitamins A, D, E, and K, the B vitamins, like vitamin C, are water soluble. Other substances such as choline and inositol found in the B complex are not considered vitamins, although they do have roles in metabolism.

B_1 (THIAMINE)

Thiamine has many roles. It helps to maintain muscle tone in the gastrointestinal tract and in so doing aids digestion and elimination. It is essential for the utilization of carbohydrates. Without it, there may be abnormal accumulations in blood, heart, and tissues, producing such symptoms as fatigue, irritability, gastric distress, and loss of weight.

The nervous system requires it. With thiamine deficiency, there are abnormal sensations such as tingling and burning of the toes, and burning of the feet that becomes particularly severe at night.

Animal studies suggest thiamine is needed for normal brain development and intelligence. The vitamin also appears to be needed for proper functioning of the appetite center in the brain. Deficiency-associated symptoms include irritability, memory impairment, mental depression, difficulty in concentration, and confusion, which can, of course, come from many other problems but when associated with thiamine deficiency clear up when thiamine is administered.

Alcoholics are particularly prone to thiamine deficiency. Alcoholic beverages contain virtually no thiamine and, with 1,600 calories in a bottle of whiskey, alcoholics eat less of foods that contain the vitamin. In addition, they have subnormal absorption of the vitamin.

Thiamine deficiency can affect most anyone. The adult daily requirement is in the range of 1 to 1½ milligrams but the total amount in the body is only about 25 milligrams. Because the vitamin is water soluble, any excess taken in is quickly eliminated in the urine. And since thiamine is not stored in reserve, deficiency can develop in a few weeks on low intake. It is probably the quickest vitamin deficiency to develop in people who, for any reason, have loss of appetite, or extended bouts of vomiting, or restrict their diets or fast because of obesity.

Pregnancy increases the need for thiamine, and deficiency apparently occurs in a surprising number of expectant mothers.

Whole-grain flours, breads, and cereals with bran virtually intact are rich in thiamine; so are liver, lean pork, and fresh green vegetables. But overcooking can destroy much of the vitamin content and thiamine is often lost when stock from meat stews and pot liquor of vegetables are discarded.

Thiamine is removed when wheat and other grains are milled. Enrichment puts it back. Federal regulations permit a manufacturer to identify flour as "enriched" if thiamine, niacin, riboflavin, and iron are added, and thirty-four states now require enrichment by law. Similar enrichment programs are in effect in a more limited way for cornmeal, some macaroni products, and rice.

But in 1974, the Food and Nutrition Board of the National Research Council, concerned that many American diets today are deficient in thiamine and other important nutrients—vitamin A, riboflavin, niacin, vitamin B_6, folic acid, iron, calcium, magnesium, and zinc—urged that enrichment programs be broadened to include all these nutrients and that they be added not just to a limited number but to all foods made of wheat, corn, and rice.

It would be advisable, too, the FNB reported, that wheat flour not be refined more than absolutely necessary for consumer acceptance because of the amounts of thiamine and other vitamins lost in milling and bleaching. The need for all this, the board noted, is accentuated by changes in American eating habits, involving increased use of snack foods. Such foods—very often sugars and starches—aside from any extra weight they may encourage, increase the need for thiamine.

B_2 (RIBOFLAVIN)

For fifty-six days in 1973, six conscientious objectors served as volunteers in a study at the United States Army Medical Research and Nutrition Laboratory at Fitzsimmons General Hospital in Denver, Colorado. They lived on a diet adequate in every way except one: It contained virtually no riboflavin.

Even before the end of the experiment, the men began to show significant personality changes. They became depressed, hypochondriacal, and even verged toward hysteria. Clearly, riboflavin had effects on behavior.

The vitamin has many functions in the body. It was discovered when a young pediatrics professor, Dr. Paul Gyorgy, at Heidelberg University, Germany, wondered whether some nutritional factor might be involved in seborrheic dermatitis, a skin condition of babies that produced abnormal oiliness and scaliness.

Gyorgy experimented with rats, feeding them different types of rations, including various chemically isolated fractions of milk. But something went very wrong with the experiments. The rats stopped growing. It turned out that something had been left out of the milk fractions. It proved to be a yellow compound in milk whey (the watery part of milk commonly separated from the thicker part, the curd, in the making of cheese), and it was named riboflavin.

Riboflavin proved to be essential for both normal growth and body maintenance, required for the proper handling of the amino acids of proteins, fatty acids, and carbohydrates.

Since then, many effects of riboflavin deficiency have been clearly established. The eyes, mouth, and skin are commonly affected.

Amblyopia—reduced visual acuity—can stem from excessive use of alcohol or tobacco or from exposure to toxic substances such as lead, benzene, carbon tetrachloride, and arsenic. But there are also nutritional amblyopias that respond to riboflavin treatment.

Riboflavin deficiency also may cause undue eye fatigue, oversensitivity to light, blurring of vision, and itching or watering of the eyes, although these symptoms may have other causes as well.

Cheilosis, or angular stomatitis, is another effect of deficiency. The corners of the mouth become pale, soft, and frayed, and narrow slits or clefts (fissures) may follow.

Seborrheic dermatitis, also known as dandruff, may start with yellowish, greasy scaling of the skin of the scalp and spread to other areas about the face and neck and even to the body. Causes other than riboflavin deficiency may be involved in both cheilosis and seborrheic dermatitis but when the vitamin deficiency is at fault, both conditions respond to supplementation.

One might suppose that riboflavin deficiency would be very rare in this country. Milk is a good source of the vitamin, but milk exposed to sunlight for 3½ hours can lose up to 75 percent of its riboflavin content. Other dairy products, and eggs, are good sources; so are organ meats such as liver, kidney, and heart, as well as other meats, and poultry, fish, green leafy vegetables, legumes, fruits, and nuts.

Sodium bicarbonate used in cooking will destroy the vitamin, and bread, fortified with the vitamin, can lose some of its riboflavin on exposure to light.

Need for the vitamin is increased in pregnancy, and a 1971 study found low riboflavin levels occurring often, particularly in the last six weeks of pregnancy. In its "Ten-State Nutritional Survey in the United States, 1968-1970, Preliminary Report to the Congress," the United States Department of Health, Education and Welfare discovered that 17 percent of Americans below the poverty level were low in riboflavin, twice the rate of better-off Americans, but the deficiency was hardly limited to the poor. The 1974 Food and Nutrition Board report urged that riboflavin be one of the vitamins included in further enrichment of all foods made of wheat, corn, and rice.

B₃ (NIACIN)

Niacin—also called nicotinic acid, niacinamide, and nicotinamide—is the antipellagra vitamin plus. Plus much more that is known and much else still being explored.

Pellagra, a nasty disease, was first identified in Italy and Spain, but then, early in this century, it was discovered elsewhere including the U.S. South among people living largely on corn.

Deriving its name from the Italian *pelle agro* for "skin, rough," it involves far more than rough skin—the dermatitis that is just one of the four Ds that characterize the disease; the others are diarrhea, dementia, and death.

Nicotine has never been found to have a health value, but in 1937 Dr. Conrad Elvehjem, then a young University of Wisconsin College of Agriculture instructor, isolated from liver extract a substance with a structure very much like that of nicotine.

He called it nicotinic acid, and in one of his early experiments with it found that it could cure—and prevent—blacktongue in dogs. And blacktongue was a kind of dog version of pellagra.

Nicotinic acid, or niacin, very quickly proved to be the specific cure and preventive for human pellagra.

But the discovery had a much greater significance. Pellagra involved dementia, and the recognition that a deficiency of a nutrient could lead to a psychiatric disorder and that making up the deficiency could cure it gave tremendous impetus to modern biological psychiatry, which holds that some (perhaps many) mental disturbances may have organic rather than psychological roots. By 1955 there were a variety of psychiatric disorders known that could, at least sometimes, develop from B₃ deficiency, and that responded to the vitamin. They included some depressions, delirium, "confusional exhaustion" (with stupor and coma), and neurasthenia, or "nervous prostration," with fatigue, appetite loss, energy deficiency, and aches and pains.

More recently, B_3 has become the subject of considerable psychiatric controversy, as it has been used in massive doses for the treatment of schizophrenia. Such use, first advocated by Drs. Abram Hoffer and Humphry Osmond in Canada—who claimed for it in numerous medical reports marked improvement in thousands of schizophrenic patients—has led to the establishment of a growing school of psychiatrists practicing "orthomolecular psychiatry" in the belief that schizophrenia and other disturbances are biochemical anomalies rather than genetic, psychogenic, or environmental in nature. In effect, because of an inborn difficulty in making proper use of some nutrients, including B_3, many people suffer mental and behavioral disturbances that may respond to doses of nutrients massive enough to make up for the difficulties in handling ordinarily adequate amounts.

In addition, B_3 is involved in carbohydrate metabolism and in many biochemical reactions in the body. It plays a role in the release of energy, is needed for the normal functioning of the central nervous system, and for maintaining the integrity of the skin and mucous membranes.

Because of certain of its characteristics, B_3 has been studied for a variety of therapeutic possibilities.

For one thing, it lowers the levels of cholesterol and other fatty substances in the blood and, for that reason, it might be beneficial in protecting against subsequent heart attacks in patients who have already experienced one attack.

Some recent studies in England suggest that a derivative of B_3 may possibly be of value immediately after a heart attack. The B_3 related compound, called NAA, in early trials seemed to have some protective value against heart rhythm abnormalities, which are hazards soon after a heart attack occurs.

Nicotinic acid, along with Dilantin, an anticonvulsant drug, has recently been used by Dr. Brian F. McCabe of the University of Iowa Hospitals and Clinics to overcome the chronic burning tongue syndrome, a previously vexing problem described by victims as almost a pain like that after accidentally sipping scalding hot coffee.

B_3 is a good vasodilator, or agent, that can expand contracted blood vessels. And that should make it useful in peripheral vascular disorders in which blood supply to the extremities is impaired. One such disorder is chilblain, with painful reddening of fingers, toes, or ears by exposure to cold. Another is Raynaud's disease with its intermittent attacks of blanching or blueness of the fingers precipitated by cold or emotional upsets. By expanding blood vessels the vitamin should help get more blood through, which it does, but the effect is too brief.

Recently, however, investigators have been working with an experimental drug, a nicotinic acid derivative called tetranicotinoylfructose, which, once in the gut, turns into nicotinic acid and then is absorbed more gradually; it has a longer-lasting effect than the parent compound. Results thus far in both chilblain and Raynaud's disease are considered promising.

B_3 is present in many foods, including fish, organ meats, whole-grain breads and cereals, and enriched breads and cereals. Substantial amounts occur, too, in eggs, milk, poultry, lima beans, and peanuts.

You are likely to find the niacin content of foods often expressed as niacin equivalents. The reason is that tryptophan, one of the amino acids of protein, can function as a provitamin, and can be converted in the body into niacin. Cow's milk, for instance, may contain 12 milligrams of niacin equivalents per 1,000 calories, 1.2 milligrams of them due to niacin itself, and the remainder to tryptophan. (Sixty milligrams of tryptophan are equivalent to 1 milligram of niacin.)

But B_3 deficiencies occur. They may develop as a consequence of prolonged diarrheal disease. In addition, both cirrhosis of the liver and chronic alcoholism are capable of causing deficiency of the vitamin.

Simple dietary deficiency—just not enough intake of foods containing B_3—can occur and is enough of a threat so that the Food and Nutrition Board in 1974 advocated including B_3 along with the other nutrients it recommended for increased fortification of all foods made of wheat, corn, and rice.

B_6 (PYRIDOXINE)

All vitamins, by definition, are potent substances, indispensable in minute amounts for normal body functioning. But even now, many remain somewhat mysterious, all their roles not yet known.

One of the most mysterious could well be B_6, or pyridoxine. Quite recently, investigators of the Harvard Laboratory for Stone Research tried giving ten milligrams of pyridoxine a day to 149 chronic urinary stone formers, all with histories of forming the painful, chill-, fever-, nausea-producing stones for at least five years. The study went on four and a half years. And although none of the patients was known to be outrightly deficient in B_6, their stone production dropped from an average of 1.3 to 0.10 per patient per year.

It was another new use for B_6, one of a remarkable variety.

The vitamin was first identified in 1934 by Dr. Paul Gyorgy whose work with rats while he was seeking to learn more about seborrheic dermatitis in babies led to the finding of vitamin B_2. Subsequently, Gyorgy went back to the rat studies. Now he placed rats on a diet lacking the whole vitamin B complex as it was known then. But he supplemented the diet with required amounts of B_1 and B_2, the only two identified B vitamins. In this way he could find out if there might be any other essential members of the B family.

After a few weeks on the diet, the rats developed scaly sores. They came, Gyorgy was convinced, as the result of a missing ingredient, which he labeled B_6; it was subsequently isolated from liver and yeast and, in 1939, synthesized in the laboratory.

B_6 came into the spotlight in 1952 when a commercial infant formula found to be causing convulsions in babies was recalled and reformulated—and still caused convulsions. The mystery was solved when a Food and Drug Administration scientist guessed that possibly excessive heating during the preparation of the formula might be destroying an essential ingredient. It turned out that B_6 was indeed destroyed, that infants recovered quickly when given injections of B_6, and that when B_6 was added to the formula no further cases of convulsions developed.

Not long afterward, a possible relationship between mental retardation and increased need for B_6 was indicated when, in mentally retarded children suffering from convulsions, increased amounts of the vitamin ended the convulsions in many cases.

Soon radiologists were finding a use for B_6; it helped relieve nausea from X-ray treatment of cancer. Obstetricians determined that B_6 was of value for nausea of pregnancy.

More recently, the vitamin has been found to be effective and safe in suppressing lactation after childbirth in women who do not nurse their babies. It has also been used for women who suffer outbreaks of acne just before their periods. In one study 72 percent of those taking fifty milligrams a day for one week before and during their periods were relieved of premenstrual flare-ups.

Breath-holding spells in a child, although benign, can provoke parental anxiety since the child can turn blue, and if the spells are prolonged enough there may even be convulsive movements. Not long ago, a pediatrician reported using B_6 effectively in more serious cases of breath-holding, in a forty-milligram dose once a day for children up to two years of age and twice a day for older children. And his experience, he suggests, indicates that there may be a definite metabolic disorder in breath-holding children stemming from B$_6$ deficiency.

Of late, some research indicates that some people may be B$_6$ dependent, requiring far greater amounts of the vitamin than others do.

The usual dietary intake for an adult is about 1½ to 2 milligrams a day. But at the Institute for Child Behavior Research in San Diego, a study of 800 psychiatric child patients indicated a need for the vitamin varying all the way from 5 milligrams to 400 a day. And Dr. Bernard Rimland of the institute has reported promising results with high dosage levels of certain vitamins, including B$_6$, in problem children—those found by parents and teachers to be extremely difficult to handle, or abnormally aggressive.

B$_6$ dependence—in the sense of need for larger-than-normal amounts —may be fostered by some drugs. In some patients receiving antituberculosis drugs, when neuritis in arms, legs, hands, and feet developed, the drugs were found to be combining with B$_6$, causing it to be eliminated in the urine, with resulting deficiency. The neuritis disappeared when large amounts of B$_6$ were given.

Oral contraceptives, too, appear to cause derangement of vitamin metabolism. As many as 34 percent of Pill users show mild to moderate depression, irritability, lethargy, and fatigue. Investigators have lately reported marked improvement of such symptoms in as many as 75 percent of women receiving fifty milligrams of B$_6$ daily.

Anemia may be induced by deficiencies of iron or various vitamins. But in one form that affects mostly men, the anemia is real enough—capable of producing lack of energy, easy fatigability, and even such symptoms as vertigo, headache, ringing in the ears, spots before the eyes, and irritability—but there is no deficiency of any nutrient. These men, otherwise healthy, apparently develop the anemia as the result of a special need for large amounts of B$_6$, and all symptoms may disappear with doses of B$_6$ ranging from 50 to 200 milligrams a day.

B$_6$ is known to be needed for normal handling of proteins and carbohydrates. It may also be required for fat handling. Recently, in animal studies, Japanese investigators have found that consumption of sizable quantities of fatty foods promotes deficiency of the vitamin, and their findings suggest that, possibly in man as well as animals, as fat consumption goes up, more B$_6$ is needed. Although it remains to be proven, the idea has occurred to some researchers that conceivably people who eat a lot of fat may be able to counter the atherosclerotic effects of the fat at least to some extent by getting more B$_6$ in their diet.

Aside from special needs for large amounts by people who may be B$_6$

dependent, is B_6 deficiency common among others? There is increasing evidence that it is.

It has been estimated that, as a general average, the requirement is for about 3.5 milligrams a day and that that amount is about 2½ times as much as many if not most people ordinarily get.

B_6 is widely distributed in foods. Rich sources are beef liver, kidney, pork loin and ham, leg of veal, fresh fish, bananas, cabbage, avocados, peanuts, walnuts, raisins, prunes, and cereal grains.

But vegetables lose some B_6 in freezing, and high temperatures of sterilization for canning destroy the vitamin. Cereal grains lose 80 to 90 percent of their B_6 during milling so that our commonly used flours and breads and other food products made from those flours are almost always low in the vitamin.

Thirty years ago, with the realization that highly milled and refined flours lost essential ingredients, provision was made for "enriching" them with four of the lost ingredients—iron, thiamine, niacin, and riboflavin. But no attention was paid to B_6 and other lost nutrients. The 1974 Food and Nutrition Board report called urgently for added enrichment.

B_{12}

B_{12} is in many ways unique among vitamins and all compounds familiar to medicine.

It is the most complex vitamin—known to be required for red blood cell formation and for normal nerve cell growth and maintenance and, of late, suspected to have other still largely unexplored functions affecting body activities in many ways.

Yet, the amount of it required is almost incredibly minute: A single microgram—one millionth of a gram, a gram being only one twenty-eighth of an ounce—in the diet can suffice.

In its first trial, upon becoming available in 1948, one injection of it in an almost microscopic amount restored to health within a few weeks a patient with far-advanced deficiency and almost at the point of death.

Far-advanced deficiency can lead to pernicious anemia, so called because it once was almost invariably fatal. Until 1926, nothing at all could be done for it.

But in 1922, Dr. George H. Whipple of the University of Rochester, discovering that dogs sometimes developed a somewhat similar disease, found that feedings of large amounts of beef liver could save the animals. Shortly, Drs. George R. Minot and William P. Murphy of Harvard tried liver in human patients and in 1926 could announce success. All three men received the Nobel prize in 1934 for their work.

When liver extracts became available, they represented some improvement—at first, not much. A daily injection of about a teaspoonful had to be given, a not entirely painless injection.

By 1935 there were purified extracts that could be injected daily in relatively small amounts with less discomfort, but not all patients tolerated them well.

Finally, in 1948, came the isolation from liver of some bright red crystals of vitamin B_{12}.

B_{12} deficiency can occur for any of several reasons. The principal sources of the vitamin in the diet are liver and other organ meats; beef and pork; eggs, milk, and milk products. Although, in theory, it is possible to get all essential nutrients without eating meat, eggs, and dairy products, B_{12} is the exception. It is difficult, if not impossible, to get even the minute amount of required B_{12} on a very strict vegetarian diet.

But deficiency can occur even on a diet adequate in B_{12}. The complex vitamin requires the presence in the gut of a substance called "intrinsic factor" if it is to be transported across the mucous lining of the intestine for absorption.

Intrinsic factor, produced by cells in the stomach, is normally plentiful in stomach juices. But in pernicious anemia, there is no intrinsic factor. The stomach cells fail to produce it. The failure may occur at any age; most commonly, it develops after about age fifty, and there is a tendency for the failure to run in families.

The failure also occurs in some people who have had partial stomach removal and in all who have had complete stomach removal for ulcer or another reason.

Deficiency can also occur when intrinsic factor secretions are normal. Some bacteria in the gut are fond of B_{12} and if they happen for any reason to multiply out of hand they may leave little of the vitamin for the host.

And an intestinal tapeworm, *Diphyllobothrium latum*, can sop up B_{12}. The larvae of the worm develop in the flesh of some freshwater fish and are destroyed by thorough cooking. But if freshwater fish is eaten raw or only partially cooked, the worm may gain access to the gut and grow to as much as a thirty-two-foot length.

Whatever the cause, B_{12} deficiency is insidious in onset.

Early symptoms can vary. Often, at first, there may be only a little soreness of the tongue and a few mild, unalarming pins-and-needles sensations of the hands or feet. At some point, gastrointestinal symptoms—quite mild at first but progressively intensifying—may turn up; among them, some impairment of appetite, diarrhea, episodes of nausea, or abdominal pain.

The lining of the mouth may become pale, sometimes even greenish yellow, except for the tongue which may be bright red. The mouth may also burn, itch, or sting, and there may be discomfort upon drinking hot or cold liquids.

As deficiency persists, other symptoms may develop: weakness, shortness of breath, or palpitations (heartbeats so unusually rapid, strong, or irregular that the victim becomes very much conscious of them). At some point, nervous system symptoms develop: impairment of memory, dulling of mental awareness and acuity, difficulty in concentration. There may also be disturbances of normal bladder and bowel control, persistent numbness and tingling of the extremities, unsteadiness in walking, especially in the dark.

Provided the symptoms of B_{12} deficiency are recognized for what they are—and the earlier the better in order to avoid any possible irreversible damage to nerves—vitamin B_{12} can produce dramatic improvement.

When the cause of deficiency is a tapeworm or overgrowth of bacteria, B_{12} will provide relief while the cause is treated: the tapeworm with deworming (anthelmintics) agents; the bacteria with antibiotics.

When intrinsic factor is missing, deficiency can be overcome and a body B_{12} reserve created and maintained by injections of fifty to a hundred micrograms of the vitamin every one to seven days for two to four months. The injections, of course, circumvent the lack of intrinsic factor. Thereafter, a monthly injection may be required, although in some cases, once an adequate body reserve has been built up, the vitamin may be taken by mouth and enough may be absorbed from the gut to be adequate.

FOLIC ACID

This B vitamin has come in for increasing attention recently and has become a matter of considerable concern—deservedly. Even as research has been establishing the multifaceted importance of folic acid, it has become apparent that deficiency of it is common.

Of all vitamin deficiency anemias, folic acid deficiency anemia is most prevalent. And, going beyond anemia, the deficiency may affect pregnancy and, in many undesirable ways, the outcome of it.

Also known as folate and folacin, the vitamin got its name from the Latin *folium*, or leaf, in 1941 when it was inauspiciously discovered to be a factor in spinach leaves required for the growth of some bacteria.

But several years later, it was found, along with B_{12}, in liver extract and became quickly established as an essential vitamin.

If a body cell is to divide normally, there must be a doubling of DNA (deoxyribonucleic acid), the material of the chromosomes that carry genetic information, so that each of the two resulting cells has its quota. Along with B_{12}, folic acid is essential for DNA production. So it is needed for the formation of new red blood cells to replace those that wear out and for cell replacement in other tissues that wear out, such as the lining of the gastrointestinal tract.

Folic acid also is required for many metabolic activities and has a role in nervous system functioning.

In many fascinating animal studies, researchers have been able to highlight the vitamin's activities.

Omit folic acid from the diet of female rats as early as the ninth day after conception and the fetuses stop developing and disappear, removed by absorption. Omit it after the eleventh day and young are born—but with skeletal deformities, underdeveloped kidneys or lungs, heart and blood vessel malformations, or extreme brain deformities.

Evidently, the vitamin is required for normal development of every organ and system of the body, raising the question: With folic acid deficiency so common (as we shall see) among pregnant women, could this be an important reason for some congenital defects in human babies?

Recent studies at the Massachusetts Institute of Technology raise another important question. For some time, researchers have been noting that diet may have a vital influence on resistance to disease; that, for example, children receiving added protein have greater resistance to rheumatic fever; that children and adults with vitamin A deficiency are more prone to respiratory and genitourinary diseases.

But the MIT studies, by Dr. Paul M. Newberne, now link a mother's dietary deficiency in pregnancy with her children's susceptibility to infections even long after birth. Offspring of mothers deficient in folic acid and B_{12} were found to have abnormally small thymus glands. The thymus, a gland high in the chest, early in life produces a chemical agent that stimulates the body to produce infection-combating cells called lymphocytes. And the gland itself becomes a kind of processing center for defense cells from bone marrow that normally reside in lymph nodes and spleen waiting to act when disease threatens.

All of which suggests that some nutrients, especially folic acid, are needed for proper development of the thymus before birth, and if the nutrients are not available, the gland is defective.

Do such studies apply to humans? Indications that they do come from other recent investigations in which women with folic acid deficiency anemia were found to have a depression of immune system defenses that was overcome when they received folic acid.

"Even a subtle impairment in the immune system," says Dr. Newberne, "may open a child to disease later in life. The many unexplained illnesses in children, and the wide variation among children in susceptibility to illness, may very possibly be explained by what their mothers eat during pregnancy."

In both men and women, folic acid deficiency can lead to anemia because of abnormalities in red blood cells. Symptoms are often insidious to begin with. At some point, the victim becomes aware of easy fatigability and weakness. Irritability may also develop, and, in some cases, sleeplessness and forgetfulness.

Severe deficiency may lead to intestinal malabsorption so that other vital nutrients cannot be properly introduced into the body. Ovaries and testes sometimes may be affected, leading to infertility. And whether or not the deficiency is causative, it is often associated with skin disorders such as psoriasis, rosacea, and eczema.

A deficiency of folic acid is all too easily induced. Body stores are small, about five to ten milligrams, enough for a month. The vitamin is found in many plant and animal tissues, the richest sources including yeast, liver, and green vegetables, with moderate amounts in dairy foods, meat, and fish.

But folic acid is destroyed by heat. Cooking, especially boiling, and the heat preservation in canning, can destroy up to 90 percent of it. The vitamin is also unstable when exposed to air and to ultraviolet light and declines steadily in storage. So a deficiency may occur not only when leafy vegetables, fresh foods, and liver are lacking in the diet but also when they are stored too long under bad conditions or cooked too long or overly processed.

Deficiency can also occur in pregnancy as the result of a greatly increased need for the vitamin—three to six times. World Health Organization studies have found folic acid deficiency present in up to one-half of all pregnant women in the world, and U.S. studies indicate American women are no exceptions.

Intestinal malabsorption—in celiac disease, for example—can cause folic acid deficiency. The disease, involving intolerance for wheat and rye cereals, produces intestinal lining changes that hinder transfer of some nutrients through the lining into the body.

Some drugs can produce the deficiency. Among them: methotrexate, sometimes used for cancer and severe psoriasis; pyrimethamine, an antimalarial agent; and phenobarbitone, phenytoin, and primidone, which are used for epilepsy.

These drugs—and oral contraceptives as well—may deplete folic acid, and folic acid supplementation may be required.

There is increased recognition now among informed physicians that many people—especially all women in pregnancy—should have folic acid supplementation as a preventive measure; and that it may be needed by others using drugs that can interfere with folic acid as well as those whose daily diet does not include at least some meats or uncooked leafy vegetables.

BIOTIN

Like many other vitamins, biotin owes its discovery to the strange effects due to a lack of it.

In this case, there was even more than the usual mystery. If you happen to put rats on a diet high in raw egg white, bizarre disturbances develop: hair falls out, skin becomes scaly, muscular control is lost, eye troubles develop, and before long the rats die.

Puzzled investigators looked into raw egg white. It contained avidin, a protein, which was lost when egg white was cooked. Avidin, it turned out, hooked onto some essential nutrient so it could not be absorbed. The nutrient proved to be biotin.

And, as studies with human volunteers who went through a period of biotin deficiency induced with raw egg white quickly established, the vitamin is important to humans as well as rats.

The volunteers suffered skin eruptions, appetite loss, severe nausea, muscle pains, lassitude, depression, even hallucinations, all of which disappeared when biotin was restored.

Under usual circumstances, biotin deficiency is an uncommon problem.

Not only is the vitamin widely distributed in nature—present in minute amounts in many foods, particularly egg yolk, liver, kidney, milk, and yeast, and in cauliflower, legumes, and nuts—our intestinal bacteria, needing it for their own use, produce it and we get much of the biotin we need from them.

Occasionally, however, biotin deficiency may occur with use of oral antibiotics which, in the process of combating disease bacteria, may kill off many of the harmless biotin-producing microbes in the gut, too. Often, it appears, the biotin-producers can be encouraged to multiply again with the aid of an intake of generous amounts of yogurt or of acidophilus culture.

PANTOTHENIC ACID

Royal jelly is rich in it and royal jelly is the material that transforms bee larvae into queen bees capable of laying eggs and reproducing. Which suggested that pantothenic acid could have something to do with reproduction—and all the more so when an even richer source of it was found to be codfish ovaries.

Animal studies did, indeed, show the vitamin to be important for reproduction. When pregnant rats were deprived of it, their fetuses stopping developing and were resorbed. In other pregnant rats, given a bit of it, half the fetuses were resorbed and half the baby rats actually born were deformed. In still other pregnant rats, given more adequate quantities, though not fully adequate, 95 percent of baby rats were born and very few were deformed.

Might increased pantothenic acid intake help prevent human reproductive failures? No definitive studies to determine this have been carried out, perhaps because pantothenic acid as its name suggests (*pantos* from the Greek for all) is found in all living cells, plant and animal, and so in all food, and it has been assumed that deficiency must be rare.

But Dr. Roger Williams, who discovered it, believes that the human body requires large amounts (human muscle tissue, for example, contains twice as much as muscle tissue of other animals), and that while it is difficult to eat anything at all, even a snack, without getting some of the vitamin, it is wishful thinking to suppose everybody always gets enough.

In his book, *Nutrition Against Disease*, Williams writes: "I would be willing to give ten-to-one odds that providing prospective human mothers with fifty milligrams of this vitamin per day would substantially decrease the number and severity of reproductive failures."

Williams was intrigued by another aspect of pantothenic acid. Where an ordinarily female bee larva becomes an infertile worker with a life-span of just a few weeks, the same larva fed royal jelly with its high pantothenic acid content not only becomes fertile but also has a life-span of six to eight years or more.

That led him to the study mentioned earlier in which he fed a daily extra of pantothenic acid in the drinking water of one group of mice and found that it extended their average life to 653 days compared with 550 days for a similar group not receiving the supplement. As he has noted, that does not make pantothenic acid a panacea for aging. Rather, he believes, it suggests that while many mice in the pantothenic acid-treated group were getting all the vitamin they needed in the regular chow diet, and the supplement did not benefit them at all, some may have had systems with greater requirements for it; their lives were prolonged, thus increasing the average life-span of the whole group by nearly 19 percent.

And Williams would bet, too, that on a purely statistical basis, if a large number of babies got twenty-five milligrams of extra pantothenic acid daily during their lifetimes, their life expectancy would be increased by at least ten years.

For a long time, clear-cut pantothenic acid deficiency was difficult to produce in humans—until a material, omega-methylpantothenic acid, was found to antagonize the vitamin's effects when fed, and so could produce deficiency. With deficiency came such symptoms as fatigue, lethargy, general malaise, headache, sleep disturbance, nausea, and abdominal discomfort.

In animals, in whom more profound deficiencies could be produced than would ever be tried in humans, incoordination, muscle spasm, and brain inflammation developed.

From such studies it became apparent that pantothenic acid plays a role in the utilization of many nutrients and the production of energy, and is needed to maintain the integrity of the nervous system and normal functioning of the gastrointestinal tract. It is also required for normal functioning of the adrenal glands atop the kidneys. The adrenals are involved in stress, may be depleted as the result of excessive stress, and some, not yet definitive animal and human studies suggest that stress may be withstood better when large amounts of pantothenic acid are available.

While virtually all foodstuffs contain small amounts of the vitamin, dried yeast, eggs, liver, organ meats, and legumes are particularly good sources. Pantothenic acid is present in wheat bran but the bran is largely removed from wheat during milling and processing to produce the flour used for bread and other products, and there has been no requirement for restoration of pantothenic acid by enrichment of the flour.

The vitamin also can be destroyed by excessive cooking.

THE VITAL MINERALS, KNOWN AND SUSPECTED

Among the forty-odd nutrients known to be essential to man—including the carbohydrates, fats, amino acids, and vitamins—are well over a dozen essential minerals, plus still other minerals not yet finally established as essential but thought very likely to be.

Two essential minerals alone—calcium and phosphorus—represent 3 percent of total body weight. Their importance—and that of two others present in lesser but still relatively large amounts, sodium and potassium—has long been well known, although that has not prevented deficiencies.

The four "big minerals" are sometimes also called macronutrients, while the other essentials are called micronutrients, or trace elements, because they are present in very tiny amounts. Only forty years ago, just two trace elements were known. Now more than a dozen are.

CALCIUM AND PHOSPHORUS

They often work together. Both go into the formation of bones and teeth. Both are needed for adequate functioning of the nervous system. Calcium is required for the transmission of signals over nerve paths. Phosphorus goes into the making of a chemical, ATP, short for adenosine triphosphate, sometimes referred to as a kind of body spark plug because, in effect, it sparks the release of energy from glucose for such activities as muscle movement.

Calcium is needed also for normal blood clotting while phosphorus is needed for the metabolism of some carbohydrates.

The Recommended Dietary Allowance set by the Food and Nutrition Board is for one gram each of calcium and phosphorus per day. For most Americans and Europeans, getting that much calcium depends a good deal on an adequate intake of milk, cheese, or yogurt. A cup of milk, whole or skim, contains about 290 milligrams; a cup of yogurt, about 295; the calcium content of cheeses ranges considerably from 30 milligrams an ounce in Camembert and 89 in Blue or Roquefort to 167 in Limburger, 262 in American Swiss, and 323 in Parmesan.

Clams and oysters contain calcium, about 113 milligrams to half a cup. And some vegetables, such as cooked collard or turnip greens, contain about the same amount per half cup. Kale, pink canned salmon, and sardines are good sources, too. But while such vegetables as spinach, beet greens, chard, and rhubarb have substantial amounts of calcium, they also have oxalic acid, which makes the calcium content unavailable for absorption.

Phosphorus is available in many foods, especially protein foods, and Cheddar cheese, beef, pork, sardines, tuna, peanuts and peanut butter, Brazil nuts, cottage cheese, milk and peas are rich in it.

An excess of calcium—hypercalcemia—is possible. Excessive amounts of vitamin D can increase absorption of calcium beyond normal. Some peptic ulcer patients after prolonged use of large amounts of milk and antacids may become hypercalcemic. The consequences: loss of appetite and constipation proceeding to nausea, vomiting, and abdominal pain and, sometimes, later emotional disturbances, confusion, muscle weakness, and even psychosis.

Much more common is deficiency of calcium, but very rarely phosphorus. A United States Department of Agriculture survey in 1965 revealed that infants and young children and most men were getting daily requirements of calcium but almost all women and girls over the age of eight and many young and adolescent boys and older men were getting inadequate amounts.

SODIUM AND POTASSIUM . . .
AND THE BODY'S SALTY INTERNAL SEA

The ocean was the mother of life. There the first primitive forms originated and when life moved to the land it took the sea with it. In every land animal, including man, the sea is very much present in the form of fluids and dissolved salts.

Fluids account for 70 percent of the human body by weight. Plasma, the fluid carrier of blood cells, accounts for 5 percent; fluid between tissue cells—called interstitial fluid—accounts for 15 percent; and the intracellular fluid, the liquid within cells themselves, makes up half of body weight.

In this internal sea, salt is a vital constituent. And its concentration in the extracellular fluids—both the plasma and the interstitial—is like that of the salt in seawater. The salt in the body is enough to fill several saltshakers.

Salt, of course, is sodium chloride. When dissolved in fluid, it forms sodium and chloride, which are electrolytes, so called because they have electrical charges that allow them to carry current.

Sodium and chloride are the principal electrolytes in interstitial fluid. It is the chloride from salt that goes into the making of hydrochloric acid in the stomach, part of the digestive fluids.

The movement of sodium in and out of nerve fibers is involved in the triggering of nerve impulses. Sodium is also needed for muscle contraction —even the beating of the heart depends upon a proper balance of sodium with other minerals (potassium and calcium).

Sodium has other important functions. Just as we work best when external conditions are suitable, so body organs work best when external conditions are constant and the body seeks to maintain constancy. Sodium goes into sweat, which helps to reduce excessive body heat when that occurs.

Another critical function is to regulate the vital exchange of water between the cells and the surrounding fluid.

One of the most important internal conditions that must be held constant is the pH of body fluids. The pH is a measure of acid-alkaline balance. Body fluids tend to be just slightly alkaline with a pH value of 7.35 to 7.45. Sodium plays a vital role in maintaining the pH within that narrow alkalinity range.

Several decades ago, a fad arose concerned with eating "properly" to maintain the body's alkalinity. It was supposed that proteins and carbohydrates must never be eaten together; otherwise acidosis would result. The fact is that no matter what is eaten, the body normally maintains the proper pH.

Salt intake can vary widely. In addition to salt we add at table, some sodium occurs naturally in fresh vegetables such as artichokes, beets and beet greens, carrots, kale, dandelion and mustard greens, spinach, and Swiss chard. It is present in milk, eggs, cheeses, and meats. Canned vegetables are rich in it. It is in baking powder and soda, in the flavor intensifier monosodium glutamate, and in the preservative sodium benzoate.

Although only one gram or less of salt intake daily may be needed, we commonly take in as much as fifteen grams a day, with some variation from day to day.

No matter. Under normal circumstances, the kidneys make certain body salt content holds steady. The kidneys determine what is to be excreted in the urine.

Within normal bounds, no matter how much or how little salt is taken into the body, the salt concentration in the blood and the total amount in the body do not vary. If virtually no salt is taken in, no salt will be excreted; if much is absorbed, the kidneys increase their excretion rate.

How the kidneys handle salt is controlled from a distance. Several powerful hormones from the endocrine glands, especially an adrenal gland hormone called aldosterone, which stimulates the reabsorption of salt, regulate the work of kidney cells.

Even as the kidneys determine what happens to salt, they determine what happens to water. For every movement of salt in the body brings about movement of water and when the kidneys return salt to the blood, they also return water. So the kidneys are very much guardians of the internal sea and of chemical balance, not just waste-removing organs.

Salt balance can be upset. Excessive sweating removes large amounts of salt as well as fluid. Sweat initially may contain in each quart almost half the usual daily intake of salt. Over a period of time, even if sweating should rise to as much as a quart an hour, and even though the amount of salt taken is not increased, the body acclimates itself through a sharp fall-off of salt loss in both the sweat and urine.

But for the short term, excessive perspiration can lead to dehydration and heat exhaustion, with such symptoms as headache, weakness, dizziness, nausea, and muscle cramps. Then, water alone is not enough to establish equilibrium. Salt tablets or in emergencies half a teaspoonful of salt in a glass of water or tomato juice may be used and even repeated several times at ten-minute intervals in order to replenish salt, which then helps retain water for rehydration.

With efficient conservation of salt by normal kidneys, a salt deficiency virtually never develops as the result of low salt intake alone. But the kidneys, as the result of disease or drugs, may fail to conserve salt in normal amounts. An adrenal gland disorder may cause kidney wastage of salt. In such situations, salt solutions will be used while the underlying problem is sought for and corrected.

An upset in salt balance—on the salt retention side—may be involved in high blood pressure, or hypertension, which affects more than 20 million Americans. That salt might be involved in hypertension could be shown easily enough. For example, in people with a tendency to elevated pressure, an injection of salt solution quickly raises pressure further.

Once, heavily restrictive salt-free diets, unpalatable and difficult to live happily with, had to be used. With the advent of modern diuretic drugs—capable of promoting salt and fluid elimination—such very strict salt-free diets have become rare although many physicians urge moderation in salt intake.

Some diuretics, in the process of promoting excretion of salt and fluids, also lead to loss of potassium (called hypokalemia). Potassium, like sodium, is an electrolyte, but unlike sodium, it is chiefly present within cells. Potassium depletion may show itself in muscle weakness, cramps, diarrhea, vomiting, loss of appetite, apathy, and listlessness and, in severe cases, irregular heartbeat and heart muscle weakness. Potassium depletion requires special attention to an intake of foods rich in the mineral and, in some cases, to potassium supplementation.

Potassium is widely distributed in foods, especially in meats, milk, vegetables, and fruits. Oranges, tomatoes, and bananas are good sources.

MAGNESIUM

For some years investigators in the United States and abroad have been noting a relationship between the hardness and softness of water and the incidence of coronary heart disease and heart attacks. In communities with hard water supplies, the heart death rates are lower.

And if there is a causal relationship between water composition and heart deaths, the factor responsible presumably is something toxic in soft water or something beneficial in hard water. If the latter, two of the most likely factors are calcium and magnesium, since they are mainly responsible for the hardness of most water supplies.

When they first looked into the whole question, a team of University of Toronto researchers examined the blood levels of both minerals in residents of soft and hard water communities and, finding no difference, had no reason to believe that residents in soft water areas were suffering from a less than optimal intake of either calcium or magnesium.

But in 1975, they found something to change their minds. Instead of looking in the blood, they looked in the heart muscles of people autopsied because of accidental deaths in soft and hard water areas. They found no significant differences in the mean concentrations in the heart muscles of calcium and other minerals, but there was a significant difference in concentration of magnesium, much lower in those who had lived in soft water areas.

As they reported, the results "are compatible with the belief that the relatively high death rates in some soft water areas may be due to a suboptimal intake of magnesium, and that water-borne magnesium exerts a protective effect."

Magnesium used to be listed in nutrition books as a trace mineral, needed in only minute amounts. No longer. In 1968 the Food and Nutrition Board finally established a recommended allowance for magnesium— 400 milligrams, which definitely takes it out of the trace mineral class with requirements of just a few milligrams.

Magnesium is now known to be involved in many aspects of body chemistry. It is needed for the activation of a number of enzyme systems involved in the use of other minerals, some vitamins, and even proteins. It is required for both nerve and muscle activity.

Severe deficiency of magnesium may be manifested by muscular irritability or twitching, muscle cramps and muscle spasm, weakness, forgetfulness, irritability, depression, even mental confusion, and convulsions. And the deficiency has been associated with accelerated and irregular heartbeat and coronary heart disease.

The mineral is plentiful in seafood, meats, nuts, whole grains, and wheat bran, and is moderately available in leafy green vegetables, fruits, and dairy foods.

Is magnesium deficiency widespread? Nobody really knows, but there is some concern that it may be. Increased softening of water supplies may be responsible to some extent. Another significant factor could be the use of highly refined flour. Minerals as well as vitamins are lost in the heavy milling of flour, which involves the stripping away of virtually all the mineral- and vitamin-rich bran.

When flour and bread "enrichment" was instituted, it called for the restoration of just a few vitamins and one mineral, iron, and bakers had the option, which some chose to use, of adding calcium to the bread, even up to three times as much as was lost in milling the flour. But no provision was made for adding magnesium.

Not only was an important source of magnesium cut off when flour became highly refined, but in addition, because the need for magnesium increases as calcium intake increases, the consumption of large amounts of calcium-enriched bread could create a calcium-magnesium imbalance.

THE TRACE ELEMENTS: IODINE AND IRON

They were among the first to be recognized. The one can make the difference between an idiot and a savant, and the other between suffocation and life.

We need just extremely tiny amounts of iodine, on the order of 150 micrograms (millionths of a gram) a day. The micronutrient is absolutely essential for the functioning of the thyroid gland and it is impossible to overemphasize the importance of the thyroid, a small, butterfly-shaped organ located in the neck and weighing under an ounce.

It is the thyroid that controls metabolism. Minute thyroid hormone secretions, something less than a spoonful a year, are responsible for much of the body's heat production. They help maintain the circulatory system, are necessary for muscle health, heighten sensitivity of nerves, affect every organ, tissue, and cell of the body.

Severe thyroid deficiency can produce a cretin child—skin thick, dry, wrinkled, and sallow; tongue enlarged; lips thickened; mouth open and drooling; face broad; nose flat; dull, apathetic, dwarfed, mentally retarded —unless the deficiency is overcome.

In adulthood severe deficiency can mean myxedema—progressive slowing of mental and physical activity; masklike face; dry, scaly skin;

coarse, brittle hair; thick tongue and lips; slow, thick, clumsy speech; joint pains and stiffness.

And even mild or moderate thyroid deficiency may produce many varied symptoms and signs: weakness, dry skin, slow speech, memory impairment, weight gain, hair loss, hoarseness, appetite loss, joint pain, slowing of mental activity, and much more.

The thyroid gland is a factory, and to do its manufacturing of hormone secretions it needs raw material, iodine. It is the principal user of iodine in the body, and when iodine from the diet is absorbed from the gut into the blood, the gland plucks the iodine from the blood passing through and incorporates it into its hormone secretions.

When, lacking adequate iodine, thyroid gland production slumps, signals come from elsewhere in the body, exhorting the thyroid to increase production and, trying to oblige, the gland may increase in size in a kind of blind effort to add to its output even though it cannot increase production for lack of raw material. The gland may enlarge until a noticeable lump may appear in the throat—a goiter.

There are goiter regions all over the world. No continent is free of them. Generally, they are the mountainous and inland areas of the globe. A high incidence of goiter is found in the Himalayas in Asia, in the regions of the Alps and the Carpathian and Pyrenees mountains in Europe, and in the high plateaus of the Andes in South America. In North America the goiter zone is the Great Lakes basin and the area of the Saint Lawrence River, extending westward through Minnesota, the Dakotas, and the neighboring Canadian territory as far as the Northwest, and including Oregon, Washington, and British Columbia. This great belt extends an arm southward in the Rocky Mountain area and another in the Appalachian area.

Through the ages in such high and inland areas the soil has yielded most or all of its soluble iodine content to water on the way to the sea. In areas close to the sea, the soil as well as drinking water is usually rich in iodine. Fruits and vegetables grown in such soil contain iodine in abundance and this is equally true of seafood.

The most important discovery in relation to goiter was that it could be prevented by adding iodine to community water supply in goiter regions or administering it in the form of tablets or drops, or making it available in the form of iodized salt. Today, use of iodized salt is the most widely accepted method of goiter prevention.

We know now that only one-fifth of an ounce of iron stands between us and suffocation since iron must go into the making of hemoglobin, the pigment in the red blood cells that transports oxygen from the lungs to all cells of the body. And we know now—but only very recently—that iron has other roles to play not just in the red cells but in every cell of the body.

The consequences of iron deficiency can be many and varied.

Anemia is one. With it may develop not only such well-known symptoms as pallor, weakness, and fatigability, but others not so well known as being anemia-linked: irritability, heartburn, flatulence, vague abdominal pains, neuralgic pains, and heart palpitations. And there may be still others, seemingly bizarre.

Why do some women eat dirt or clay? Because of iron deficiency, Washington University investigators found not long ago. Why do some people, men and women, crave ice and eat ice cubes by the trayful? Again, iron deficiency anemia, Air Force physicians recently established.

Can long-continued iron deficiency affect the heart? With the aid of the powerful electron microscope, investigators recently have noted in animals changes in heart muscle fibers, leading to heart enlargement, with the enlargement reversed slowly after the iron deficiency is corrected.

Can iron deficiency account for irritability and lack of appetite in many infants and even possibly for learning impairment in some children? Studies by investigators in Philadelphia and New Orleans suggest this.

And the possibility that the deficiency may be the reason why some children chew on plaster and paint chips and develop lead poisoning is suggested by studies by Dr. Philip Lanzkowsky, professor of pediatrics at the State University of New York, Downstate Medical Center, Brooklyn.

Iron deficiency is remarkably common.

The ten-state survey mentioned earlier not only found 25 percent of those living below the poverty level suffering from iron deficiency but also 12 percent of the nonpoor and supposedly well fed.

The well fed? Apparently, many people are well fed except for iron. A few years ago, a United States Department of Agriculture survey of food consumption in representative American households revealed that generally protein intake was high, higher than recommended allowances, but inadequate intake of iron was common. Among adolescent girls and women ranging through age fifty-four, iron intake was 30 percent or more below recommended allowances of eighteen milligrams a day, and that was also true in women over sixty-five. Iron in the diets of infants and children under three years averaged 50 percent below recommended allowances.

As many as 60 percent of all American women, it has been estimated, may have some degree of iron deficiency, and millions have severe degrees with symptoms that may be blamed on other factors.

The fact is that total body iron amounts to only about half a gram in infancy and in adulthood is only about five or six grams, roughly a fifth of an ounce.

Of the total, 70 percent is in use at any one time, leaving only 30 percent to be stored as reserve. That makes for a slim margin of safety.

Each day a healthy person who is experiencing no abnormal bleeding loses about one milligram of iron in urine, sweat, and cast-off cells. That loss must be made up by diet.

A good diet contains only about six milligrams of iron per thousand calories, and only five to ten percent of the iron in food is absorbed and the rest is excreted.

Thus, with a good diet providing twelve to eighteen milligrams in the two thousand to three thousand calories that make it up, the 5 to 10 percent absorption rate would give the body just about enough new iron to counter the normal loss of the old.

But many women and girls who should have at least eighteen to twenty milligrams of iron daily—because as much as twenty-eight milligrams may be lost in menstrual blood—get much less. Many, concerned about keeping calories and weight down, get far below their iron requirements on the basis of total caloric intake.

Quite possibly, the disappearance of iron cooking utensils in modern society may be contributing to an increase in the prevalence of iron deficiency. Iron cooking pots, once standbys in homes and food processing plants, used to add iron to the diet but now have been largely replaced by aluminum and stainless steel ware.

Nevertheless, a good diet can help prevent iron deficiency. Meats are good sources, most of them providing 2 to 3 milligrams of iron per 3-ounce serving. Liver is an especially good source. Beef liver provides 5 milligrams in a 2-ounce serving; calves' liver is half again as rich in iron as beef liver, and pork liver has twice the iron of calves' liver. Liverwurst, made from liver, is a good source and so is chicken liver, although it has less iron than beef liver.

An egg contains a milligram of iron. Oysters, sardines, and shrimp provide 2½ to 5 milligrams per 3-ounce serving. Most green vegetables provide 1 to 4 milligrams per cup, and other good sources include dry beans, nuts, prunes, dates, and raisins, each containing about 5 milligrams per cup.

Blackstrap molasses has long been popular in some circles as an iron source. A by-product of sugar processing and long used to enrich livestock fodder, it contains 2.5 to 3.2 milligrams of iron per tablespoon and gets it as a contaminant from the kettle used in boiling sugarcane. But certainly molasses is no essential in the diet, considering all the other less exotic iron sources in ordinary foods.

Iron deficiency in young children should really be no problem but it is a common—and frequently neglected—one. In a Chicago study, 75 percent of infants up to eighteen months old were found to be suffering from iron deficiency anemia. A National Academy of Sciences study of 2,150 children found poor diagnosis, poor treatment, often no treatment at all. The investigation disclosed that less than one-fourth of the general run of physicians even bothered to check young children for anemia. And although two-thirds of the doctors in hospitals, clinics, and prepaid group practices said they checked, a study of their charts found that almost two-thirds of youngsters with tests indicating anemia were not diagnosed as being anemic and not treated.

Although iron-containing milk formulas that could do much to eliminate the problem have been available for a decade, and the American Academy of Pediatrics has recommended their wide use, a recent academy survey found that less than 30 percent of formulas prescribed by American physicians contain iron.

THE TRACE ELEMENT CHROMIUM

It is a commonplace industrial metal, one that, in substantial amounts, gives a new car body glitter.

But only very recently has come the knowledge that chromium in tiny amounts is indispensable in the human body, and there is mounting evidence that this trace mineral may be essential if diabetes and heart attacks and the atherosclerotic, artery-choking disease that produces the attacks are to be avoided.

After a meal, when glucose from food reaches the bloodstream, insulin is secreted by the pancreas to take the excess glucose out of the blood and store it. In animal studies, Dr. Walter Mertz, now chief of the United States Department of Agriculture's Vitamin and Mineral Nutrition Laboratory, Beltsville, Maryland, established that in chromium deficiency the rate at which glucose is removed from the blood is halved. Fully effective glucose handling evidently requires the presence of *both* insulin and chromium. Before long, it was clear that chromium is an essential part of an organic complex called the glucose tolerance factor (GTF). GTF potentiates the effect of insulin, and when GTF activity falls off with a decrease in chromium, insulin effectiveness is also diminished.

Almost at the same time that Mertz was investigating chromium in diabetic rats, Dr. Henry A. Schroeder in the unique Dartmouth Medical School Trace Element Laboratory in Brattleboro, Vermont, was beginning extensive studies of the effects of trace elements fed to rats and mice from weaning until natural death.

One of the elements was chromium, although at the time Schroeder had no reason to think the mineral might be essential for health. In usual scientific fashion, Schroeder divided rats into two groups, feeding one chromium in small doses while the other group received no extra chromium and their diet contained little of the element.

Four years later, when the last of more than a hundred rats receiving chromium died, it was something of a record for rat longevity. Surprisingly, too, at death, the chromium-fed animals showed no fatty deposits in their aortas in contrast to the substantial deposits found in other rats.

Moreover, Schroeder in this and other investigations noted that in animals on a low chromium diet both blood cholesterol and sugar levels were abnormally high but when chromium was given, both levels were healthily low.

The effect of chromium on both levels seemed significant to Schroeder. As he pointed out, although the role of fats and cholesterol in atherosclerosis had come in for great emphasis, it is also true "that practically everybody with clinical atherosclerosis of moderate severity has a mild form of diabetes, and the long known fact that people with moderate and severe diabetes have especially severe atherosclerosis, from which most of them die, links the two disorders of fat metabolism and sugar metabolism together and demands a search for a single causal factor basic to both."

But could the animal studies apply to humans?

It would be necessary, first of all, to show that chromium deficiency is common in humans, and particularly common in those on Western diets with great proneness to the diseases and not common in others—Africans, for example—who are not prone.

Studies did show this. When chromium concentrations in the tissues of Americans and those of foreigners were compared, chromium was found in the tissues of children in both groups but could not be detected in almost one-fourth of Americans over age fifty while it was present in almost all (98.5 percent) foreigners. Other studies established that generally Africans have twice as much chromium in their bodies as do Americans.

Soon Schroeder was investigating the reasons for chromium deficiency in Americans and other Westerners. Virtually all babies, he found, are born with a healthy reserve of the metal but the reserve drops with age.

And Schroeder could, after more studies, offer an explanation for the marked drop.

When we eat sugar—and also starches that are split in the intestine into sugars and absorbed as such—blood sugar rises. In response, more insulin enters the blood and simultaneously chromium levels in the blood increase as the metal is mobilized from body stores to help the insulin handle the increased blood sugar content. After performing its function, the chromium in the blood reaches the kidneys where about 20 percent of it is excreted.

If the sugar and starch in the diet contain adequate amounts of chromium, enough is absorbed to make up for the urinary loss. But if the sugar or starch contains little chromium, a net loss results and body reserves are depleted.

And the fact is that the sugar and starch most common in our diet are very low in chromium. While raw sugar contains 36 micrograms of chromium per 150 grams, refined white sugar contains only 3 to 4. Schroeder has calculated that if we consume 150 grams of refined white sugar a day, there will be a net loss of about 8.75 milligrams of chromium in the urine in a year—more than the body's total content—unless the chromium is replaced from other sources. (Actually the average American consumes not 150 but 208 grams of sugar a day from all sources, including even bread which contains up to 8 percent sugar.)

And other than sugar, the major source of carbohydrates in our diet is refined white flour. Whole wheat contains 175 micrograms of chromium per 100 grams but refined white flour contains only 23. So white flour may cause depletion of body chromium just as does white sugar.

As Schroeder has pointed out, if anyone set out deliberately to develop atherosclerosis, he could hardly do better than what many of us do—drink coffee all day long with several spoonfuls of sugar and cream; use marmalade and jams on breakfast white toast along with refined breakfast foods with sugar and cream, eat white bread sandwiches and a slab of pie for lunch, more bread and pie for dinner, and maybe a sticky, sweet liqueur or two afterward.

Schroeder's suggestions for preventing further depletion of body chromium and helping to restore reserves include recognizing that, in addition to vegetables and fruits, fish and meats contain chromium, with shellfish and chicken being especially rich in it. He also urges avoidance as much as possible of refined white sugar and all foods and beverages containing it (including jams and jellies, candies, sweet cakes, pies, cola drinks containing glucose, and other sweet manufactured products) and avoidance as well of refined white flour as much as possible in favor of whole wheat and other whole grains, unpolished rice, whole rye, oats, and corn.

OTHER VITAL TRACE ELEMENTS

Total them up, the weights of all the trace elements in the human body, and the combined figure, according to the best estimates today, amounts to something between twenty-five and thirty grams, about an ounce or less.

It has been a long wait for research techniques precise enough to identify the tiny quantities of many elements—they are now detectable down to just a few parts mineral to one billion parts body tissue—and to provide some understanding of their role in metabolic processes.

Currently, it appears that the vital trace elements function through the cells, either as parts of enzymes that catalyze metabolic activities or as triggers for activating enzymes.

Actually, more than sixty trace elements have thus far been found in living organisms, from bacteria to man. Some are clearly established as being vital to man; others are suspected of being so—on the basis of strong evidence; and still others, among the known and the still unknown, may well be vital.

Copper is clearly essential. It is a part of many enzymes. It is involved in the normal development of bone and muscle and in the functioning of the central nervous system. And it also works with iron to form hemoglobin, the red blood cell pigment that carries oxygen.

Some investigators now believe that chromium, zinc, and, in special instances, copper may be deficient in the American diet. Healthy adults eating a well-rounded diet are not likely to develop copper deficiency but people with kidney disease or celiac disease sometimes have low copper levels in their blood. (See the following trace metals chart for recommended daily allowances of copper and its sources.)

One unpleasant consequence of copper deficiency—and also of zinc deficiency—in both adults and children can be taste distortion, once thought to be entirely psychological but now known to be correctable when supplements of whichever element is responsible are provided.

Zinc today is under increasingly intensive study. The mineral is necessary for growth, sexual maturation, and as a component of many vital enzymes. And it has come into increasing use as a therapeutic agent.

It has been used successfully to speed the healing of wounds; in adult dwarfs it has led to some gains in height, along with normal sexual maturation (previously lacking) and improved learning ability; and in middle-income children with histories of poor growth and appetite, it has restored their appetites and tastes, and their growth rate improved.

That zinc depletion can cause mental changes—poor memory, depression, disorientation—and that these can be overcome by zinc supplementation has been shown in recent work at the Baylor College of Medicine.

When mothers are zinc deficient, offspring may have learning disabilities, according to animal studies by Dr. Harold H. Sandstead and other investigators of the Department of Agriculture's Human Nutrition Laboratory in Grand Forks, North Dakota. For still unknown reasons, the effect on learning has been apparent only in male offspring.

Cobalt's principal function is as an essential constituent of vitamin B_{12}. Only 0.043 micrograms a day are needed, the smallest amount of any substance known to make the difference between health and disease, and it would be difficult not to obtain that amount in a diet containing a moderate amount of meat.

Fluorine is an important aid in preventing dental decay. Along with calcium and vitamin D, it also stimulates bone formation. And there is some evidence that it is helpful in preventing osteoporosis, the loss of mineral substance from bone that not uncommonly in older people leads to greater proneness to fractures. It may work both by retaining calcium in bone and by forming a firmer crystalline structure of bone. Fluorine is found in many foodstuffs, with tea and seafoods especially rich in it.

Although no human role has yet been definitively established in humans for a number of trace elements, they have proved essential to animals and are believed likely to be for man:

Selenium is believed to protect membranes and other fragile structures from oxygen damage, much as vitamin E does.

Manganese deficiency in rodents leads to growth retardation, seizures, and impaired lactation. The mineral is believed to be part of a number of enzyme systems and to be required for normal bone formation, nervous system functioning, and reproduction.

Molybdenum-deficient chickens show growth failure and early death.

Nickel deficiency in experimental animals has led to abnormal liver changes, increased fetal mortality, poor growth, and changes in hair coat.

Vanadium deficiency in animals has led to reduced body growth, increased blood fat levels, altered bone development, and impaired reproductive performance.

Silicon is necessary for proper bone calcification in animals.

Tin, from the evidence in animals, may be important in the structure of proteins and in various body reactions.

TRACE ELEMENTS: NEEDS AND SOURCES

ELEMENT	Recommended Daily Allowance [1]		SOURCES
Chromium	20-15 mcg. [2] estimated		Whole grains, meats
Copper	2 mg. estimated		Organ meats, shellfish, nuts, dried beans, peas, other legumes, cocoa, raisins, copper cooking utensils, drinking water
Fluorine	1-3 mg. estimated		Various foodstuffs, tea and seafoods especially rich. Reliable source: municipal water supplies fluoridated at 1 part per million, equal to 1 milligram per quart
Iodine	130 mcg. (male), established	100 mcg. (female)	Iodized salt, seafood, plants grown in iodine-rich soil
Iron	10 mg. (male), established	18 mg. (female)	Liver, meats, eggs, green leafy vegetables, legumes, nuts, whole-grain and enriched breads, flours and cereals, dried fruits, iron cooking utensils
Manganese	2.5-7 mg. estimated		Whole grains, vegetables, fruits, nuts
Molybdenum	45-100 mcg. estimated		Organ meats, cereal grains, legumes
Nickel	less than 0.6 mcg. estimated		Whole grains, vegetables, legumes, fruits
Selenium	unknown		Meats, seafoods, whole grains grown on selenium-rich soil
Tin	less than 1 mg. estimated		Meats, whole grains, vegetables, legumes, fruits
Vanadium	0.1-0.3 mg. estimated		In many foods. Present in adequate amounts in any normal diet
Zinc	15 mg. (male), estimated	15 mg. (female)	Liver, meats, seafoods, eggs, milk, whole grains

1. Set by Food and Nutrition Board, National Research Council/National Academy of Sciences. In Recommended Dietary Allowances, 8th Edition, 1974, Washington, D.C.
2. Mcg. means microgram, equal to one-thousandth of a milligram, one-millionth of a gram. Mg. means milligram, one-thousandth of a gram, a gram being one twenty-eighth of an ounce.

PUTTING IT ALL TOGETHER: COMPLETE NUTRITION

Nutrition is complex, and as such should serve as a guard against fads that put emphasis on this or that particular nutrient as if it were something special.

No nutrient is special or preeminent. All nutrients are interrelated. All, together, are jointly constructive.

Moreover, if one is missing, supplying enough will be effective but too much can be harmful. Increase calcium intake to abnormally high levels, for example, and you may induce zinc-deficiency symptoms. Increase molybdenum levels excessively and there may be an effect on copper, leading to retarded growth and a reduction in hemoglobin production. An excess of phosphorus in the diet can curb iron absorption.

In short, an excess of some one nutrient can interfere with the activity of one or more other nutrients.

Ideally, complete nutrition should be supplied by the seven major food groups.

THE BASIC SEVEN, NOT FOUR

Although foods can properly be classified into seven groups, what has long been promoted is the Basic Four grouping. People have been exhorted to use each day foods selected from each of the four groups: meat (for protein); milk (for calcium); fruits and vegetables (for vitamins and minerals); and breads and cereals (for energy).

But there are shortcomings to that oversimplified set of groups. Are all fruits and vegetables alike? Hardly. Consider vitamin A content, for example. While a mango contains 8,000 international units of the vitamin and an apricot contains 5,000, a banana has 400, an orange 290, and an apple only 120. As for vitamin C, an orange, with 75 milligrams of C, is fine, and a mango has a useful 55 milligrams, but an apricot, an apple, and a banana hardly have enough to help avoid scurvy.

The "protein group" idea misleads many people into thinking that cereals furnish no protein when, in fact, they are the major source throughout the world. And the "energy group" distinction has been criticized because it suggests to many people that all foods in it are much like sugar in contributing calories and very little if anything more.

The Basic Four concept lumps together foods that are nutritionally different and cannot be substituted for each other. Even if you followed it devotedly, you could still be deficient in some vitamins and in other nutrients.

Far more pertinent to complete nutrition is the use of a seven-group daily food guide:

1. Milk or milk products.
2. Meat, fish, poultry, eggs, nuts, dried beans, and peas.
3. Green, yellow, and leafy vegetables.
4. Citrus fruits, tomatoes, raw cabbage, and salad greens.
5. Noncitrus fruits, potatoes, and other vegetables not included in group 3.
6. Bread, cereals, and pasta.
7. Butter, margarine, or vegetable oil.

Milk or milk products include cottage cheese, yogurt, cheeses, and ice cream, and contribute calcium, vitamins B_2, B_{12}, and A, many minerals (but not iron), and protein. Low fat milk can be substituted for whole milk.

Meat, fish, poultry, and the other foods in group 2 contain large quantities of protein. Fish and poultry have less fat than most meats. Eggs contain virtually all vitamins and minerals but large amounts of cholesterol. Liver is rich in iron and vitamin A but also cholesterol.

Green, yellow, and leafy vegetables—excellent sources of minerals and A, B, and E vitamins—include spinach, kale, Swiss chard, watercress, collard, mustard and turnip (the greens), and carrots, pumpkin, squash of various types, and yams (the yellows).

Citrus fruits, tomatoes, raw cabbage, and salad greens contribute vitamin C. Lettuce, cabbage, and salad greens provide somewhat less of the vitamin than do tomatoes, oranges, grapefruit, tangerines, and other citrus fruits.

Potatoes and other vegetables and fruits that include broccoli, Brussels sprouts, green peppers, cauliflower, berries, cherries, melons, and peaches contribute vitamin C, minerals, some protein, and energy.

Bread, cereals, and pasta provide proteins, iron, and B vitamins as well as carbohydrates. They help fill energy requirements. Enriched flour and cornmeal offer vitamins B_1 and B_2, niacin, and iron. And whole-grain flour, bread, and brown rice contain other B vitamins, minerals, and desirable dietary fiber.

Butter, fortified margarine, and vegetable oil provide vitamin A as well as calories.

Anyone getting at least one food from each of the seven major food groups each day could be eating a well-balanced diet and, if varied choices were made from each group, the likelihood of getting everything needed in adequate and well-proportioned amounts would be increased.

But there can be problems.

THE TWENTY PARTIALS, NOT "THREE SQUARES"

If the research had not been quite serious, the results could seem unbelievable. It concerned differences between how people think they eat and how they actually eat (and was reported in 1974 to an American Medical Association special symposium on nutrition after being carried out by a team of investigators under the direction of Dr. Paul A. Fine, psychological consultant to many major food companies).

It showed that the typical American mother, asked to describe her family's eating pattern, will reply that it is the traditional three squares a day, with after-school snacks for the children. But when Fine's investigators asked housewives to record actual consumption as it happened, the eating pattern was indeed something else again.

Three out of four families do not eat breakfast together and many eat no breakfast at all, and as for the hallowed evening meal together, it can take place "as seldom as three days a week or less" and may often be as brief as twenty minutes.

Snacking is the pattern from early morning to bedtime, and even then it does not end. "People cannot sleep—they are restless—they are hungry. They get up and raid the leftovers they would not eat at dinner."

Which makes for an average of about twenty "food contacts" a day in the family instead of three squares. The "American mainstream," Fine reported, feeds on "Oreos, peanut butter, Crisco, TV dinners, cake mix, macaroni and cheese, Pepsi and Coke, pizzas, Jell-O, hamburgers, Rice-a-Roni, Spaghetti-O's, pork and beans, catsup and instant coffee."

Not long after that symposium, the *New York Times* reported that recent meetings of nutritionists have been marked by an air of defeatism; that "the plague of munchies is new"; that it was something of a "remarkable understatement" when at one meeting Professor Paul A. LaChance of Rutgers University observed that "currently, the food industry is catering to the American way of life but not to the 'betterment' of the consumer. . . . Can the situation be improved without necessitating radical changes in food habits?"

The *Times* despaired of such radical changes: "The nutritionists and government agencies are collaborating with the industry to 'fortify' the munchies with the minerals and vitamins now missing from the American diet. This gives manufacturers an additional selling pitch for junk foods; appealing to the guilt complex of the mainstream mother, they can tell her that these wafers or slices or bars contain 'all the vitamins and minerals required.' "

Unfortunately, that may not be true at all—for there is no guarantee whatever that at the present time all the essential vitamins and minerals present in natural foods are known, and many investigators are virtually certain that more remain to be discovered.

Nor has the record of the food processors been admirable in restoring to foodstuffs what is processed out of them.

THE PROCESSED OUT AND UNREPLACED

We eat very little in the way of whole grains today; some of us get none at all. We eat breads, rolls, pastas, and a wide variety of cakes and confections made of highly refined flour.

The refining of flour removes 80 percent of the zinc and iron, 88 percent of the manganese, and 62 percent of the molybdenum that is present in whole wheat. It removes other minerals and many vitamins.

It also removes the dietary fiber, which is something much more than just mere roughage, and now (as we will see in the next chapter) is finally being recognized as essential, as much as vitamins and minerals.

Yet, flour "enrichment" has been and remains today a very partial kind of restoration of what has been removed from flour; out of the many elements removed in processing, enrichment is largely limited to putting back just four: iron and the vitamins B_1, B_2, and B_3.

GUIDELINES ON CONSERVING NUTRIENTS

Vegetables and fruits. Wash them quickly; do not soak; do not overdo peeling but cook them whole, with skins on, whenever possible. Peeling and slicing causes as much as a 50 percent loss of vitamin C.

Avoid thawing frozen vegetables and fruits until you are immediately ready to cook them, or they lose nutrients. Short storage of fresh fruits and vegetables before preparing and serving is also mandatory.

Do not drain the liquid from canned vegetables; it contains 40 percent of the vitamin C, as much as a third of B_1 and B_2; cook with it and save what is left for soups and sauces. Remember, too, that as much as half the vitamins in a can of fruit are in the liquid.

Be skimpy in trimming such leafy vegetables as lettuce and cabbage; nutrient concentration is greatest in outer rather than inner leaves.

Do not overcook frozen vegetables; they are already parboiled. The same for canned goods; just heat and serve.

Drop fruits and vegetables into already boiling water (at high temperature—because of the effect of an enzyme system in the foods—there is less destruction of vitamin C), cover, bring to boil again, and cook only until firm and tender. Better yet, use a steamer so vegetables don't soak in water.

Do not use baking soda in cooking yellow or green vegetables; it destroys vitamin B_1.

Meats. The higher the temperature in cooking, the greater not only the shrinking and drying but also the loss of nutrients. Cook at moderate temperatures—300 to 350 degrees—and do not overcook. That includes pork which, because of the risk of trichinosis, many people "cook to death." Trichinae are destroyed at 140 degrees and pork cooked at 325 degrees for 30 minutes a pound is safe—and also more nutritious.

Roasting and broiling are the best ways of cooking meat from the standpoint of nutrient retention, and in broiling, in addition, much of the fat drips off and can be discarded. Frying may actually double the calorie count.

Fish and shellfish. Broil or bake fish at 400 degrees, leaving on the skin (and even head and tail until you serve, if you are cooking a whole fish) to prevent loss of juices and nutrients.

Steam lobsters and crabs in their shells to help preserve nutrient content. An exception is shrimp, which can be shelled since cooking time is only three to five minutes, minimizing nutrient loss.

Cereals and pasta. Simmer rice, barley, and other cereals in no more than about twice as much water as cereal. Cook pasta in already boiling water, drain, and serve.

NUTRITIONAL INSURANCE

Vitamin supplements are in widespread use. Are they necessary? And if so, are the types used adequate—or even rational?

Theoretically, it should be possible to get all the nutrients one needs in a balanced and varied diet.

But if it is possible, it is not always easy in an age of snacking behavior and of convenience foods in which vitamins and other nutrients have been processed out.

Which is why large numbers of people on their own, and an apparently increasing number of physicians, consider that supplementation of the diet is desirable in many cases.

But supplementation has to be understood for what it is intended to do—make up for inadequacies—and what it cannot do. And choosing the supplement needs care.

Micronutrient supplements do not—cannot—take the place of food. They are no real substitutes for a balanced, varied diet. They do not, of course, contain any, let alone a balance, of the necessary proteins, fats, and carbohydrates. Nor can they contain, ipso facto, any of the still-unknown vital nutrients that may be present naturally in foodstuffs.

The best vitamin-mineral preparation available today may still be as basically unsophisticated and inadequate as has been the "enrichment" programs for foods first devised several decades ago.

Nevertheless, some surveys have shown that more than 60 million Americans believe supplements are necessary and about 49 million use them regularly.

Even if they are using them as supplements rather than substitutes, a large proportion of users, however, could well be getting considerably less than they are hoping for. In a check of a thousand vitamin preparations, the American Medical Association's Council on Foods and Nutrition found only seven that could be considered rational.

In a new book, *Physicians' Handbook of Nutritional Science*, published in 1975 as a guide for the medical profession, Dr. Roger Williams considers the problem of what should properly be in a supplement designed to provide "nutritional insurance" for most people.

He notes that one of the most widely used present-day supplements, its name almost a household word, and quite representative of many other widely used supplements, contains nine vitamins. But it contains nothing at all of vitamin E, vitamin K, biotin, and folic acid, and no consideration is given to minerals or trace elements.

"Nutritional insurance," writes Williams, "cannot be perfect, but if it is to be used, it should be as comprehensive as feasible."

He also observes that formulating a good "nutritional insurance" supplement is no simple matter, "and it is a matter of judgment just which of the manageable nutrients are most likely to be deficient in the diets of the general population and what amounts of each should be supplied."

In the *Handbook*, based on a career lifetime of research as well as the findings of many other researchers, Williams suggests a vitamin formulation and a mineral formulation to be used daily by those who need insurance. "These formulations," he emphasizes, "are subject to change when new information becomes available. No infallibility is claimed."

By checking the ingredients listed on the labels of various vitamin and mineral preparations readily available on the market, you may be able to combine several to approximate the Williams's formulations. At least one pharmaceutical firm in California has brought out a "Vitamin and Mineral

Insurance Formula" so patterned along the lines of Williams's suggestions that three tablets a day provide the quantities of all recommended ingredients. Other similar preparations may become available and, if you wish, your druggist may obtain one of them for you.

But, remember, no supplement can replace—nor may it be inevitably essential in the presence of—a balanced and varied diet.

Williams's suggested formulations are:

VITAMINS

Vitamin A	7,500 units
Vitamin D	400 units
Vitamin E	40 units
Vitamin K (menadione)	2 milligrams
Vitamin C (ascorbic acid)	250 milligrams
Thiamine	2 milligrams
Riboflavin	2 milligrams
Vitamin B_6	3 milligrams
Vitamin B_{12}	9 micrograms
Niacinamide	20 milligrams
Pantothenic acid	15 milligrams
Biotin	0.3 milligram
Choline	250 milligrams
Inositol	250 milligrams
P-aminobenzoic acid	30 milligrams
Rutin	200 milligrams

MINERALS

Calcium	250 milligrams
Phosphate	750 milligrams (equivalent to 250 milligrams phosphorus)
Magnesium	200 milligrams
Iron	15 milligrams
Zinc	15 milligrams
Copper	2 milligrams
Iodine	0.15 milligram

MINERALS

Manganese	5 milligrams
Molybdenum	0.1 milligram
Chromium	1 milligram
Selenium	0.02 milligram
Cobalt	0.01 milligram

Although primarily meant for adults, the suggested vitamin and mineral supplements can be used without change for teen-agers as well, Williams says. For younger children, the amounts can be halved and for very young children they can be reduced to one-third the adult quantities.

7 The fiber finding

THE GERMANS like to say *Der Mensch ist was er isst*—Man is what he eats.

Nature over the course of millions of years—in trial and error, through the evolutionary process of natural selection—matched complex body chemistry to slowly changing diet.

But in the last hundred years or less—hardly any time at all in the evolutionary scale—one of the most drastic of all food alterations has taken place. What our grandparents called roughage, or bulk, has largely disappeared from the diet in the United States and many Western countries: To an astonishing degree, refined cereals have replaced the unrefined, and our bread, cakes, pastas, and everything else made from wheat, rice, and maize have become technological products.

Mounting evidence suggests that it may be because of this, to no small extent, that colorectal cancer—cancer of the colon and rectum—has been increasing rapidly and now is the most common major cancer in the United States, topping in incidence both lung and breast cancer, and second only to lung cancer in deadliness.

Moreover, the evidence suggests that it might well be the dearth of fiber in the modern Western diet that is largely responsible for other common intestinal problems—including appendicitis, constipation, polyps, spastic colon, and hiatus hernia—that are almost unknown in areas of the world not yet using our Westernized diet. There are even indications that a significant role in heart disease and obesity may have to be assigned to our smooth, very largely fiber-free diet.

Only in the seventies has any real attention been focused on dietary fiber—long neglected because it has been assumed to be totally unnecessary: inert, undigested, and without nutritional or any other value.

Curiously, dietary fiber is more than roughage; in fact, it is not roughage at all; and although it may have no nutritional value and is not even absorbed from the human gut, it has much to do with the environment of the gut and through that can exert profound influences even outside the gut.

To a very great extent, we owe our new insights into the importance of fiber to a pioneering cluster of scientists in England, many of them physicians with experience as medical missionaries in Africa where they could see what Western doctors ordinarily are not privileged to see: a dearth of many of the most troublesome and even dread diseases of Western civilization. A leader has been Denis Burkitt, British surgeon, mission surgeon, discoverer and prime treater of a previously mysterious cancer that bears his name (Burkitt lymphoma), Fellow of the Royal Society, Britain's select honors group; winner of awards from many countries, including America's highest medical honor, the Lasker Award; and now a member of the British Medical Research Council. Burkitt and his British Fiber Gang, as it has sometimes been called, have of late swollen to become a worldwide Fiber Gang of distinguished researchers of many disciplines, including medicine, physiology, and nutrition.

A SEARCH FOR CULPRITS

Many possible causes have been considered for colorectal cancer. Certainly, heredity, endowing some people with a proneness, could be involved, as it is in many other diseases. A failure of the immune system might be influential, for it is that system in the body that is designed to help protect us not only against infectious agents but also against the almost routine development—and, with the immune system's help, quick disposal—of abnormal cells that could become malignant.

But clearly environmental factors had to be significant. Colorectal cancer is not universally common. Its incidence is highest in developed countries, lowest in the underdeveloped. While the American incidence rate runs to 51.8 cases per 100,000 population, it is only 3.5 per 100,000 in Kampala, Uganda. All told, colorectal cancer accounts for only 2 percent of all malignancies in Africa but it accounts in Great Britain for 12.5 percent and in Connecticut (with the world's highest rate) for 14.7 percent.

Noteworthy, too, is the fact that the ancestors of American blacks came from villages where even now there is virtually no colorectal cancer, so there is hardly a hereditary propensity. Yet, today's American blacks are fully as prone to the disease as are whites.

Nor is it only a matter of colorectal cancer. Wherever the incidence of that disease is low, so is the incidence of other bowel disorders such as appendicitis, polyps, ulcerative colitis, diverticular disease, and hemorrhoids. And there is the currently observable phenomenon that Denis Burkitt sums up: "In Uganda, you do not get appendicitis if you do not speak English." It holds for other parts of Africa: Among Africans who move from native villages and traditional diets to urban areas and modern Westernized diets, colorectal cancer and all other bowel disorders begin to zoom up.

WHICH DIETARY FACTOR

If it is a dietary factor that is involved, several could be blamed and have, in fact, come under suspicion.

Beef consumption? It has been noted that the Scottish death rate from colorectal cancer is 19 percent higher than for the rest of Great Britain and the Scots eat 19 percent more beef. Japanese in Hawaii have a higher colorectal cancer death rate than Japanese at home, and the switch from the traditional vegetable-and-fish-heavy Japanese diet to a diet heavy in beef has been suspect.

Fat consumption? Rather than beef, it is the fat in beef and the fat in other meats, the high content of fat in the Western diet, which some investigators think may be a culprit.

For Burkitt and many other researchers now, refined cereals seem far more likely to be responsible.

In rural Africa a major portion of the diet is made up of coarsely ground grains, very commonly lightly processed corn (maize). Such grains are high in fiber. It is present naturally and has not been milled out. Typically, a rural African consumes about twenty-five grams of maize and other cereal fiber a day. But an urban African now gets only about five grams—still more than what an average American gets.

Since about 1880, in less than a century, American and European consumption of whole-wheat flour and the fiber contained in it has dropped to a fifth of what it was and, according to some estimates, to only one-tenth.

It was about 1880 that modern roller mills for the milling of flour came into use. To be sure, the refining of flour from cereal grains goes back a long way. The early Egyptians used it. The aim was to remove as much as possible of the outer coat of the wheat kernel in order to get a white flour that could be made into bread or cake with a smoother taste than could be obtained from coarse whole flour.

In a process called bolting, flour was filtered through cloth, and because of the extra labor cost, the resulting white flour was usually only for the wealthy; the poor ate unrefined grain.

But with the roller mill, not only could flour be more highly refined; the cost of refining came way down. Refined flour, and the products made with it, became available to everyone. The bran and the germ that the mills extracted became offal to be fed to animals, which thrived on it.

Not until about 1920 was it even realized that most of the vitamins and minerals were to be found in the so-called offal.

Actually, the wheat grain is a tiny seed growing in clusters at the top of its stalk. And the seed is much like an egg. Left alone, the seed will grow into a new plant just as an egg will grow into a chicken. And like an egg, the grain has three main parts. There is the bran, the hard outer shell, which serves as protection for the softer inside and is rich in vitamins and minerals. There is, secondly, the white of the seed—the endosperm— which is largely protein and starch. Finally, there is the germ of the seed which, like the yolk of an egg, is a storehouse of nutrients, especially vitamin B_1, minerals, and important fatty acids.

Refining involves removal of parts of the seed as the wheat grain is crushed to a fine flour. Different types of flour are produced according to the extent to which the various parts of the grain are retained. Whole-meal flour has a 100 percent extraction rate, meaning that it contains all the ground grain, nothing removed. White flour today is of 70 to 72 percent extraction, the endosperm being retained while the germ and bran are removed.

When, some fifty years ago, there dawned the realization of the loss of nutrients with loss of the germ and bran, "enrichment" programs were begun. But the knowledge of what was lost was incomplete. Then, and even now, flour and bread could be considered "enriched" if thiamine (B_1), riboflavin (B_2), niacin (B_3), and iron were restored. Much more recently has come the realization—even if without a concerted action to do anything about it—that much more was lost in refining: vitamin A, vitamin B_6, the vitamin folic acid, and such minerals as calcium, magnesium, and zinc.

Now it is fiber's turn. Only very recently has come the realization of the importance of the loss of fiber involved in the refining of flour.

Of the diseases that plague us today, many are relatively new and have arisen or become common only since the introduction of modern refining techniques.

Coronary heart disease, for example, was considered a rarity by Sir William Osler in 1910 and was still newsworthy in 1925 when a British physician, Sir John McNee, described with some excitement two cases of this "rare condition" he had seen in the United States. Appendicitis was first described earlier in the nineteenth century but appeared to become common after 1880. Diverticular disease has become a major problem only in the last fifty years, hiatus hernia only in the last thirty years. Hemorrhoids and tumors of the colon also appear to be recent developments. So, too, gallbladder disease, which has increased 350 percent in the records of the Bristol Royal Infirmary in England.

In wartime the incidence of many of these diseases dipped noticeably. To make wheat supplies go further, particularly in England, extraction rates were increased. The more bran and germ left in the flour—no matter that it was not so white and smooth anymore—the more bread and other products to be gotten from a given quantity of wheat. In England a study has shown a steady rise in deaths from diverticular disease and heart disease until the start of World War II in 1939, then a check in the deaths, followed by rising patterns again when white bread later returned to the market.

WHY SHOULD FIBER MAKE A DIFFERENCE?

Many centuries ago, Hippocrates, the father of medicine, admonished the citizens of Athens that it was essential that they pass large bulky motions after every meal and that to ensure this they had to eat abundantly of whole-meal bread, vegetables, and fruits.

Hippocrates was intuitively right. We now know that dietary fiber is important, among other things, because it very significantly affects the size of stools, the transit time—the time required for material to move through and out of the gastrointestinal tract—and even the bacterial environment of the bowel.

Burkitt and other investigators, collecting stools from primitive people and comparing them with those from economically privileged groups, discovered striking differences. The stool weights of rural Africans commonly ranged up to 150, 250, and 350 grams—three times the weights for whites.

By having subjects swallow with their meals dyes or special plastic-coated tablets that served as markers, the progress of an individual meal through the GI tract could be followed and the transit time determined. In native Africans, transit time was as little as one-third that for whites.

The repeated studies clearly demonstrated that on a diet low in fiber, stool bulk is significantly reduced and transit time significantly lengthened.

And there were differences in the gut flora—the bacterial populations of the bowel. Some bacteria can convert bile salts normally entering the intestinal tract into a known cancer-provoking chemical, deoxycholic acid. Few such bacteria were present in African stools; many such were found in British and American stools.

The difference in incidence—a high rate of colorectal cancer in Americans and the British, a low rate in native Africans—was a fact. The three differences—in stool bulk, transit time, and bacterial populations—offered an explanation.

For the higher the concentration of a cancer provocateur and the longer the time it has in which to act, the more likely it is to do harm. And in Westerners on a low fiber diet, the provocateur is not only present in greater quantities, its concentration is greater as well because the stools are smaller—and, because of the slower transit time, it is held in contact with the intestinal lining longer.

Is lack of cereal fiber the only factor in colorectal cancer? No investigator claims that. But it does have to be considered seriously. And it warrants very serious consideration as a significant factor in other gastrointestinal diseases which, as with colorectal cancer, are rare among primitive Africans but common in the West.

FIBER LACK AND OTHER GASTROINTESTINAL DISORDERS

Constipation and diarrhea. The stools, small, hard, lacking in bulk; the slow movement of them; the accumulation of gas—these are the characteristics of constipation and they are also characteristic of a low fiber diet. And, although there is still far too much recourse in the West to such measures as laxatives and purgatives for the treatment of constipation, it has been known for years that adding fiber to the diet—often in the form of a bran cereal for breakfast—is a simple, effective measure.

To demonstrate this scientifically, a study was carried out with a group of schoolboys, aged fifteen to nineteen years, at an English boarding school, and with adult members of the school staff. When measurements were made while the subjects were on the normal school diet that included white bread, stool weights were as low as 39 grams and the mean transit time was 64.5 hours, better than 2 1/2 days; these were small, slow-moving stools. Within three weeks after a switch to an average of two slices of whole-meal bread instead of white and the addition of two heaping dessertspoonfuls of unprocessed miller's bran daily, transit times were shortened 29 percent and stool weights increased by 21 percent.

As a report in the British medical journal, *The Lancet*, noted: "This simple expedient [of restoring fiber to the diet] might well do more to 'keep the doctor away' than the proverbial apple."

Even as that study was being carried out, another at the Bristol Royal Infirmary in England was producing unexpected results. Not surprisingly, the Bristol investigators found that adding fiber to the diet helped people with constipation. But they were surprised to discover that the addition helped others with nonspecific diarrhea, diarrhea not associated with any specific infection or disease.

They worked with a group of otherwise healthy people bothered by either constipation or nonspecific diarrhea. All were eating the usual low fiber foods. Transit times were measured and then all received either a high fiber diet containing whole-meal bread or continued on their usual diet but with the addition of about thirty grams, approximately one ounce, of separated, unprocessed bran a day.

As expected, the bran or high fiber diet reduced transit times, which were initially three days or even longer, benefiting the constipated. But the bran or the diet also slowed the initially rapid one-day transit time in the patients with diarrhea.

It came to this: With the addition of fiber, most subjects had a two-day transit time whether their initial transit time had been either slow or fast. That suggested that somehow dietary fiber normalizes bowel behavior and that foodstuffs from which fiber is removed, such as white flour, induce abnormal bowel behavior.

Appendicitis. What could dietary fiber deficiency have to do with appendicitis? Man carries such vestiges of his prehuman past as body hair, wisdom teeth, muscles that move his ears, and the vermiform appendix. The appendix, you will recall, is a blind alley appended to the large intestine. Any stool material that flows into the appendix normally is dumped right back into the mainstream.

Constipation produces increased pressures in the bowel. The pressures affect the wall of the appendix. As far back as the 1930s, American studies had demonstrated that sustained pressures even for as little as six hours brought about changes in the wall.

Appendicitis occurs when bowel bacteria multiply in the appendix, invading the lining, producing infection and inflammation. A low fiber diet can lead to constipation, increased pressures in the colon and increased pressures in the appendix, which could damage the appendix lining, setting it up for ready invasion by bacteria.

Diverticular disease. This, too, stems from abnormally increased pressures in the colon. A diverticulum—from the Latin for "to turn aside"—is an outpouching, or sac, protruding outward from the intestinal lining into the intestinal wall. There may be scores, even hundreds of diverticula—benign at the start and sometimes remaining so. But the pouches can trap feces, and about 20 percent of those with diverticula develop inflammation, or diverticulitis, which may produce pain in the lower left abdomen, nausea, vomiting, distention, chills, and fever. Medical treatment often helps but surgery sometimes is required.

Once patients with diverticular disease were placed on low fiber, no roughage diets with the idea that such diets would be beneficial. They were not and many physicians abandoned them, telling patients to eat as they chose.

Today, there has been a 180-degree turnaround, and high fiber diets are being prescribed for those with diverticular disease and as a likely means of avoiding it in others.

The man who did more than anyone else to change the whole outlook for diverticular disease is Neil Painter, a surgeon at Manor House Hospital in London. Earlier, in pioneering work at Cambridge University, Painter had measured colonic pressures in diverticular disease and coupled the pressure measurements with X-ray movies of the colon. With the combination of the two, he could establish that the pressures were abnormally high and also that they occurred as the walls of the colon had to clamp down hard in efforts to move along the small, hard stools of diverticular disease patients who commonly had long histories of constipation. And it was this high-pressure clamping down that pushed hard on the lining of the colon so that eventually the lining pushed through the muscular wall of the colon, forming more pouches.

Then in 1967 Painter began a study that lasted through 1971. Seventy diverticular disease patients were put on a high fiber diet. They ate bran cereal, porridge, whole-meal bread, fruits, and vegetables. They were also told to take two teaspoons of unprocessed bran three times a day.

Bowel habits changed dramatically. The formerly constipated passed soft motions regularly and easily, no longer straining at stool. And with the diet change, symptoms of diverticular disease were relieved in 88.6 percent of the patients, even in those with colic so severe that they had been considered candidates for surgery to remove the affected portion of the colon. None required surgery.

Spastic colon, irritable colon, irritable bowel syndrome. These are all names for the same very common problem, a kind of unexplained bellyache. The symptoms can be very variable: abdominal distress is common and may take the form of generalized abdominal distention, cramps, sharp, almost knifelike pains, or deep dull pain. Other common complaints include nausea, heartburn, excessive belching, constipation or diarrhea, or one alternating with the other.

In the course of his studies, Neil Painter has determined that irritable colon affects as many as 60 percent of all patients who seek help at GI clinics. And he has also determined that it is not the colon that is somehow abnormal and irritable but rather that the colon is being irritated, and that it is the lack of dietary fiber that is the irritant. Painter has reported excellent results in treating many irritable colon patients with a high fiber diet. His work has been confirmed in the United States by Dr. J. L. Piepmeyer, a United States Naval Reserve medical officer at Beaufort, North Carolina, Naval Hospital, who has reported that 88 percent of patients with irritable colon have responded within three weeks to the use of eight to ten teaspoons of bran a day.

Hiatus hernia. This is one of the most prevalent defects in the gastrointestinal tract in the Western world. It involves a defect in the diaphragm, the dome-shaped muscle that separates the chest from the abdominal cavity. The esophagus, or gullet, passes through the diaphragm. And the defect occurs at the point in the diaphragm, just above the stomach, where the esophagus passes through.

Through the defect, part of the stomach may enter the chest cavity, either intermittently or constantly. Often, a hiatus hernia produces no symptoms. But not uncommonly it is associated with reflux, an abnormal return flow of gastric juices from the stomach to the esophagus, which can produce such symptoms as heartburn and burning pain in back of the breastbone.

What does lack of dietary fiber have to do with hiatus hernia? Recent studies show that straining at stool, associated with constipation caused by lack of fiber, raises pressures within the abdomen, pressures that can exert tremendous force upward so that, after many years, the defect in the diaphragm is created as the stomach is pushed upward. The studies suggest that resort to a high fiber diet may be helpful in relieving symptoms of hiatus hernia and could well help to prevent its development.

Hemorrhoids, varicose veins, and deep vein thrombosis. All three of these conditions—common in Western countries but rare among native Africans—can be related to lack of dietary fiber, the work of Denis Burkitt indicates.

Varicose veins and hemorrhoids are both conditions in which veins become dilated and engorged, in the one case in the legs and in the other inside or just outside the rectum.

Deep vein thrombosis is the grave problem. A blood clot, or thrombus, forms in a deep vein in the leg. As it increases in size, it may obstruct the vein, causing swelling, pain, or tenderness. Eventually, the clot may stop growing, become firmly attached to the vein wall and, over a period of months, the body may respond to the vein blockage by forming new vessel pathways to bypass the blocked area.

But a major risk is that at some point during the time when the clot is not firmly attached to the vein wall it may break loose, travel in the bloodstream to end up lodged in and blocking a major lung vessel. Then, it is a pulmonary embolism that can kill and does kill thousands annually.

Deep vein thrombosis, an American study has shown, occurs in 20 to 30 percent of all patients undergoing surgery and is no less common in severe medical illness.

Many explanations have been proposed for the three conditions. For example, man's erect posture has been blamed for varicose veins since the condition occurs only in humans. Other proposed causes have included hereditary weakness in vein walls or valves, prolonged standing, pregnancy, and constrictive clothing. Hemorrhoids, too, have been attributed to erect posture, heredity, prolonged standing, and even horseback riding.

But such explanations do not explain at all why African villagers rarely get the conditions. The recent work of Burkitt and others suggests that what can explain varicose veins and hemorrhoids in Westerners and their virtual absence in African villagers is the dietary difference and the resulting straining at stool in Westerners. The straining with its increased pressures can dilate both the veins about the rectum and the superficial veins in the legs. The straining also can produce abnormal changes in the deeper veins in the legs, predisposing them to cause blood to stagnate and clots to form when there is immobilization during serious illness or surgery.

Is there any evidence that a high fiber diet can help in treating or preventing the three conditions? Recently, many patients have discovered that a high fiber diet helps to relieve hemorrhoids. And in recent months, a number of hospitals in England have begun to feed their patients high fiber diets and are reporting that the prevalence of deep vein thrombosis has been greatly reduced.

HEART DISEASE

Cholesterol, of course, has been associated with heart disease. The higher the blood cholesterol levels, the higher the risk of coronary artherosclerosis, which all too commonly leads to heart attacks.

A relationship between blood cholesterol levels and fiber in the diet has been uncovered by many investigators: the more fiber, the lower the cholesterol concentration.

In investigations supported by the British Heart Association, Dr. Hugh Trowell, formerly consultant physician to the Ugandan government, has determined that in all Africans remaining on native diets with high dietary fiber intakes the blood cholesterol levels are low and coronary heart disease uncommon—but that among Africans in urban areas adopting Western patterns of living and diet, both the cholesterol levels and incidence of coronary heart disease increase.

In many animal studies, the addition of fiber to the diet has been shown to reduce serum cholesterol. Fed a cholesterol-rich diet but also given fiber-rich alfalfa at the same time, rabbits have been protected from increased blood cholesterol levels.

Some studies suggest similar protection in man. In an Indian study, adding 156 grams of butter to the diet led to elevated cholesterol levels in the blood but when fiber was also added, the cholesterol levels fell by 20 percent. In a Netherlands study, when men who had been eating about 10 ounces of bread daily were given, as replacement for some of the bread, about 5 ounces of rolled oats, a rich fiber source, the mean serum cholesterol level fell from 258 to 226.

In a study at the Bristol Royal Infirmary in England, when bran was fed to a group of subjects, aged thirty-six to sixty-three, there were significant declines in serum triglycerides, blood fats that have been linked along with cholesterol to coronary heart disease.

OBESITY

In 1973 in the *Lancet*, Dr. Kenneth W. Heaton of the University of Bristol and the Bristol Royal Infirmary set out a totally new explanation of why obesity is so common in modern civilization.

Many explanations have been offered in the past—genetic predisposition, emotional problems, glandular disorders, and, of course, just plain eating abnormal amounts of food.

The problem could well be, Heaton proposed, simply intake of an abnormal *type* of food.

Although carbohydrates are widely considered to be fattening and their restriction is an integral part of almost all weight-reducing diets, in primitive societies carbohydrate intake is much greater than in the West and obesity is rare.

If this seems paradoxical, it isn't at all, Heaton noted, when it is realized that in primitive societies, unlike sophisticated societies, carbohydrates are not eaten in refined form but rather in unrefined, with much or all the fiber intact, as in home-pounded rice, coarsely sieved maize, and unprocessed bananas and plantains.

Fiber, Heaton reported, is a natural obstacle to obesity because it is a natural obstacle to excessive nutrition. Fiber is not absorbed by the body; it provides no calories. And to the extent that fiber is eaten, other nutrients with absorbable calories are displaced from the diet.

Fiber also requires chewing, which slows down food intake. And the chewing, beyond its slowing effect, has another that helps to limit intake. Chewing, as we have seen, promotes increased secretion of saliva in the mouth and gastric juice in the stomach; and the saliva joins the gastric juice and helps to distend the stomach, promoting a feeling of fullness, or satiety.

Moreover, fiber tends to cut down a bit on the absorptive efficiency of the small intestine so that some of the caloric energy that otherwise would be absorbed goes into the stool instead. In one study in Bristol, a group of young women received three different diets, one very low in fiber, the second moderate, the third high in fiber. As the amount of fiber went up, so did excretion of fat and energy, and energy in the stool is not energy-convertible-to-fat in the body.

"Overnutrition," says Heaton, "is not normally due to overeating, to eating too much food. It is due to getting too much out of food. It is due to satisfying a normal appetite with food that has an artificially high energy/satiety ratio. In practice, this means refined carbohydrate.

"Unrefined carbohydrate foods," he goes on, "should be nonfattening, since their energy/satiety ratio has not been tampered with. Bread should be nonfattening if it is whole-meal bread. [It is hard to believe that grass seeds, that is, wheat grains, are fattening!] Whole-meal flour contains 9 percent fewer calories per gram than white flour and it is 4 percent less absorbed. May I, therefore, make a plea to include whole-meal bread routinely in weight-reducing diets?"

ON GIVING YOURSELF ENOUGH FIBER

If dietary fiber eventually were proved to be valuable for only a few problems (treating and preventing constipation and diverticular disease, for which the evidence seems virtually conclusive) and perhaps less valuable or even of little value in combating some of the other problems (obesity, appendicitis, colorectal cancer, hiatus hernia, varicose veins, hemorrhoids, deep vein thrombosis, heart disease, for which the evidence is highly suggestive if not yet proved conclusive), obviously returning dietary fiber to the diet would be a wise step.

One way to increase the fiber in your diet is to eat more vegetables and fruits. There is, naturally, no fiber in meat, fish, fats, milk, sugar, or alcoholic drinks. But vegetables and fruits do contain varying amounts.

Among vegetables and fruits that are particularly useful because of their high dietary fiber content are mango, carrot, apple, Brussels sprouts, eggplant, spring cabbage, corn, orange, pear, green bean, lettuce, winter cabbage, pea, onion, celery, cucumber, broad beans, tomato, cauliflower, banana, rhubarb, old and new potato, and turnip.

As much as possible, try to eat these and other kinds of fruits and vegetables in generous amounts—preferably raw or cooked only lightly.

Seeds such as whole sesame seeds and sunflower seeds along with seed-filled berries such as raspberries, blackberries, and loganberries contain high dietary fiber.

Some but far from all breakfast cereals are fiber rich. You can choose from a number of high fiber cereals: oatmeal, the old-fashioned, slow-cooking kind, not the "instant"; whole-grain wheat cereals designed to be cooked; shredded wheat; cereals labeled as being all bran or made up of a goodly percentage of bran.

An important step is to substitute bread made from whole wheat or whole rye flour (100 percent extraction) in place of white bread. Because many brown breads are not whole meal, do not depend upon color alone but establish from the labeling or by inquiry (from the manufacturer if necessary) that the bread is, in fact, made from whole wheat or whole rye flour.

Where, in the kitchen, you now use white flour and products made with it, use instead as much as possible whole-meal flour—whole wheat or whole rye of 100 percent extraction. And here again make certain from the labeling or by inquiry that it is indeed 100 percent extraction.

If you are inclined to do so, you can make your own whole-meal bread, biscuits, and cakes using whole-meal flour. Similarly, you can make waffles, griddle cakes, and French toast with whole-grain products. And they lend themselves to use in producing pizzas, tortillas, and the shells for enchiladas and tacos.

You can also use whole-meal flour instead of refined flour or corn-starch for thickening sauces and stews, whole-grain bread or breadcrumbs in many dishes—for example, for preparing ground beef for meat loaf, hamburgers, and German meatballs; in chicken, veal, and lamb patties; and in such other dishes as stuffed cabbage, sauerkraut balls, and pork balls in tomato sauce.

Use brown unpolished rice where you can; it retains its bran coat and full complement of vitamins and minerals. Use whole-meal spaghetti and macaroni in place of the routine kind; if they—and brown rice as well—are not available elsewhere, they may be found in health food stores.

You may be inclined to add unprocessed bran to your diet. This is the bran removed during the milling of refined flour, also available in health food stores when not available elsewhere.

Unprocessed bran, a couple of teaspoons at a time, can be added to cereals, soups, sauces, puddings, or can be taken dry and washed down with a glass of water or fruit juice. It can also be added to whole-meal flour and used in baking.

Because of considerable publicity, something of a mystique has grown up about bran. It is no panacea. It does help to restore fiber to the diet. But it is no substitute for the restoration of fiber—intact, as it occurs na-turally—in cereals, flours, breads, fruits, and vegetables. It is when it is part of the original food that dietary fiber is most effective in contributing to the health of the digestive tract and to combating obesity and possibly diseases outside the digestive tract such as coronary heart disease.

8

Is it true what they say about cholesterol? sugar? coffee? salt? milk?

ONE OF the great unsolved riddles of medicine is the cause of coronary heart disease. Hypotheses and theories, however, are numerous and not without consequences.

Somewhat tongue in cheek, an editorial entitled "The Martyred Meal" appeared not long ago in the *Journal of the American Medical Association.*

Before diet became suspect as a possible cause of coronary heart disease, it noted, "breakfast was a meal of invigorating abundance. Cream-drenched cereal, buttered toast, eggs, coffee, and, for those to whom the laws of Moses or strictures of Mahomet did not apply, bacon or ham—all were parts of a harmonious whole that might have inspired a memorable 'still life.'

"The picture underwent drastic changes. These began more than a decade ago when evidence from different countries pointed to an association between fat consumption and mortality from coronary disease. The changes continued with each new 'discovery' in the realm of food-coronary interrelationship, and various components of the breakfast ensemble disappeared one by one.

"First to go was the egg, its very color betraying the offending cholesterol. Next went the fatty bacon and lipid-laden milk products, leaving behind them the bleakness of dry toast and the drabness of black coffee.

Somewhat unexpectedly, sugar followed suit when studies by Yudkin in the United Kingdom and Kuo and Bassett in the United States deflected some attention from dietary fat to dietary sugar by suggesting that the latter is the major causative factor in the rise of blood lipid level and the increased incidence of coronary heart disease.

"Sugarless and creamless coffee—the lone survivor of the ghost town that was once breakfast—also appears to be on its way out. Paul [Oglesby] and colleagues found in their epidemiologic survey a positive association between coffee intake and incidence of coronary disease. . . .

"The traditional breakfast is out! Even the customary postprandial cigarette is a coronary suspect. All that may be left as a reminder of past glory is the morning paper habitually glanced at between bites and sips. If front page news and stock market reports are kept out of sight [emotional stress is high on the list of coronary culprits], a newspaper can still be read with impunity."

But is diet really *the* cause, or a prime cause, of coronary heart disease? If so, is cholesterol in the diet (and fats, too) the culprit? Or sugar? Or coffee? Or salt? Or, to add still another, milk, which has come in for some blame?

THE GREAT—AND CONTINUING— CHOLESTEROL CONTROVERSY

High blood cholesterol can accompany high cholesterol and high fat (especially saturated, or hard fat) intake.

European studies showed that during World War II, with reduced intake of such foods as eggs, butter, and meat, deaths from coronary heart disease were reduced. In the United States during the war there was no great change in dietary patterns and there was an increase in heart disease deaths.

Exactly what constitutes a normal blood cholesterol still is not clear. But it is generally agreed that 300 milligrams (per 100 milliliters of blood) is dangerous. In the famous Framingham study, the risk of developing heart disease tripled in people with levels about 220 and became six times as great when the level exceeded 260.

Such studies led to making blood cholesterol measurements routine in thorough physical examinations in the United States, especially for men over forty. And they led, too, to an idea so strong—that strictly controlling the intake of foods high in cholesterol and saturated fat can prevent atherosclerosis and heart attacks—that many of us, whenever we indulge in eggs, marbled steaks, oysters, lobsters, butter, and cream, do so with guilt feelings.

Although high cholesterol levels and heart disease often may be associated, and although many thousands of physicians adhere to the cholesterol theory of heart disease, a cause and effect relationship has not been definitively proved. Nor is there conclusive proof that lowering blood cholesterol by means of diet alone does in fact reduce the risk of coronary heart disease. And there is some worry among many responsible scientists that the present near-fanatical concern about and focus on such diet control—besides taking some of the pleasure out of life—may also take away from a focus on other factors.

THE MATERIAL

Though it is commonly considered a culprit, cholesterol is a vital material. From it are derived cortisone and other important hormones of the adrenal gland, sex hormones, and bile constituents needed for the digestion of fats. Moreover, cholesterol is present in every body cell and may help to regulate the transport in and out of all nutrients and waste products.

Part of the cholesterol in the body comes from food but more of it is produced in the body, and, in fact, is one of the most complex chemicals synthesized in the body.

Coronary artery disease, which leads to heart attacks, is also known as coronary atherosclerosis, *athero* meaning soft swelling and *sclerosis* meaning hardening. Deposits build up in the coronary arteries feeding the heart, reducing the blood supply to the heart muscle.

And cholesterol is included in the deposits.

But how responsible is a high level of cholesterol in the blood for the deposits? And what is the role of diet in inducing the high level and the laying down of the deposits?

There is no question that many statistical studies have shown a correlation—in general—between high blood cholesterol and high incidence of atherosclerosis.

But the pattern is not airtight.

Coronary atherosclerosis occurs, quite commonly, in men who have normal blood cholesterol levels. The blood cholesterol level does *not* continue to increase with age in men past the age of fifty, while the death rate from coronary heart disease continues to increase. Blood cholesterol levels are almost identical for men and women but the coronary heart disease rates are much different for the two sexes. There is a lack of correlation between blood cholesterol levels and the degree of atherosclerosis found at autopsy in persons dying from noncoronary heart disease.

In a study at Baylor University of 1,700 patients hospitalized for surgical treatment of atherosclerosis because of its severity, Dr. Michael De-Bakey and a research team found that eight out of ten had cholesterol levels within the normal range for Americans.

That low blood cholesterol does not necessarily protect against coronary atherosclerosis is shown by studies of Trappist monks. Trappists have a lower incidence of the disease than the general population of the same age. They live on a frugal vegetarian diet and may have much lower blood cholesterol levels than the general population or other monks. But still, with their low blood cholesterol, Trappist monks do get coronary artery disease. Moreover, a comparison of Trappists living on their usual restricted diet and Benedictine monks showed no differences in the rate of heart attacks; the Benedictines ate an ordinary diet. The heart attack rate in both groups was less than in the general population so there may be something in the way monks live that provides some protection against coronary atherosclerosis, but it does not appear to be in what they eat.

A NEW LOOK AT THOSE ANIMAL FEEDING STUDIES

Feeding studies in animals have been used to indict dietary cholesterol. But while, without question, the studies were serious and well intended, there is some question about their validity.

Dr. Mark D. Altschule of Harvard criticizes them on several grounds. For one thing, he notes, the amounts of cholesterol that must be fed to induce atherosclerosis in animals are unrealistically large and the levels to which blood cholesterol must be raised are equally unrealistic, rarely if ever found outside the laboratory.

For example, in man or dog, a cholesterol blood level of 400 is very high. But in dog-feeding experiments, the cholesterol blood level had to be raised to 4,000 before atherosclerosis developed.

Moreover, recent studies have cast new light on the atherosclerosis produced in animals by experimental cholesterol feeding. In none of the reported experiments, Dr. Altschule observes, were the large amounts of cholesterol given in the form in which cholesterol occurs naturally in foods but rather as crystalline cholesterol or as heat-dried egg-yolk powder.

The chow for the experiments was produced in batches for use over many days or weeks. Cholesterol as it normally exists in the body combined with other substances is stable; crystalline or powdered cholesterol in a bottle is not: Once exposed to air it forms a number of other compounds, some of which are injurious to artery linings.

Significantly, says Altschule, a normal artery lining allows cholesterol in the form of lipoprotein to move through in both directions equally but when the lining is damaged, the movement of cholesterol through it into the artery wall is greater than from the wall back into the bloodstream, and this unbalanced movement, once a lining is damaged, occurs even when blood cholesterol levels are normal.

And in recent studies using crystalline cholesterol or heat-dried egg-yolk powder, artery lining damage was detected within just two to three days after the start of the experiments in animals, long before blood cholesterol levels rose above normal.

To Altschule, that means that "it is not cholesterol feeding but rather the feeding of oxidized cholesterol products not normally occuring in food that produces the atherosclerosis in the test animals." And he is concerned that "the finding that dried egg yolk develops substances that damage artery linings may have some bearing on human atherosclerosis. Dried egg yolk is widely used in commercial baking of bread and in the preparation of cake mixes and dried soups. The widespread use of commercially baked products and other 'convenience' foods containing dried egg yolk may explain why populations of undeveloped countries are more prone to atherosclerosis when they achieve civilized status or move to developed areas."

AND THE MATTER OF FATS, SATURATED
AND UNSATURATED

Commonly, today, people are eating "special" margarines and distinctive vegetable salad oils and cooking oils on the theory that these are full of polyunsaturated fats (see also chapter 6)—the "good" fats as opposed to the "bad" saturated fats—and such a change in diet is good for heart health and the way to stave off coronaries.

But how valid is this?

A number of investigators very strongly question the validity and some have grave reservations about possible hazards in going overboard on unsaturated fats.

Commonly, it is supposed that vegetable fats are all desirably unsaturated while animal fats are virtually all saturated and this includes animal fats found in eggs, butter, and cheese, with some fat-oriented protagonists including the fats in meat and others not including them.

But that is not so. Cocoa butter, for example, contains the same mixture of fatty acids found in animal fats. Some vegetable fats such as coconut oil contain a fatty acid, lauric acid, in amounts large enough to be potentially poisonous if such fats were to make up an unusually large proportion of a diet.

Moreover, some saturated fatty acids such as stearic acid have never been charged, as have others, with raising blood cholesterol levels, and stearic acid is a chief component of meat fat.

So any blanket statements about vegetable versus animal fat and the development of high blood cholesterol levels and atherosclerosis are without real meaning.

But, beyond that, by a process called hydrogenation, unsaturated vegetable oils can be changed to saturated. And, according to a study reported in 1973, the change does not make any difference in their role in cholesterol metabolism. According to that study, despite all the talk otherwise, the evidence is that cholesterol events in the body are no different whether saturated or unsaturated vegetable oils are consumed.

Is there any conclusive evidence that diets high in vegetable oils are beneficial?

Studies in birds and rats have shown that when the animals are deliberately given extremely large amounts of cholesterol, their blood levels of cholesterol become greatly elevated. Adding polyunsaturated fats to the diet then improves the blood cholesterol levels but has no beneficial effect on the development of atherosclerosis.

In 1969 a review of studies in man also found no beneficial effect despite claims to the contrary. And in 1973 an editorial in the *American Heart Journal* pointed out: "It is known that polyunsaturates have increased in the 'average' American diet almost three-fold over the past three decades without the slightest decrease in heart disease mortality—which result logically could be expected to follow if this food did, in fact, exert a positive clinical effect."

ILL EFFECTS?

There is some growing concern among scientists that diets quite high in vegetable oils may carry potential risks.

When polyunsaturates are heated, as in family cooking, they tend to become resaturated, thus defeating the purpose for which they are espoused. The resaturation becomes greater if a fat or oil is reused, a common household practice. And heating an unsaturated oil, particularly corn oil, to 200 degrees for fifteen minutes (less than usual cooking temperatures and times) has been found to increase atherosclerosis in animals.

In infants, excessive intake of unsaturated fatty acids has been found to cause vitamin E deficiency and anemia. Whether a similar problem may develop in adults is not yet established.

Other studies suggesting, but not definitely establishing at this point, that high intake of vegetable oil could have other undesirable consequences have been appearing.

In one, men on a high polyunsaturated fatty acid diet were found to have a 65 percent greater incidence of cancer than other men on a standard diet.

In another, 78 percent of a group of patients who deliberately forced polyunsaturates showed signs of premature aging of the skin.

If much remains to be learned about the upper limits of tolerable intake of unsaturated fatty acids, it also appears that much is yet to be learned about what happens when polyunsaturates are prepared for market.

Recently, Dr. F. A. Kummerow, professor of food chemistry at the University of Illinois, found that margarine producers often use a process that converts a large proportion of polyunsaturated fats from the naturally occurring form to another somewhat chemically different, or "trans," form. And, at least in swine, Kummerow found, the trans form actually increased blood cholesterol levels and the development of atherosclerotic deposits. According to Kummerow, there are margarines on the market that contain as much as 36 percent of fatty acids in the trans form compared with 2 to 6 percent in butter.

A NEWER CONCEPT

Some scientists now believe that peculiarities in blood flow may lie at the heart of the atherosclerosis problem.

Recent studies indicate that, regardless of age and sex, atherosclerosis occurs with a spotty distribution in arteries, and while the size and number of the patchy deposits may vary, the distribution pattern does not. The patches occur in arteries in certain areas—along the inner side of curves in the vessels, downstream from where the arteries divide or branch, and at points where the arteries are held rigidly in position by fat tissue or by scar tissue.

Such a distribution would suggest that the characteristics of blood flow in these areas could be involved. Because of the manner in which blood flows along the inner side of curves, patches could be expected there and at the other sites as well. At such sites, as the blood flows, pulsed by the heartbeat, static pressure dips and rises, producing a pulling or lifting effect. In response to the pulling, extra cells proliferate in these areas, producing thickenings, and, it is believed, setting the stage for patches to form and in time grow.

And, in fact, in animal experiments, when pronounced curves have been produced artificially in arteries, atherosclerosis has developed where none usually occurs.

Much of the work on the relationship of blood flow to atherosclerosis has been done by Dr. Meyer Texon, a member of the medical examiner's staff in New York County.

His work also indicates that fat in the tissues around arteries fixes them rigidly in position and, in doing so, produces blood flow alterations that lead to atherosclerosis. That helps to explain why excessive body weight is a risk factor in atherosclerosis.

Texon's work also helps to explain how high blood pressure and cigarette smoking are involved as risk factors. When blood pressure is elevated within arteries, the circular layer of muscles in the artery wall thicken; at the same time, the longitudinal layer of muscles also increases in size and becomes elongated—and when arteries elongate, they can fit in a fixed space only by becoming tortuous, and the curves of these tortuous arteries can become sites for atherosclerotic patches.

The evidence indicates that cigarette smoking is damaging to artery linings because of the content of carbon monoxide in the smoke. Carbon monoxide appears to accelerate development of atherosclerotic patches so that they increase in size more rapidly than they otherwise would.

But how does all the cholesterol get into atherosclerotic patches? For one thing, damaged cells, whether in the arterial wall or in the lung, kidney, or liver, always come to contain more than normal amounts. So some of the cholesterol in the patches may well be formed by injured artery wall cells.

Recently, too, Dr. Elspeth Smith of Aberdeen, Scotland, has shown that the first change during the development of atherosclerosis is the appearance in the artery wall of a gelatinous-looking mass of cells along with some fluid from plasma; the fluid contains lipoproteins that carry, among other things, cholesterol.

Then, later in the course of atherosclerosis development, other changes occur, and there may be a great increase in the amount of free cholesterol, apparently the residue remaining after body attempts to destroy the cholesterol-carrying lipoprotein in the gelatinous mass. If this is the case, and the masses of cholesterol found in atherosclerotic areas consist of the debris from the body's defensive efforts to try to get things back to normal after the appearance of the initial gelatinous lesion, then the cholesterol masses have nothing to do with cholesterol in the diet.

WHAT DOES IT MEAN?

If, as the evidence suggests, the primary cause of atherosclerosis lies not so much, if at all, with cholesterol or fats in the diet but with artery injuries from blood flow disturbances that tend to occur at certain sites determined by artery arrangement and curvature, hereditary factors, of course, enter into the picture since the basic arrangement and curvature are largely matters of inheritance.

But if heredity cannot be changed, other risk factors can be. Among those that seem most important to avoid or eliminate: obesity that may fix arteries in fat and distort them; high blood pressure that can lead to formation of tortuous curves; and cigarette smoking that can accelerate patch growth.

Coming on top of such recent findings is another reported in 1975. In a study of cardiovascular disease in Tecumseh, Michigan, 4,057 adults were interviewed to assess the frequency of consumption of 110 different foodstuffs. The average weekly consumption of foods high in fat, starch, sugar, and alcohol was determined for each participant and the total daily caloric intake was estimated.

For both men and women, blood cholesterol and fat (triglyceride) levels showed no correlation with the types of diet consumed. But significant correlations were found linking blood cholesterol and fat levels with body fat.

"This study," its authors, Drs. Allen B. Nichols and Leon D. Ostrander of the University of Michigan School of Medicine, noted, "suggests that hyperlipidemia [high levels of cholesterol and fat in the blood] is more strongly associated with body fat and presumably quantitative overnutrition than with proportions of fat, starch, sugar, or alcohol in the diet."

SOME SPECIAL CASES

Late in 1974, the National Heart and Lung Institute undertook to support a special seven-year study, which will be carried out in twelve major medical centers. It is designed to assess the effectiveness of measures for reducing elevated blood cholesterol levels in preventing or slowing down the development of premature atherosclerosis.

It is being carried out with some four thousand men, aged thirty-five to fifty-nine, who have not yet developed obvious signs or symptoms of coronary heart disease but whose risk of doing so is increased by a blood-lipid (fat) disorder called Type II hyperlipoproteinemia.

The disorder is characterized by abnormally high blood levels of low-density lipoproteins, the major carriers of cholesterol in the blood, and hence by elevated blood cholesterol. While it may possibly be related to cholesterol-rich diets, it can also be due to such disorders as hypothyroidism (low thyroid gland functioning), kidney or liver disease. Often, it is a hereditary disorder. The hereditary form, called familial Type II, is transmitted as a dominant trait so it occurs with high frequency among the children and brothers and sisters of affected individuals.

Type II hyperlipoproteinemia is one of the most common blood-lipid abnormalities and also one of the most dangerous because of a high risk of premature atherosclerosis. Depending on blood cholesterol level, a Type II subject's risk of symptoms or death from coronary heart disease ranges from 2½ to more than 10 times that of persons with normal blood cholesterol.

Although it is known that elevated cholesterol can be lowered by diet to some extent and that more substantial reductions can be achieved by supplementing the diet with a cholesterol-lowering drug, cholestyramine, what is not known—and what the study is designed to help find out—is whether treatment to correct the blood-lipid abnormality will reduce risk of coronary heart disease sufficiently to justify the trouble and expense to the patient.

SWEET AND DANGEROUS?

For centuries, sucrose—the technical name for sugar from cane or beets—was sold only by apothecaries who measured out the granules by the ounce. Only the rich could afford it and even they could not splurge because the supply was short. In Elizabethan times, the total consumption for all of England was only about eighty-eight tons a year.

It was only when, less than a century ago, Latin America went in for sugarcane cultivation and Europeans worked out a process for refining sugar beets that production of table sugar began to soar. In 1850, total world production was about 3.5 million tons; by 1950, it was up to 35 million; now it is more than 70 million. And in Western industrialized nations, the per capita consumption per year is up to 140 to 150 pounds, more than 2 pounds a week.

The huge and ever-growing consumption has long been of concern—at first, largely in connection with dental disease.

One of the earliest mentions of an association between sugar and dental decay was by a sixteenth-century German traveler who remarked on the black teeth of Queen Elizabeth who had a great fondness for sweetmeats made from sucrose extracted from cane.

Many factors may enter into decay but at the heart of the process is the activity of bacteria in a sticky film, called plaque, which forms on the teeth. The bacteria, which produce acid that attacks the dentine, thrive on sweets, particularly sticky sweets that are held against the teeth.

In Sweden twenty years ago, studies with volunteers demonstrated that dental decay activity rises with the addition of sugar to the diet—and rises even further when the sugar is taken in the form of sticky foods such as toffee between meals.

Fifteen years ago, a study of children of faculty members of dental schools in Great Britain found that the youngsters who were restricted from eating sweets at bedtime and between meals had the least number of decayed, extracted, or filled teeth, and this was confirmed by larger studies made of children in London in 1971. Researchers have been able to produce decay in previously decay-free monkeys by feeding them diets high in sweet biscuits, jams, and the like.

Recent research suggests that sugar may be a factor in producing periodontal, or gum, disease. In a 1972 study, when sugar was omitted from the diet of a group of young men, the extent of plaque declined to significantly lower levels than before, and plaque is known to be involved in triggering periodontal disease.

IN OBESITY

Sugar has come in for indictment as a major factor in the obesity problem. It is certainly not the only factor; no one particular food, whether potatoes, or meat, or bread, or milk shakes, or anything else, is the sole culprit.

Obesity is a matter of an excess of caloric intake over calorie burnup. But commonly now a startlingly large proportion of daily calories, 500 or more, about 20 percent, come from sugar. Of the 525 pounds of food consumed in the United States, and in many other Western nations, per capita yearly on a dry basis, sucrose makes up one-fifth.

Sugar is called an "empty calorie" food since it contains no proteins, vitamins, or minerals, and provides only energy—calories. "Now that most of us are leading less active lives there is less and less reason to have something in the diet that gives only energy or calories," says Dr. Ruth Leverton, science adviser to the United States Department of Agriculture.

Perhaps the best-known antagonist of sugar is a British authority, Dr. John Yudkin, a biochemist and physician who was professor of nutrition and dietetics at London University from 1954 to 1971.

Many people, Yudkin is convinced, could lose excessive weight simply by giving up or severely restricting sugar. If, he likes to point out, you take just one spoon of sugar in each cup of coffee or tea and drink only five cups a day, you could drop more than ten pounds a year by eliminating the sugar in your coffee or tea.

Moreover, Yudkin emphasizes, sugar does more than contribute to obesity in and of itself. "We have developed a liking for it," he points out, "that can increasingly be satisfied by a wide range of foods and drinks that many of us find almost irresistible. We take them more and more even though we don't need them. Some of the high amount of fat we eat comes about because of the use of sugar with fat in such foods as cakes, ice cream, and other sorts of confectionery. Sugar thus becomes a fat-carrier as well as providing calories itself."

DIABETES AND HEART DISEASE

Does sugar, aside from possibly contributing to diabetes and heart disease via obesity, do so directly? Various studies suggest so.

Diabetes, the number one cause of blindness in Western nations, has risen dramatically. Fifteen percent of adults, every fifth or sixth person, is diabetic. The reason now appears to be a combination of genetic tendency and the consumption of sucrose.

There have been many studies to suggest this but the immigration of Yemenites to Israel during the past few decades has provided Israeli researchers with a particularly clear indication of the effects of diet on diabetes.

In 1975 Dr. A. M. Cohen of the Hadassah Medical School in Jerusalem described to the American Chemical Society meeting in Chicago what is almost certain to become a classic epidemiological case study.

When Yemenites arrived in Israel, the incidence of diabetes among them was low. There has been little intermarriage since so that the Yemenite gene pool probably has remained stable. No sucrose was used in the traditional diet in Yemen but the consumption increased to the level of

Western Jews within a short time. And within a few years after immigration to Israel, the diabetes incidence among Yemenites matched that of other Israelis.

Dr. Cohen and his co-workers, going beyond this study, undertook laboratory experiments and found that animals on the Yemenite no-sugar diet for two months remained normal while some of those on a Western high-sugar diet developed symptoms of diabetes.

The animals that developed the symptoms were probably genetically susceptible. "And this is undoubtedly true of humans," he says. "Eating sucrose can bring on diabetes in the genetically prone person. On the other hand, proper dieting—cutting the consumption of refined sugars down to 5 percent of total carbohydrates, not 50—can prevent the onset of diabetes in the genetically prone."

Currently, Cohen says, "There is no way to tell who is genetically prone to diabetes and who isn't. Therefore, we must all be careful about the consumption of sugar."

The Yemenite and other investigations also suggest that increased sugar consumption could be related to the coronary heart disease problem.

Dr. Cohen has reported that over a period of time after arriving in Israel, the immigrants became increasingly prone to coronary heart disease. In those in Israel ten years or less, there was little of the problem, but incidence was sharply increased in those in Israel twenty-five years.

Some researchers also point to the people of Saint Helena who have a high incidence of coronary heart disease. Yet they eat less fat than Americans or British, smoke less than people in most Western countries, and are not physically inactive since Saint Helena is very hilly and there is little mechanical transport. "There is only one reasonable cause of their prevalence of coronary disease; the average sugar consumption in Saint Helena is around 100 pounds per person a year," argues Dr. Yudkin.

In 1957 Yudkin reported a study of death rates from coronary disease in 15 countries in relation to the average intake of sugar. The annual coronary death rate per 100,000 persons, he noted, increased steadily from 60 for an intake of 20 pounds of sugar per year to 300 for 120 pounds per year, and then more sharply to about 750 for 150 pounds per year.

In 1964 and 1967 Yudkin and his co-workers reported the results of two studies of the average intake of sugar during a period of some years before they had developed the disease of 65 men with heart attacks or peripheral arterial disease and also of 58 men of whom some were healthy and some were hospitalized with other diseases. The mean sugar intake of the men who developed heart attacks or peripheral vascular disease was 140 pounds per year and that of the others was 80 pounds.

Yudkin's work was criticized on the ground that his method of determining the intake of sugar, by questioning patients within three weeks after hospitalization about normal eating habits, was unreliable.

There is still much skepticism among scientists about a direct link between sugar consumption and diabetes and coronary heart disease. But that does not mean that its excessive consumption does not play a role.

Perhaps the views of many scientists are summed up accurately and succinctly by Sir Richard Doll, Regius Professor of Medicine at Oxford. "I am not," says Sir Richard, "a believer in the hypothesis that sugar is a specific cause of either. But I think sugar does come into the picture because it makes it easier to eat too much, and if we lower total intake of food, we are more likely to avoid coronary heart disease and diabetes."

Meanwhile, added insights into the possible role of sugar in diabetes and coronary heart disease have come from work (chapter 6) on the depletion of body chromium by sugar and the importance of chromium in determining blood levels of both cholesterol and sugar.

Nor do the charges against excessive sugar consumption end there. Recently, at the University of Bristol in England, Dr. Kenneth W. Heaton, working with laboratory animals, has found that "all diets which have been successful in producing gallstones in such animals have contained a high proportion of refined sugar or refined starch."

Dr. Yudkin has reported being able to help many people with dyspepsia, himself among them, through diet low in sugar. In one of his studies, he used stomach tubes to sample the gastric juices of young men volunteers before and after they went on a high sugar diet for two weeks. The results indicated that a sugar-rich diet causes an increase in both acidity and digestive activity of the gastric juice, "the sort of change you find in people with such conditions as gastric or duodenal ulcer."

Recently, in the United States, nutritionists have been providing advice for a sugar-loving public on how to manage well with less. Among the suggestions:

If you must have a sweet dessert, try fruit with a little liqueur. Instead of cakes, try fruit and cheese or crackers and cheese. For baking, use half the sugar recommended in some recipes, and train yourself and the family to like things that taste less sweet. The retraining may not be as difficult as you imagine. Toasting bread helps to break down carbohydrates and gives the bread a sweeter flavor.

A homemade milk shake without added sugar that may well be as sweet as you could wish is suggested by Mena Dows, former secretary of the American Nutrition Society: Use bananas with well-mottled skin, indicating they are very ripe. Chill in refrigerator with skin on, then peel and place in plastic bag and freeze. Cut a banana into one-inch cubes, add half a cup of milk plus half a teaspoon of vanilla, then homogenize in a blender for twenty seconds. Old bananas are sweet and a milk shake made with them can be expected to be sweet indeed.

COFFEE: FRIEND OR FOE?

Americans today are not quite up with Voltaire, a king of coffee drinkers, who consumed more than fifty cups a day. But we do drink up 50 percent of world production, averaging about sixteen pounds per person per year.

For a time, a heavy dark cloud loomed over coffee in terms of heart attacks. In 1963 came one of the first reports indicating a possible positive association between coffee and coronary heart disease. And in 1972 and 1973 came other reports suggesting that people who drink more than five cups a day have about twice as great a risk of having a heart attack as people who do not drink coffee.

But then in 1974 came two important contradictory studies.

To be sure, coffee—or, more accurately, the caffeine in coffee—is known to accelerate the heart rate, raise the blood pressure, interfere with sleep, and elevate blood levels of fatty acids. But if such circumstantial evidence is impressive, is it enough to incriminate coffee as a risk factor in coronary heart disease?

The 1974 reports provide some reassurance that it is not.

One was based on an analysis of multiphasic health checkup questionnaires completed by 197 men aged 40 to 79 years some time before they suddenly died. Comparison with data on other men comparable in age and other characteristics culled from 250,000 computerized multiphasic health checkup questionnaires showed no significant increase in the incidence of sudden death from heart attacks among those who drank coffee even in excess of six cups a day.

The other report came from the Framingham study, begun in 1949, one of the most intensive investigations into heart disease ever conducted. Careful records of daily coffee consumption were kept for a 12-year period in this continuing study that involves almost 4,500 men and women in the Massachusetts community. No significant differences were found between coffee drinkers and noncoffee drinkers with regard to onset of coronary heart disease—or the development of such heart disease manifestations as chest pain angina pectoris or heart attacks. The researchers also reported finding no significant relationship between coffee consumption and the development of stroke and other heart and blood vessel problems not related to coronary heart disease. The data also showed that coffee drinking had no significant effect on high blood pressure or blood cholesterol levels, which had been suggested in some earlier studies.

But if the case against coffee as a factor in coronary heart disease is no longer all black, what of its relation to other problems?

Ulcers? The caffeine in coffee does tend to stimulate stomach acid secretion. The stimulation appears to be mild and transitory in healthy people but may be sustained in those with ulcers, suggesting that people disposed to ulcers may be more sensitive and could do with moderation.

Heartburn? In some people, it may contribute to heartburn. The mechanism seems to be twofold. Even as caffeine stimulates stomach acid secretion, it produces a slight decrease in the grip of the sphincter, or circular muscle, in the esophagus near the entrance to the stomach, and the decrease may be enough to allow some of the acid secretion to flow back out of the stomach and into the esophagus, producing heartburn.

But for many if not most people coffee has its values. It smells and tastes good, and produces mild euphoria, lessened fatigue, and increased alertness, as Dr. R. B. Johnson, head of the Gastroenterology Branch at the National Naval Medical Center and assistant professor of medicine at George Washington University, reports.

CAFFEINISM

A new and significant finding relates not just to coffee but to excessive intake of caffeine via other beverages as well, including tea and cola drinks, and, in addition, caffeine-containing medications, including headache tablets containing caffeine.

The finding: Large amounts of caffeine can produce symptoms mimicking those of a psychiatric disorder: chronic anxiety. And tranquilizers and other drugs then may be used when the need is not to add new drugs but simply to reduce the intake of caffeine.

Among the symptoms of "caffeinism" are restlessness, irritability, insomnia, headache, muscle twitching, racing pulse, flushing, lethargy, nausea, vomiting, diarrhea, and chest pain.

Individual sensitivity varies but for some people as little as 250 milligrams of caffeine a day may be enough to cause trouble. And while that amount is considered fairly large, many people exceed it almost daily. For example, three cups of coffee, two caffeine-containing headache tablets, and a caffeine-containing cola drink may be consumed in one morning, providing about 500 milligrams of caffeine.

It was Dr. John Greden, then of Walter Reed Army Medical Center and now a professor at the University of Michigan, who brought the problem to light at a 1974 American Psychiatric Association meeting, along with some dramatic cases of people who benefited when their caffeinism problem was recognized and their caffeine intake reduced.

One, a young nurse married to an army physician, sought help because of a three-week history of light-headedness, tremulousness, breathlessness, headache, and irregular heartbeat. When examination disclosed nothing physically wrong, she was referred to a psychiatric outpatient clinic with a diagnosis of anxiety reaction attributed to worry that her husband would be sent to Vietnam.

But the young nurse refused to accept the diagnosis and, in fact, was the first to suspect a possible dietary cause and in about ten days managed to link her symptoms with coffee consumption. She had started making coffee by a different method that she found superior and so had been drinking ten to twelve cups a day, containing more than a thousand milligrams of caffeine. Her symptoms disappeared within thirty-six hours after she stopped drinking coffee. She was later challenged with caffeine twice, and each time the symptoms returned only to disappear when the caffeine was eliminated.

Another case involved a thirty-seven-year-old military officer referred for psychiatric help after a two-year history of chronic anxiety. His symptoms occurred almost daily and included dizziness, tremulousness, apprehension about job performance, restlessness, frequent diarrhea, and persistent sleep problems. Three complete medical examinations turned up no explanation. Tranquilizers had little effect.

Finally, it was discovered that he drank at least eight to fourteen cups of coffee a day and often drank hot cocoa at bedtime. He liked only cola soft drinks and drank three or four a day. He was incredulous at the idea that caffeinism might be causing his problems and was unwilling at first to cut down on coffee, cocoa, and colas, but finally gave in. A few weeks later, he reported marked improvement.

SALT

One of the most pervasive health problems is high blood pressure—hypertension—which affects upward of 23 million Americans alone. Hypertension has been clearly established as a major risk factor for coronary heart disease and stroke.

Even several millennia ago, Chinese physicians had some insight into hypertension and its consequences and even discerned some connection between salt in the diet and elevated pressure. In 2600 B.C., a classic Chinese treatise on internal medicine contained a passage noting that "if too much salt is used in food, the pulse hardens, tears make their appearance, and the complexion changes."

As noted earlier, only one gram or less of salt daily may actually be needed by the body, but the average American salt intake is about fifteen grams a day. It is present naturally in small quantities in many foods—milk, eggs, cheeses, and meats. It is in baking soda and powder, in monosodium glutamate used to intensify flavor, and in the preservative sodium benzoate. And, of course, it is added to many foods—both at the table and by food manufacturers and processors.

Is there any real modern evidence that excessive salt intake may cause hypertension? For more than twenty years, some investigators, notably Dr. Lewis K. Dahl of Brookhaven National Laboratory, have been working on the concept that it may—and that hereditary factors may determine who will and who will not tolerate a high salt intake.

Dahl's interest in salt came about indirectly. In 1948, aware that a rice-fruit diet was being used with some good results to treat hypertension, he began to wonder what was the ingredient in the diet that lowered pressure. In four years of studies, Dahl and other investigators determined that it was not any special ingredient at all in the diet but rather the very low salt content. That was double-checked when, in trials, salt was added to the diet and there was no beneficial effect on hypertension.

Dahl's thinking soon went a little further. If a low salt intake could lower blood pressure, might a high salt intake be a cause of hypertension?

He was soon noting—and has continued to note ever since—that of the many hypertensive patients he saw, he never encountered a new one who was on a low salt intake.

The custom of adding salt to food is ancient. But the appetite for salt, Dahl points out, is an acquired one, and some people acquire an enormous appetite for it.

There have been attempts to argue that there must be an inborn salt appetite—witness the long treks animals sometimes make to salt licks. Quite likely, the argument has been, the appetite simply continued in man.

But only herbivores make such treks. "The omnivores and carnivores," Dahl notes, "may go to licks, too, not in search of salt but in search of herbivores! The salt hunger of the herbivores, furthermore, is often due to true salt deficiency; with a few exceptions, all plants are low in sodium. In areas far removed from the sea, the soil can become leached of salt. The plants will, therefore, have extremely low sodium content."

Dahl is convinced that salt appetite in man is acquired and when it leads to excessive intake, the large salt consumption is not at all a reflection of body needs.

Because in the United States and many other countries, large amounts of salt are consumed almost uniformly from childhood to old age, it is difficult to establish clearly how much of an influence salt intake is in hypertension in a given individual because the factor is common to all. In man, Dahl acknowledges, it is possible to state only that there is a relationship between salt intake and elevated pressure, but in the laboratory rat, the cause and effect relationship is clearly demonstrable.

Over the past two decades, Dahl has worked with more than 32,000 rats. Thousands developed hypertension as the result of chronic salt feeding. As the work progressed, Dahl noticed that the response of rats ranged all the way from no effect to gradually increasing pressures to rapid, sharp elevations. Even after consuming a very high salt diet for most of their lives, about one-quarter of the animals showed no elevation of pressure at all. The remaining three-quarters developed elevations of varying degrees, including 2 to 3 percent dying of hypertension after just a few months on salt.

Since this suggested hereditary influences, genetic variances, Dahl and his co-workers began to mate members at either extreme of the response range and within a few generations had two colonies, which they have since kept breeding and studying.

In one colony, the rats—of the R, or resistant, strain—generally showed little harmful effect from high salt intake; the average pressure in the group was not significantly increased. In the other colony—the S, or sensitive, strain—even moderate amounts of salt in the diet led to marked pressure elevation and with high salt intake death occurred in a few months.

The experiments established that heredity can be a critical determinant for experimental hypertension. Clearly, at least in rats, when heredity is appropriate and some other critical factor such as high salt intake is introduced, hypertension is more likely to appear than if there were genetic resistance.

If the same thing applies to man, as well it may, Dahl suggests, at one extreme there should be people with such strong genetic predisposition that only little in the way of an environmental stimulus such as salt intake can lead to hypertension; at the other extreme there should be those so weakly predisposed by heredity that they could fail to become hypertensive even after long and intense exposure to an environmental stimulus such as salt. But most people could well fall in between, having only a modest predisposition and liable or not to develop hypertension, depending upon the severity and duration of an inciting factor such as salt intake.

In fact, many studies have shown the influence of heredity in human hypertension. For one thing, pressures of identical twins, with exactly the same inheritance, have been found to resemble each other much more than those of nonidentical twins. And among patients diagnosed as being hypertensive at a mean age of 36 1/2 years, it turned out that 44 percent of the parents had been hypertensive whereas in another group of subjects of the same age and free of hypertension, only 14 percent of the parents were hypertensive.

Especially where there is a family history of hypertension, Dahl advises, salt intake should be limited.

MILK

Can milk possibly be a factor in atherosclerosis?

For years, the Masai, an East African tribe of cattle herders, have been a puzzle to investigators. Despite a diet consisting largely of meat, blood, and milk, high in saturated fat and cholesterol, atherosclerosis is virtually nonexistent among the tribesmen.

The phenomenon has been explained on the basis that the Masai are extraordinarily physically active, commonly walking up to sixty miles a day.

But the explanation broke down with the finding that lumber-producing men in Finland actually exercise more than do the Masai, yet have the world's highest death rate from coronary heart disease.

If, then, the virtual immunity of the Masai to atherosclerosis is not due to exercise, what is it due to?

The most recent—and controversial—explanation not only of Masai immunity but of Western proclivity has been proposed by Dr. Kurt A. Oster, head of cardiology in a Bridgeport, Connecticut, hospital, and a Fellow of the American College of Physicians, the American College of Cardiology, and the American College for Clinical Pharmacology.

Dr. Oster believes that atherosclerosis is caused by homogenized milk, which the Masai do not drink but many Finns and many of the rest of us do.

Although attention has centered on saturated fats and cholesterol in the diet, the per capita intake of fats in the United States has not increased in the past seventy years—in the early part of the century, people ate pork, now it is beef—while the incidence of atherosclerosis has increased markedly. So atherosclerosis does not appear to be related to fat consumption, Oster argues. But something else has changed in the past three-quarters of a century: a physical characteristic of cow's milk. Now it is homogenized.

How does homogenization enter into the picture?

Dr. Oster believes that an enzyme called xanthine oxidase is the damaging agent in atherosclerosis. It is present in the body, especially the liver, but not normally in the walls of blood vessels. In atherosclerosis, the xanthine oxidase attacks artery walls and, as a defense mechanism, plaques are laid down.

Cow's milk contains the enzyme and is the only important food containing it that is nearly universally consumed.

In unhomogenized milk, Oster says, the xanthine passes through the intestinal tract and is not absorbed into the body. But homogenization breaks down the particle size of fats and other materials to one micron so that they will remain in an emulsified state. This minute size, according to Oster, allows xanthine oxidase to be absorbed, enter the arterial system, and be desposited on arterial walls.

Oster suggests that prevention lies in either consuming milk in its natural, unhomogenized state, as do the Masai, or in boiling milk to destroy the enzyme.

To what extent Oster's theory is valid is yet to be established. It does seem to offer an explanation of why the Masai can consume so much fat and cholesterol and have so little heart disease.

And there appears to be some additional buttressing for it in a set of figures on the coronary heart disease death rates and milk consumption and type of milk used in various countries:

**CORONARY HEART DISEASE DEATH RATE
AND MILK CONSUMPTION—1967°**

Country	Deaths per 100,000	Milk Intake lbs/person	Homogenized	Preboiled
Finland	244	593	33%	No
U.S.	211	273	Almost all	No
Canada	187	288	Partly	No
Austria	88	327	Occasionally	No
Italy	78	137	12%	—
France	41	230	Negligible	Yes

Interestingly, the French—prodigious eaters of cheese, butter, and eggs—rank at the bottom of the list.

° H. Rosenberg, *The Doctor's Book of Vitamin Therapy*, New York: G. P. Putnam's Sons, 1974.

9

Dining in the lab:
Is our food deteriorating?

THE CHEMICALS WE EAT

MANY OF our foods today may leave something to be desired for those with sensitive palates, but the big publicized controversy is over the chemicals in foods, those that find their way in or are deliberately added.

Because many American eaters are nervous, business at health food stores has been booming since the 1969 cyclamate ban, and booms still more each time an additive is charged with being harmful.

Perhaps adding somewhat to the anxiety is a theory advanced by a San Francisco allergist that many children now classed as hyperactive-learning disabled or with minimal brain dysfunction actually are genetically constituted so that their bodies have no natural defense against synthetic colors and flavors in foods—and that these, along with foods with a natural salicylate radical (similar to aspirin's acetylsalicylic acid), may trigger wild behavior or difficulty in coordinating. Whether or not controlled studies support the charge, the theory has meant a bad press for the food industry.

Reacting to a bad press, some food firms have rushed to add the word "natural" to their labels for various products—cereals, yogurts, soups, salad dressings, even beer.

But if there are numerous, increasingly vocal critics of our foods, there are also critics of the critics and of the emerging "eating natural" philosophy.

The pro-additive group charge that the eating-natural philosophy has alarming economic, medical, and nutritional implications and is based on false premises.

They assert that, for one thing, any idea that "artificial" foods alone contain chemicals that natural foods do not is—or should be—patently ridiculous. When, for example, you eat eggs, melon, and coffee for breakfast, you are consuming, among other things, such naturally present chemicals as methanol, acetaldehyde, ovomucoid, anisyl propionate, and malic acid.

They also argue:

● that "natural" does not necessarily mean better. Vitamin C, they note, is the same whether you squeeze it or synthesize it.

● that many natural foods, if unpreserved, can sometimes permit development of dangerous growths, as, for example, the molds (aflatoxins) that may develop on peanuts, wheat and rye products, and are known to be carcinogenic in animals and suspected of playing some part in human liver cancer.

● that many natural foods contain chemicals potentially poisonous if consumed in large amounts: The solanine in potatoes which, in excessive quantities, can inhibit nervous system impulse transmission; the hydrogen cyanide in lima beans, deadly in excess. But, when taken in moderation in a balanced and varied diet, they are helpful rather than threatening to health.

● that we know more about the additives to foods—which make up less than 1 percent of what we consume in a year—than we do about most of our natural products.

● that such additives keep our food supply plentiful, attractive, inexpensive, nutritious, and pleasing; reduce food loss caused by spoilage; and have helped almost eliminate scurvy, rickets, goiter, and botulism.

● that food quality is an emotional issue; that the rush to the "natural" today is being fostered by almost daily statements of self-appointed consumer advocates making a career out of criticizing food technology—aided by food laws so written that a single animal experiment using large doses of an additive and reporting a health problem can be enough to produce a ban or an inordinate amount of attention.

Critics of additives reply that such arguments offer all the factors in favor of chemical food additives while remaining silent about their dangers; that most artificial food colorings, for example, are synthesized from coal tar, which has been proved for many years to induce cancer, yet the colors have not been subjected to long-term tests for carcinogenicity; that two insecticides, aldrin and dieldrin, were used until recently to protect the wheat crop and were consumed in bread, and that after both were shown to induce cancer, it took four years of legal battles to stop their production and sale; that human milk now contains five times more aldrin and dieldrin and forty-five times more DDT than cow's milk; that in this country chemicals added to foods are assumed to be harmless until proved otherwise; that cyclamates were thus absorbed by consumers for twenty years before being removed from the market; and that saccharine has replaced the cyclamates as an artificial sweetener even though 5 to 7 percent of saccharine added to the diet of rats produces cancer.

Certainly, the problem of chemicals in our foods is not a simple one.

Every food, no matter what it is, in its natural state consists only of chemicals. Many thousands of those chemical substances have been identified; undoubtedly, many more, quite likely an even larger number, have not been.

While a goodly number are known to be important for normal body functioning, the largest number have no known function, at least none yet recognized.

It is also a basic fact of toxicology—an axiom—that whether or not a chemical component of food has a valuable function, it can, like any other known chemical, have harmful effects if consumed in excessive amounts.

By experience, over the course of millennia, man has learned what he can eat, which natural products he can absorb in his diet, with safety—including the many chemical substances with known potential for toxicity, such as arsenic, lead, cadmium, copper, iron, tannic acid, safrole, nitrates, and estrogenic materials. The consumption of foods containing normal levels of these substances has never been known to cause injury—even though some that are known to be nutritionally essential are present at levels even closer to known toxic levels than would today be allowed for food additives or pesticide residues.

Moreover, some components naturally present in foods—estrogenic substances, for example—today would not be allowed in any amount as food additives because of suspicions about their tendencies to produce malignancies, mutations, and possibly fetal abnormalities.

Most of our common natural food materials have been accepted as safe on the basis of their long history of use without producing obvious injury; they have never had scientific study and evaluation. But well-informed scientists recognize that there could be a question about whether any of the natural dietary components such as estrogens, arsenic, cadmium, or sodium chloride could possibly contribute in any way to degenerative diseases or shortened life-span.

What then is practical?

"Intake of a variety of foods is obviously the best insurance against absorption of toxic amounts of any single food component," according to both Dr. Julius M. Coon (chairman of the Department of Pharmacology at Thomas Jefferson University, Philadelphia, past chairman of the Panel on Food Safety of the First White House Conference on Food, Nutrition, and Health) and Professor John C. Ayres (chairman of the Food Sciences Division of the University of Georgia College of Agriculture, who was also a member of the Panel on Food Safety).

They also urge investigation to get full knowledge of the amounts of potentially toxic substances present in natural foods and the relationship between these amounts and those that might be actually harmful. And they consider this information to be important to the food industry, "which has the obligation to avoid concentrating toxic substances in its processing of foods or in its production of new foods from materials derived from natural products."

Even plant geneticists and breeders, looking for ways to improve upon plant food products, need to be wary of any harmful changes that could occur in toxic component content of any new plant varieties they may develop. And this is hardly an academic warning. In 1970 a new variety of potato was developed and seemed promising—until it turned out that it had substantially increased amounts of toxic solanine alkaloids and the Department of Agriculture stopped further development.

In their analysis, Coon and Ayres add another vital reason to have more information on the natural levels of toxic substances in foods. It would provide standards on which to assess the significance of man's addition of the same or similar substances in efforts to improve foods or through environmental pollution.

The food industry, they warn, must not oversupplement its processed foods with those essential nutrients, such as some vitamins, minerals, and amino acids that can be toxic in excessive amounts.

And the dangers of monkeying with foodstuffs without adequate testing can be considerable. One unfortunate example was a kind of epidemic in the mid-sixties among apparently healthy Canadian, American, and Belgian men in their middle years who suddenly dropped dead and turned out to have had only one thing in common: a love of drinking beer. Postmortem studies showed that the men had a peculiar destruction of heart muscle.

It also turned out that about a month before the epidemic broke out, some beer makers had begun to add the metal cobalt to improve foam quality. In 1968 investigators, studying the effect of cobalt additives in animals, reported that when rabbits received cobalt in beer, their hearts developed a "moth-eaten" appearance, with many of the same characteristics as those found in the hearts of the unlucky beer drinkers. On the other hand, when the cobalt was given without the beer, there were no such changes in the animals' hearts. Evidently, it was not cobalt but rather the combination of cobalt and beer that caused the trouble, something that might not have been suspected at all without careful testing.

PRUDENCE IN THE FACE OF IGNORANCE

In recent years, a number of restrictions have been placed on certain pesticides and food additives.

DDT has been drastically restricted because it has accumulated in the environment, has apparently interfered with reproduction of some forms of wildlife, and in laboratory animals fed large amounts it has produced liver tumors.

Cyclamates, artificial sweetening agents, were banned on the basis of some suggestive, but not definitive, evidence that they might have cancer- or mutation-producing effects or might lead to fetal abnormalities.

Baby food makers gave up using the flavor enhancer monosodium glutamate when it was reported to produce some brain cell damage in infant mice.

Coumarin and safrole, natural flavoring agents, and agene, a flour bleaching agent, were discontinued when very large doses were shown to have toxic effects in experimental animals.

In all these cases, there was no evidence that their presence in foods had ever caused any adverse effects in humans.

Actually, these substances were withdrawn not because they had been convicted of causing harm in man but because of ignorance and as a matter of prudence.

What does it mean when a food additive or residue, present for many years without producing any obvious damage, is found to cause serious trouble when fed to animals in doses far beyond those consumed under any circumstances by humans?

Often, it is simply not known whether the same effect would ever occur in man even with excessive doses. It is not known whether man might be more sensitive or resistant to the substance. It is not known either whether, if man were sensitive to the substance, the effect would be the same or different and at what dose there would be no effect at all.

So, out of ignorance and as a matter of prudence, it may be banned.

Actually, as scientists point out, no group of people have been studied scientifically throughout a lifetime exposure to any dietary substance, so ultimate safety has not been established conclusively for any substance.

So, even though DDT has been in our food for two decades with no evidence of injury to human health and saccharine has been used for eighty years by millions with no indication of injurious effects, there is no certainty that there have not been unrecognized ill effects or that ill effects would not come to light with further continued use.

Coon and Ayres size up the problem well: "Long-delayed harmful effects, especially when they are of infrequent occurrence or when they are manifested as the common illnesses of mankind, are extremely difficult to attribute to their specific causes. Injury due to unrecognized causes may have been the result of substances that have long been thought safe for use in foods. We are forced, therefore, to be concerned about the possibility that some items lurk in our diet among the food additives and pesticide residues that may play a role in the production of cancer, birth defects, and genetic damage, and of various endocrine (glandular), cardiovascular (heart and blood vessel), special sensory and mental disorders that plague mankind."

It is a complex problem, all the more so because, as noted earlier, the composition of common natural foodstuffs is even more complicated and chemically unknown as yet than is the residue and additive composition, and many known ingredients of natural foodstuffs have toxic potential, so that they could even be more suspect than the residues and additives.

But that does not mean, as Coon and Ayres emphasize, that we can afford to relax precautions about the additives and residues; on the contrary, it means just the opposite. "The presence of many unavoidable toxic chemicals placed in our diet by nature is compelling reason for us to avoid adding any more, even though it may be only a small percentage increment," they say.

SAFETY IN NUMBERS

It is often claimed that the use of insecticides is essential if we are to produce enough food to meet our needs. It is also claimed that the use of various additives is necessary if food, once available, is not to spoil and is to reach consumers in good condition.

One may accept these claims as valid even while pondering the necessity perhaps for using more additives and treatment procedures to produce nutrition-poor and tasteless convenience foods.

In any case, if the very number of chemicals used in producing and processing seems alarming, it may, in fact, contrary to common impression, help make them safer.

For one thing, the greater the variety of insecticides used in raising food crops, the less likely that any one will appear in harmful levels in foods. That applies to food additives as well, as the Joint Food and Agriculture Organization-World Health Organization Expert Committee on Food Additives recently pointed out. The basis for the concept is simple enough: The body has only limited ability to tolerate any single chemical but far greater capacity to tolerate small amounts of many different chemicals. This is what enables us to get along well on a normal, well-balanced and varied diet of foodstuffs containing only their natural chemicals.

FOOD POISONING

The dramatic incidents, of course, make the headlines: a planeload of air travelers hospitalized after a stopover during an international flight; one hundred or more children sick after a school cafeteria lunch; dozens of people ill after a church supper or picnic.

But that is only the tip of the iceberg. It may well be that the food supply today is safer than ever before: The risk for reported food illnesses in the United States is about one illness for 7 million meals consumed; yearly, fewer than four hundred outbreaks are recorded by the National Center for Disease Control. But public health authorities are convinced that food-borne diseases are grossly underreported, that the number of major outbreaks is at least seven times greater than the reported less-than-four hundred, and that millions of cases of food poisoning a year occur in homes.

In a Gallup poll, two-thirds of American housewives interviewed proved to be unfamiliar with the most basic and simple precautions to prevent salmonellosis, a common form of food poisoning estimated to account for 2 million cases of illness per year.

If reported food illnesses are indicative, salmonellosis and staphylococcus-caused illnesses are about on a par in frequency; they are outdone slightly by *Clostridium perfringens* food poisoning.

Fortunately, the vast majority of food poisoning incidents are relatively mild and commonly are not even reported to a physician. But serious cases can be fatal, particularly for infants, the elderly, or people weakened by other illnesses. Botulism is also a problem—a relatively rare one.

Salmonellosis. Salmonella bacteria are widespread in nature and often may contaminate meat, fish, poultry, and some dairy products.

Symptoms of salmonellosis include severe headache followed by vomiting, diarrhea, abdominal cramps, and fever. The symptoms usually begin within twelve to thirty-six hours after eating contaminated food and may last two to seven days. (For treatment of salmonellosis and other food poisoning, see Part Two.)

Refrigeration at 45 degrees F. will stop the growth of salmonellae that might be present in foodstuffs but the existing bacteria will still remain alive. They are destroyed by heating food to a temperature of 140, and holding for ten minutes, or to higher temperature for less time.

Perfringens. *Clostridium perfringens* is a spore-forming bacterium that grows in the absence of oxygen and grows best at temperatures in the range of 45 to 130 degrees F. Most commonly, outbreaks from *C. perfringens* are associated with meat, especially meat pies, stews, reheated meats, and gravies from beef, turkey, and chicken.

Symptoms, which usually appear within eight to twenty hours and may persist for twenty-four hours, include nausea without vomiting, diarrhea, and cramps.

Perfringens poisoning is unlikely if cooked meats are eaten promptly or if cooked meats and gravies that are to be eaten later are cooled rapidly under prompt refrigeration at 40° F. or below.

Staphylococcal (staph) poisoning. *Staphylococcus aureus* is a bacterium present virtually everywhere and especially likely to be found on human skin and in the nose and throat. It proliferates in boils and other staph infections.

Staph bacteria can be transferred to food by people with infections and by healthy people who harbor the organisms without themselves being infected. When they grow in food, the bacteria produce a toxin that can inflame the intestinal tract.

The symptoms of staph poisoning—vomiting, diarrhea, abdominal cramps, prostration—usually appear within three to eight hours after ingestion of contaminated food and last one to two days.

The organisms grow rapidly and produce toxin at temperatures between 44 and 115 degrees F., especially in pastries, custards, salads, salad dressings, sandwiches, sliced meats, and other meat products left for several hours at room temperatures.

The bacterial growth is inhibited by keeping hot foods above 140 degrees and cold foods at or below 40. Toxin is destroyed by boiling for several hours or heating food in a pressure cooker at 240 degrees F. for thirty minutes.

Botulism. Clostridium botulinum is a spore-forming organism that grows and produces toxin in the absence of air, such as in a sealed container. The spores, which are extremely heat resistant, are harmless but the toxin is a deadly poison.

Botulism, caused by eating food containing the toxin, produces such symptoms as double vision, inability to swallow, speech difficulty, and progressive breathing paralysis. The symptoms usually appear within twelve to thirty-six hours, sometimes longer, and last three to six days. The fatality rate is high—about 65 percent.

Boiling kills most other organisms but botulism spores in food can be destroyed only in the pressure canner. More than six hours is needed to kill the spores at boiling temperature (212 degrees F.). The toxin is destroyed by boiling for ten to twenty minutes.

Botulism rarely occurs in commercially canned foods. Between 1970 and 1973, for example, with millions of cans of food sold, only two outbreaks from commercially canned products occurred while there were twenty-one incidents as the result of home-canned foods.

PRECAUTIONS

Knowledgeable shopping, adequate refrigeration and storage, proper canning procedures, good hygiene, and an understanding of danger signs should keep your food safe.

Whether you can your own food or purchase canned products, look for telltale signs of food spoilage. These may include bulging can ends, jar lids or rings; leaks from can or jar; change in color of the food; spurting liquid on opening a can or jar; a disagreeable odor, or mold. If there is the slightest suggestion of spoilage, do not even taste the food. Dispose of it so it cannot be eaten by a pet. And wash the empty can or jar in hot soapy water, rinse, and place in boiling water for fifteen minutes before throwing away—to be certain a pet will not eat any toxin that may be present.

In shopping for frozen foods, avoid any that have become soft or mushy because of improper storage in the case. Also avoid any dairy products and meats that have been left unrefrigerated for any length of time.

Do not leave perishable foods in your car on hots days; do your grocery shopping just before going home.

Use a thermometer to check temperature in your refrigerator. Perishables should be kept between 35 and 45 degrees; frozen foods at 0 degrees or lower.

Scrub hands not only before handling any food but also again after working with raw food to avoid possible reinfestation. Avoid using utensils for more than one chore without washing in between as a safeguard against cross-contamination.

Keep working surfaces clean. A laundry bleach can be a useful degerming agent.

Cook meats, especially pork, until the center reaches at least 165 degrees F.

When you stuff a turkey, cook it immediately. Then remove the dressing and store any leftover turkey and dressing separately. If the stuffing is left within the turkey, it may stay warm enough, even when the turkey is refrigerated, to permit bacterial growth.

Because broth and gravy are particularly likely to spoil, cool and refrigerate any leftovers without delay, use within a day or two, and boil for several minutes prior to serving.

Serve cooked foods without delay if possible. If hot foods have to be held for a time, keep them at 140 degrees F. or above to inhibit growth of any bacteria that might be present.

10 New views on those therapeutic diets

UNTIL THE early nineteenth century, medicine was largely based on the Greek system of Aristotle and Hippocrates and treatment under this system relied almost entirely on diet. With the arrival of potent drugs and surgery, however, the importance of diet began to decline. And particularly in very recent years, some special therapeutic diets have come in for skeptical review and their value questioned.

One prime example is the ulcer diet.

For the millions who have endured the painful periodic attacks of peptic ulcers, the traditional medical dictum has been a ban on all foods thought to stimulate the secretion of gastric juice, including red meat, fresh fruits and vegetables, and highly spiced dishes. Ulcer patients, if they faithfully followed the dictum, lived on a boring regimen of pale, soft, mild-flavored items such as milk, rice, creamed chicken, and gelatin.

Now it appears that the old caveats may be unjustified in most cases. Increasingly, physicians have been questioning old assumptions that a bland consistency, color, taste, or odor of a food as it enters the mouth has any direct relationship to the action that food may have on the gastrointestinal tract.

In fact, not long ago in the *Journal of the American Medical Association*, Dr. Robert Donaldson, a gastroenterologist at the Veterans Adminis-

150

tration Hospital in West Haven, Connecticut, contended that "the rationale behind the 'bland' diet is completely unscientific. Light-colored foods with a soft texture *seem* as if they should be gentle to the stomach, but some of them actually stimulate gastric juices."

Moreover, Donaldson added, several hospital studies of ulcer patients have shown that the traditional no-no's like spicy foods have no effect on the course of peptic disease or the quantity of acid in the stomach. Although many doctors are aware of these facts, some see no harm in indulging the ulcer patient who insists on having a restricted diet. Unfortunately, Donaldson says, the bland regimen not only may fail to help the patient's ulcer but, with its high fat content, may also increase his risk for a heart attack or stroke.

"If an ulcer patient discovers through experience that certain foods disagree with him," Donaldson says, "of course he should stay away from them. But in some cases, they upset his stomach just because his doctor has told him they will."

The only common substances that have been positively shown to stimulate gastric acid are alcohol and caffeine and they should be avoided by anyone with an ulcer, Donaldson advises. Otherwise, it now appears, the ulcer patient who wants to may feel free to feast on chili con carne, curried shrimp, or garlic-studded steaks.

Not, it should be added, that all physicians agree. There was some ruckus recently when a medical school dean criticized physicians who recommend a bland diet for peptic ulcer.

Among the replies was one from a practicing Astoria, New York, physician who remarked: "I wonder why these practicing doctors 'pay no attention to the beautifully designed and carefully controlled trials that prove bland diets to be ineffective?' Could it be that out in the field the practicing doctor has heard so many ulcer patients bemoan (after they ingested spices, coffee, alcohol, or many highly seasoned foods) their eructations, flatulence, heartburn, among many other symptoms of hyperacidity? No one claims bland diets are a cure-all, but simply part of a total regime of soothing a tension personality. . . . There is no question some therapies are outmoded. But when there are none better, let's not eliminate what we have without justifiable reason. Bland diets imply a soothing assuagement, like Grandma's touch. Even if it's only psychological, let's not knock its value—or would you recommend a peck of peppered pickles?"

Nevertheless, the scientific evaluation of therapeutic diets goes on and often upsets some hallowed traditions. It even appears now that the rigid diabetic diet is not always necessary.

THE DIABETIC DIET

In 1974 investigators compared the effectiveness of low carbohydrate diets with that of high carbohydrate diets in mild to moderate diabetes.

They divided diabetic patients into two groups. To one group, they gave a diet containing 60 percent carbohydrate and 25 percent fat; to the other, they gave 40 percent carbohydrate and 45 percent fat. After twenty weeks, they reversed the diets for another twenty weeks.

Despite the differences in carbohydrate load, control of diabetes and capacity to secrete insulin, as measured by many tests, were equally well maintained. And levels of cholesterol and fats in the blood were similarly unaffected by changes in the ratio of carbohydrate to fat.

In 1975, Dr. John Moorhouse, professor of physiology and medicine and director of the Endocrine and Metabolic Laboratory, Health Sciences Centre, Winnipeg, Canada, told the annual meeting of the Canadian Medical Association that the real issue in the management of maturity onset diabetes is control of hunger. He remarked that the first step in management is to restrict intake of calories, adding that drugs and insulin are secondary and frequently interfere with good treatment.

And he emphasized: "The conventional exchange 'diabetic diet,' rigid in timing, distribution and content is the worst possible approach to hunger control. The patient's problem is not blood sugar, lipids or pressure. It is hunger control and priority to any other matter will result in failure."

Underscoring obesity as the central medical problem in diabetes, Moorhouse said that environmental pressures are its chief cause. He saw calorie excess as indigenous to modern society because of misunderstandings about nutrition, advertising influences, and common food abuses such as the milk drinking habit, consumption of soda pop, fats added at the table (butter, margarine, salad dressing), abuse of red meats that have a high caloric density, and the use of refined foods.

Refined foods deserve special note. As we will see in the next chapter, the substitution as much as possible of unrefined foods for the refined is one of the most promising of all developments for what up to now has been virtually a totally frustrating endeavor—getting and keeping excess weight off in both diabetics and nondiabetics.

DIETS FOR OTHER GI DISORDERS

If the bland diet for peptic ulcer is now being discounted, so, for lack of evidence that they are helpful, are special diets for gallbladder disorders, regional enteritis, ulcerative colitis, diverticular disease, and other colonic disorders.

For diverticular disease, in fact, there has been a full 180-degree turnabout.

As we have noted in chapter 7, avoidance of roughage was once considered to be an important part of the treatment of diverticular disease, enteritis, colitis, and other disorders involving gastrointestinal irritability or inflammation.

On the principle that it was necessary to spare the GI tract by frequent small feedings of easily digested nutrients low in residue, diets put emphasis on sugar, milk, eggs, lean meat, refined and cooked cereal, cottage or cream cheese, strained cooked fruit or vegetables, potato, bouillon, broth, cream soups, spaghetti, and such desserts as custard, cookies, puddings, ice cream, and plain cakes. Such items as whole or raw fruits and vegetables and whole-grain cereals and breads, bran, corn, and dried legumes were to be strictly avoided.

But the recent studies noted in chapter 7 that link diverticular disease, irritable colon, and the like to a lack of adequate dietary fiber, and the reports of marked improvement in patients treated with exactly the items previously banned, including whole-grain cereals and breads and bran, have brought a marked shift in medical thinking.

CELIAC DISEASE

Two special diets—one for celiac disease and the other for lactase deficiency—are well established as valuable.

It was only in the 1950s that celiac disease was shown to be the result of a sensitivity to gluten in wheat flour and rye flour, which causes changes in the lining of the small intestine and leads to impaired absorption.

A familial condition, celiac disease can produce abdominal distention, muscle wasting, attacks of vomiting, soft, pale, and malodorous stools.

The disease can be controlled effectively with a diet that eliminates the cereal protein, gluten, by omitting all foods containing wheat, rye, oats, buckwheat, and barley and their derivatives. Rice, corn, soy, and wheat starch flour can be used as substitutes. Gluten-free bread and muffins are available commercially or may be baked, using rice, soya, or cornstarch flour.

The response to a gluten-free diet is quite rapid. The patient may feel better in a matter of days. Within about eight weeks, the intestinal mucosa usually returns to normal. The diet is lifelong.

LACTASE DEFICIENCY

Lactose is a milk sugar and lactase is an enzyme needed to convert the lactose to glucose. A deficiency of lactase leads to abdominal pain and diarrhea with the drinking of milk or the eating of milk products.

Treatment consists of the avoidance of milk and milk products. But this, unlike celiac disease, is a quantitative susceptibility and complete avoidance of milk and milk products may not be necessary—only as much as required to avoid symptoms—so that, for example, milk in coffee or tea may be allowed.

Lactose intolerance was first identified in the 1950s. Yet, many peoples appear to have recognized it intuitively. When milk products are soured or fermented, they contain very little lactose, which may be the reason why many groups in Greece, India, and elsewhere have long used cheese, cultured buttermilk, and yogurt as good sources of many nutrients but relatively free of lactose.

GENETIC IDIOSYNCRASIES

There are a number of metabolic problems traceable to inherited enzyme deficiencies, which are also treatable by diet.

Phenylketonuria (PKU) is one of the better known. It occurs in about 7 of every 100,000 births in the United States and is caused by a deficiency of a liver enzyme, phenylalanine hydroxylase, which is supposed to break down phenylalanine.

During the first few weeks of life, an infant with PKU may be unusually irritable and suffer from vomiting and epileptic seizures. If the problem is not detected and treated, the child may show moderate to severe mental retardation. There are many exceptions but phenylketonurics tend to have blue eyes, blond hair, and fair skin.

Fortunately, PKU is detectable shortly after birth by a relatively simple test that is mandatory in many states. The problem can be controlled effectively by reducing intake of the amino acid phenylalanine. One preparation that is often used is Lofenalac, which contains only 0.06 to 0.1 percent of phenylalanine as compared with 5 percent in normal dietary proteins. This is supplemented by fruits, vegetables, and cereals low in protein.

A few rare individuals suffer from hereditary fructose intolerance because of the lack of an enzyme, 1-phosphofructoaldolase, needed to handle the simple sugar fructose. Fructose occurs in ordinary table sugar and in many other carbohydrates. For an individual with intolerance, eating fructose can lead to nausea, vomiting, malaise, chest pain, tremors, excessive sweating, confusion, and even coma and convulsions. A diet eliminating fructose is required.

Galactosemia is another inherited metabolic inability. In this case, there is inability to convert the simple milk sugar galactose into glucose for lack of the enzyme galactose 1-P uridyl transferase. Unless the problem is detected, often with the help of family history, the victim may suffer mental retardation, stunting of growth, cataracts, and, in some cases, death. Eliminating milk and milk products from the diet relieves all symptoms.

GOUT

For thousands of years, gout was recognized—but not for what it really was. An attack, excruciatingly painful, was considered to be a reward for the nonvirtue of overindulgence. And even just a few years ago, books were full of cartoons of obese aristocrats suffering from painful gouty toe because of high living.

In reality, gout is an inherited disorder related to abnormal metabolism of certain compounds, called purines, in foods. Because of the abnormal body handling of purines, a purine breakdown product, uric acid, builds up in blood and body tissues.

When excess uric acid is deposited in joints, the joint tissues may become inflamed, with resulting severe pain, swelling, and stiffness. The joints usually affected are those of the lower extremities, particularly the great toe, but any other joint in the body can be involved.

The arthritis of gout can be severe and disabling if untreated and may lead to permanent deformity. There may also be changes leading to impairment of vital organs such as the kidney.

Not everyone with gout actually develops the chief clinical symptom of arthritis. In fact, most cases are without symptoms. People in sedentary work are more likely than manual laborers to have gouty arthritis.

In occasional patients, certain foods may precipitate gout attacks. In most cases, however, it is no longer considered necessary to ban many rich foods—those which have high purine content—with the possible exceptions of such items as sweetbreads, anchovies, liver, and kidney.

The mainstay of preventive treatment today is medication rather than diet. One drug, colchicine, an old one, has long been used to relieve the agony of a gouty arthritis attack. It usually stops an attack within twenty-four hours. For individuals who can predict when they are about to have an attack—through warmth and tingling in the joint—colchicine may be taken to prevent the attack.

Several drugs are available to promote excretion of uric acid via the kidneys, thus reducing the amount in the tissues. The preparations, which include probenecid, a drug first used not long after the discovery of penicillin to make a little of that antibiotic go further, are taken regularly as a means of avoiding acute arthritis attacks, and are effective in many cases.

A more recent addition to the preventive treatment of gout is a compound called allopurinol. It has the remarkable ability to block the enzyme needed for uric acid to be formed. Therefore, there is no danger of uric acid building up to be deposited in a joint. Allopurinol also stimulates the breakdown and excretion of uric acid deposits that may have already accumulated in the body.

LOW SALT DIETS

Once highly restrictive low salt diets were just about the only means of combating high blood pressure and edema, or waterlogging of body tissues, associated with heart disease, kidney disease, liver disease, and other conditions accompanied by edema.

Severe restriction meant limiting the average United States salt intake of fifteen grams, a little more than half an ounce, a day to two hundred milligrams—one-fifth of a gram—a day.

Most physicians now consider such a very low salt diet an archaic form of treatment because of the availability of modern diuretic drugs that promote the elimination of salt and excess fluids.

But many physicians still consider moderate restriction of salt desirable for hypertension and edematous conditions, such as swollen ankles. If you have any of these problems, your physician may suggest limiting salt intake. A modern salt-limiting program might allow use of a modest amount of salt for cooking purposes but a much reduced use of salt at the table; also the avoidance of very salty foods such as crackers, potato chips, pretzels, and other such obvious items.

ELIMINATION DIETS FOR SUSPECTED FOOD ALLERGY

Allergy is an abnormal and individual hypersensitivity to a substance or substances ordinarily harmless. For example, the pollen of plants is not generally harmful but some people are acutely sensitive to its presence, in which case the pollen becomes an allergen.

For some people, specific foods can be allergens, capable of causing trouble. And the troubles may be quite varied.

Food allergy can produce gastrointestinal upsets, with such symptoms as abdominal pain, diarrhea, gas, nausea, and vomiting (although, obviously, any or all of these symptoms may not be allergic reactions but caused by other problems).

Food allergy also can produce skin reactions, including hives. It is involved in some cases of asthma and migraine headaches.

Among the most common food allergens are milk, eggs, fish, shellfish, nuts, wheat, citrus fruits, tomato, chocolate, and products containing one or more of these as ingredients. Any food, however, can be an allergen.

When allergic reactions are relatively infrequent and some food is thought to be the cause, a food diary can be useful. It may clearly establish a definite pattern of reactions related to a specific food.

When reactions occur more frequently, an elimination diet may be needed. The idea is simple enough: to incriminate or eliminate certain foods as allergens by their gradual, individual addition to a basic diet composed of foods that are relatively nonallergenic.

Using elimination diets—more than one may sometimes be needed—is not so simple although it can be rewarding.

The common allergens and any suspected food must be kept out of the starting diet and nothing else must be consumed other than what the diet specifies. It is advisable not to eat in restaurants while on an elimination diet since the exact composition of all meals must be known.

Four elimination diets are commonly used. The procedure usually goes like this. The first diet is tried for two weeks. If there is no improvement in that time, a second diet is tried for another two weeks, and others, if necessary, thereafter. When definite improvement occurs, then one new food may be added every three days. Reappearance or aggravation of symptoms after a particular new food is added is evidence of allergy to that food. For double-checking, the food can be removed from the diet for several days to make certain that symptoms are relieved, and then the food can be restored again to the diet to make certain that symptoms appear again.

Diet No. 1 eliminates all pork, beef, fowl, milk, rye, and corn. It allows rice cereal products; lettuce, spinach, carrots, beets, and artichokes; lamb; rice flour (for bread or biscuits); lemon, pear, grapefruit; cottonseed and olive oil; black coffee or tea or lemonade; tapioca pudding, gelatin, cane sugar, maple sugar, salt, and olives.

Diet No. 2 eliminates all beef, lamb, milk, and rice. It allows corn cereal products; corn, tomatoes, peas, asparagus, squash, string beans; chicken and bacon; corn or 100 percent rye flour (note that ordinary rye bread also contains wheat); peaches, apricots, prunes, pineapple; corn and cottonseed oil; cane sugar, gelatin, corn syrup, and salt; but no tea, coffee, and lemonade.

Diet No. 3 eliminates all lamb, fowl, rye, rice, corn, and milk. It allows no cereals but does permit lima beans, beets, potato (white and sweet), string beans, tomatoes; beef and bacon; soybean or potato flour; grapefruit, lemon, peaches, apricots; cottonseed and olive oil; black coffee, tea, lemonade; tapioca pudding, gelatin, cane sugar, maple sugar, salt, olives.

Finally, Diet No. 4, used only if symptoms persist on the other three elimination diets, restricts the diet to only whole milk, two to three quarts daily.

Once anyone with a food allergy knows the source of his problem, he should be able to avoid trouble by avoiding the food item. But he will have to learn what packaged foods he can safely eat by careful study of the labels. And, because all ingredients are not necessarily listed on all packages, he may have to learn by experience. If, for example, he is allergic to eggs, he may discover that he runs into trouble when he eats bread, cookies, some breaded foods and meat dishes, some salad dressings, and other products that may include eggs.

11

The "habit belly" and other new insights into obesity and controlling it

FOR SOME years it has been known that people and animals who fast excrete a chemical in their urine that appears to be a fat-mobilizing substance (FMS). When FMS has been injected into animals it has increased the amount of fatty acids in their blood and the turnover rate of fatty acids in their fat tissues. And it has led to weight loss. This evidence suggested that FMS might possibly make a diet compound.

In mid-1973, at a meeting of the American Chemical Society, Drs. Maurice V. L'Heureux and Roderic P. Kwok of Loyola University Stritch School of Medicine could report some further evidence of FMS's weight-reducing potential. They found that the substance releases fatty acid in the test tube. They also found out something about how it works—by stimulating the production of cyclic AMP, a hormonal messenger, which in turn promotes the activity of a fat-destroying enzyme, lipase. And they could report that they had made some progress toward purifying FMS. It appears to be a protein, and once it is available in large, purified, identifiable amounts, it can be tested further on a large scale in animals and perhaps, eventually, in humans.

A little over a year later, also in an announcement via the American Chemical Society, came news of another possibly hopeful new approach to weight control. From ordinary uncooked kidney beans, a calorie-cutting chemical that works by blocking the body's use of starch had been derived.

Dr. John J. Marshall, biochemist at the University of Miami, who reported the chemical Phaseolamin, hastened to warn anyone who might be tempted to eat uncooked kidney beans not to do so because they also contain toxins that are destroyed by cooking.

Phaseolamin, he explained, inhibits the action of an enzyme, alpha-amylase, involved in converting starch to the blood sugar, glucose. Potentially useful to diabetics, who must control the level of blood sugar, and to the obese, who store unused glucose as fat, the compound has passed early tests.

"What we would like to think," Marshall says, "is that eventually we are going to have on our tables [containers of] pepper, salt, and another container with amylase inhibitor. And when one is going to eat potatoes, let's say, or bread, then one sprinkles some of the amylase inhibitor over the foodstuff, eats it, and then the starch is not completely utilized."

FMS or Phaseolamin—either or both—may or may not at some future time make an impression on the obesity problem, which has reached epidemic proportions.

But there are three new and apparently basic insights that could have immediate practical values: the discovery of the fat cell laydown early in life; the "habit belly" concept; and, not least of all, the concept of overeating as being not a matter very often of eating too much but rather of getting too much out of food.

THE EPIDEMIC

In the United States today, it is a rare person who is not on a diet or who does not know someone who is. Although women have been the mainstay of the diet industry, men are becoming increasingly concerned about their weight, too. Three national surveys conducted by the American Institute of Public Opinion and by the Elmo Roper organization indicate that a greater percentage of men felt that they were overweight in the most recent study than in those carried out in 1950 and 1956.

More than one-third of middle-aged Americans are at least 20 percent over their ideal body weight. And the prevalence of obesity in children has been increasing. In 1951 one study showed that 12 percent of middle-class Boston high school students were grossly overweight; by 1968, the incidence had increased to 19 percent.

In 1971 there were almost as many visits to physicians for obesity as there were for such established national illnesses as arthritis and psychoneurosis.

Dr. Neil Solomon, the Johns Hopkins University psychiatrist who coined the term "yo-yo syndrome," estimates that more than 30 million Americans are now yo-yoing on the scales in a battle against five to fifteen excess pounds.

Diet experts have long warned that these ups and downs put stress on the system. And some, including Dr. Solomon and Dr. Jean Mayer, the Harvard nutritionist, now suggest that a moderately overweight person may be better off in a holding pattern rather than a seesawing cycle.

More than a cosmetic liability, excess weight is associated with many chronic disorders and with excess mortality. Compare the figures with a normal-weight person: Anyone who is just 10 percent overweight has as much as 13 percent greater risk of dying prematurely; at 20 percent overweight, the risk goes up to 25 percent, and at 30 percent overweight, to 42 percent. The death rate for heart disease is 51 percent greater in the overweight; for stroke, 53 percent; for cancer, 16 percent; for diabetes, 133 percent; for digestive system diseases, 68 percent.

And insofar as they fail to produce permanent weight reductions, fad diets, always proliferating in this country, must get no small share of the blame for a startling phenomenon: The United States is the only nation in the World Health Organization that has shown no increase in life expectancy in twenty years.

CAUGHT IN THE MIDDLE

We are a society highly organized to "do in" the overweight in more ways than one.

The food industry increases its income by filling supermarkets with ever more profitable packaged, processed, and fast, convenience foods that tempt one and can be nibbled any time without effort or preparation.

In addition to buying this ethic of convenience, Americans are manipulated through incessant advertising to believe that they *need* the increasing quantities of goods produced by the economy.

"American society hypocritically condemns obesity, while it simultaneously acts as a pitchman for the powerful food industry," charges Dr. C. S. Chlouverakis, associate professor at the State University of New York, Buffalo, Department of Medicine, and director of the Obesity and Lipid Abnormalities Service at the E. J. Meyer Memorial Hospital, Buffalo.

Half of the advertisements interrupting children's TV programs sell food items, many of them high calorie, low nutrition junk foods. In one year alone, over half a billion dollars was spent on potato chips.

And when people become fat, their fatness is conveniently and even cunningly attributed to their own weakness, so that the economic system can remain immune from accusation.

"Ironically," says Dr. Chlouverakis, "within the scenario of an ever-increasing consumption of goods, the image of obesity as a public hazard has arisen. Suddenly society has caused us to become very weight conscious, and tells us that thinness is a virtue. The system has managed not only to avert the accusation that it generates fatness and unhealthiness, and thus survive any potential threat, but it has also managed to make the best of the situation. First, the problem of obesity is blown all out of proportion so that many more people are worried about their weight than medically need be. Then, the solution is sought within the existing economy—and in such a way as to benefit the system. Thus, an enormous industry of 10 billion dollars a year has been created with diet books, mechanical devices, health spas, fat farms, and many other reducing techniques. Of course, the products marked 'trimline' and 'low-cal' cost more than the gourmet lunches that put the extra pounds on in the first place.

"Not only does the system make billions of dollars fattening Americans up and then billions more exploiting those who try to reduce, but it also deceives those who think that the flourishing diet and reducing industry is a solution to the problem. Whereas some promoters advertise 'a five-minute total body-shaper and slimming course,' others claim that you can lose six inches off your waistline in only twenty-one days while eating the food you love. Doctor writers have joined the crusade with the revolutionary diets guaranteeing weight loss while eating five thousand calories or reducing to the 'ideal' body weight in fourteen days. None of the promises of these moneymaking diets or methods could be substantiated by evidence. Society, then, not only makes you fat, but also charges you double for the false promise of making you thin again. In this atmosphere of profiteering, exploitation, and deceit, the obese have reacted with naïveté and passivity. They are ever ready to buy a new miracle diet or device; they are equally ready to accept the blame when the promised results are not forthcoming."

"IT IS TIME TO RECOGNIZE THE FAD DIET AS A TRUE POLLUTANT OF NATIONAL HEALTH"

So says Dr. Morton B. Glenn of the New York University School of Medicine and chief of the Nutrition Clinic of the New York City Department of Health. And he is unquestionably right. But the fad diets go on.

One of the most popular, which keeps turning up under various names such as the Air Force diet, the Mayo Clinic diet, and the Drinking Man's diet—both the Air Force and Mayo Clinic disclaim it vigorously—is high in protein and fat and low in carbohydrates. The claim behind it— that protein is less fattening than carbohydrates—is denied emphatically by just about every nutritionist.

Any loss from such a diet is illusory at best, usually caused only by increased excretion of water at the beginning. Nor is this the most serious flaw. Besides a definite need for adequate carbohydrates in the diet for ready energy, the dieter also may need the B vitamins from cereals and vitamins A and C from fruits and vegetables. In addition, when the diet is low in carbohydrates, it almost has to be high in fat, which may lead to higher cholesterol levels in the blood or acidosis from the burning of too much fat, or both.

Still another hazard is that about a hundred grams of carbohydrates a day appear to be essential and if they do not get that amount, some people may develop low blood sugar (hypoglycemia) and, as a result of the lower concentration of glucose in the blood, the brain and the retina of the eye may not be properly nourished.

Some fad diets deemphasize fats as well as carbohydrates and put all the emphasis on protein and water. But with excess protein in the diet, it is possible for a person with an unsuspected kidney problem to retain nitrogen and develop elevated blood urea nitrogen levels and become uremic, comatose, and moribund.

A diet deficient in fats can be harmful, too, since the body depends upon food intake to supply several essential fats that it cannot manufacture for itself. These fats are needed for the health of all glands and especially the prostate gland in men. A deficiency of them may also lead to abnormally dry skin and scalp, reduced joint lubrication, and other body disturbances.

On the other hand, excess fats in the diet may, as some fat diet proponents have claimed, lead to weight loss, but that is because the fats in excess produce diarrhea, which provides little chance for foods to be absorbed. That is dangerous because daily diarrhea can lead to loss of essential vitamins, minerals, and other nutrients, excess loss of body fluids, and loss of essential electrolytes such as magnesium, potassium, and sodium, and if these are not quickly replaced, coma and death may result.

There are also the diets low in protein, so low that they carry the risk that the dieter will lose protein from his own body, using up muscle and organ tissue and generally weakening the body. Anyone already somewhat

weakened—by a liver problem, kidney disorder, heart disease, or anemia—
can be placed in a hazardous situation by further tissue depletion.

Fad diets may put some people in the hospital, gravely ill; or they
may kill some. But for the great majority of those who use them—perhaps
briefly attaining cosmetic near-elegance with one, bouncing up on the
scales again, taking pounds off again with another, only to rebound again,
and on and on—the long-term consequences are the major hazards.

Yo-yoing is risky since every time weight goes up it puts a load on the
cardiovascular system. And aside from the yo-yo danger, the very fact of
being overweight much more of the time than being at ideal weight means
that all the risks of increased morbidity and mortality from excess weight
have to be borne.

THE NEW INSIGHTS: THE FAT CELL PHENOMENON

Excess weight, a spare tire, becomes a case of obesity when it adds 15
percent or more to its owner's ideal weight. Many Americans eat their way
to such weights, but not until adulthood.

Many others, however, get an early start, even in the first few months
of life, toward corpulence. They are the particularly unlucky ones—fat in
the sandbox, fat through school, fat now, and facing perhaps the toughest
fight of all if they are not to die fat.

The villains for them: tiny structures called fat cells, located throughout the body, common in tissue between skin and muscles, with large concentrations in the abdomen and around such organs as the kidneys and
heart.

All of us have such cells to collect and hold fat from food intake meant
to be kept in storage for delivery into the bloodstream and burning as
energy when needed.

Whether all of us have exactly the same number of fat cells at birth is
an unknown. But two facts about the cells have become known very recently. One is that once a fat cell appears in the body, it stays there for a
lifetime although the amount of fat stored in any given cell can vary from
day to day and year to year. The second fact is that the number of these
permanent fat cells can triple or quadruple in the first few months of life.
And such multiplication of fat cells presents a considerable problem. The
baby who is fed so that there is no such multiplication will have far less
trouble with obesity throughout a lifetime than the infant fed in excess and
stuck thereafter with an excess of fat cells.

The discovery of the way infancy-formed fat cells form a base for lifetime weight problems was made by Dr. Jerome Knittle of Mount Sinai School of Medicine and Dr. Jules Hirsch of Rockefeller University in New York City.

Starting first with rat studies, they took newborn litters from various mothers and redistributed them so that some mothers had only four infants to feed and others had up to twenty-two.

After only a few days, the small litter rats, thriving on the milk abundance, were clearly growing faster than rats in the larger litters compelled to compete intensively for the milk. At that point, all the young rats were given all the food they wanted. The slim rats stayed slim; the fat rats got fatter.

When some of the rats were sacrificed, the fat rats were found to have more fat cells than the lean rats. When, next, some of the fat rats were starved down to little more than skin and bones and then sacrificed, they still had abnormally large amounts of fat cells although the cells had shrunk in size and content.

Turning to humans, Dr. Knittle studied two hundred obese children. With a special syringe he removed small amounts of tissue from under the skin. He found two-year-old obese children with double the number of fat cells of normal-weight children of the same age, and five-year-olds carrying more fat cells than normal adults.

Some investigators believe that the indestructibility of fat cells represents a survival mechanism dating back to the Stone Age when cavemen were lucky to find food once a month and, having found some, would gorge and store the food in their fat cells to be released slowly for energy over the weeks of starvation until the next big meal. Like the appendix, for which we have no known use, the fat cell survival mechanism is not needed now but it persists.

Excess fat cells do not just sit there quietly. There is some evidence that the fat cells communicate with the appetite center in the brain, although there is no understanding yet as to how. Apparently, some investigators believe the fat cells communicate a need to be filled and an excess of such cells may lead to excess appetite.

This may explain the great difficulty for people obese since childhood in keeping excess weight off. In one two-year study carried out by Dr. David Swanson at Loyola University, twenty-five patients, all obese since infancy, managed to lose as much as 150 pounds each in four months—more than a pound a day. But within two years, every one of the twenty-five was obese again.

The excess fat-cell phenomenon helps to explain their problem even though it does nothing to ameliorate it. But it does offer some guidance for avoiding such extremely difficult to combat obesity in the future.

If the final answer is not in yet on why one child accumulates more fat cells than another, there is good reason to suspect where the answer lies.

It seems highly likely then that the more food a baby eats the more fat cells he develops. But there is evidence that the fatter a child's parents are, the more likely he is to be fat. In the Boston area, a study of several thousand obese children revealed only 7 percent had normal-weight parents while 80 percent had obese parents. It is not, scientists believe, that obesity is inherited in such cases but rather that a child born into a fat family learns the family eating habits and early loads himself with excess fat.

Another influence is very much at work. In a study of 130 infants, Johns Hopkins University pediatricians discovered that although the needs of a two-month-old infant can be met adequately through formula, breast milk, or milk alone, 93 percent of the infants of that age were being fed dry cereal as well, and 70 percent were also receiving strained fruit. The mean intake of protein was almost 60 percent and total caloric intake about 30 percent above recommended allowances. The pattern remained the same—feeding to excess—when the babies were studied again at the age of seven months. A basic problem, the investigators reported, is the false conviction of many people that a fat baby is healthier than a skinny one.

In a recent study by the New York City Department of Health, the finding was that it is not the baby but the mother who molds the baby's appetite. Rather than listen to medical advice about sensible diets, the surveyed mothers acknowledged that they paid more attention to advice from relatives, to TV commercials, and even to old wives' tales.

Many physicians see at work a spirit of keeping up with the Joneses by having an infant gobble up formula to produce a better-looking growth chart—a decidedly unhealthy spirit in view of the evidence of what excessive feeding can do. One New York obesity specialist calls the intestinal tract "the biggest battleground between mother and child in early childhood," and believes that it is going to take a rather Herculean effort on the part of medical men to encourage mothers to nourish children sensibly and not excessively if millions are to be saved from a lifetime of obesity.

THE "HABIT BELLY" CONCEPT

A new approach to weight control focuses on changing eating habits through behavior therapy or behavior modification. It holds that eating too much is learned behavior, a habitual response to stimuli in the social environment, and it applies principles of psychology to change the habits that make for overeating.

It points to the fact that a newborn baby will naturally react to an inner stimulus, hunger pang discomfort, by sucking on a bottle until he feels comfortably full, then stop. But even during infancy, external cues begin to intrude and trigger eating. His mother praises him for finishing his bottle and he may do some of his eating thereafter not out of hunger but for her praise. Does he get a sweet cracker, perhaps, to ease teething pain; soon sweet may be equated with pleasure. As a toddler he may bump himself in a fall and get a lollipop to comfort him. He is forming a new habit of eating without hunger.

To an extent, virtually all of us may do some eating without hunger, but the obese are far ahead. It appears that fat people eat in large measure because of environmental cues—time of day, odors, palatability of food, and so on. They eat at the sight of food. Watching television or reading, they often nibble without thinking. They often eat simply because it is mealtime and even though not hungry finish everything in front of them. And they commonly eat when they feel depressed or bored or lonesome.

This is learned behavior and fad diets will not surmount it. When and why the behavior came to be learned is of no particular interest to behavior therapists. What is of paramount concern is developing relatively simple and practical methods of changing the behavior.

The methods vary. One physician advises his overweight patients to keep a diary of everything they eat and analyze it daily. If they overindulge at certain times, they can learn what leads them to do so, and be alert for and more resistant to the trigger or triggers. He suggests that if they experience emergency cravings during the day, they can prepare a supply of emergency foods in the morning—celery stalks, carrot sticks, radishes, cucumbers—and use them to satisfy the cravings, breaking the habit of giving in to cravings for calorie-loaded snacks. And he urges them to drink two eight-ounce glasses of iced or chilled water five minutes before each meal; if they drink water first, many people can accommodate more readily to eating less food.

At the University of Kentucky College of Medicine, Dr. Hugh A. Storrow, professor of psychiatry, has found it valuable to direct patients to remove from their homes all foods that can be eaten without preparation; to pause and lay down their utensils after each bite; never to eat when doing anything else such as reading or watching TV; and as much as possible to engage in pleasurable alternative activities, whatever they may be for an individual, whenever they get the urge to eat between meals.

Some therapists advise patients to make hunger and satiety work for them. Since it may take twenty minutes from the start of a meal for the stomach to begin to signal satiety feelings to the brain, they urge stretching a meal to half an hour or more. One trick, some suggest, is to lay down knife and fork and sit quietly for thirty seconds. This can be tried at first toward the end of a meal when appetite is already blunted. Gradually, the number and duration of each pause can be lengthened until eventually there are several interruptions of two minutes each during a meal.

At the University of Pennsylvania, Dr. S. B. Penick and a Department of Psychiatry team have used behavior modification techniques with great success. They also ask patients to keep detailed daily records so that they become aware of how much they eat, and the speed and circumstances associated with eating. Because most obese people habitually eat in different places at many different times during the day, patients are encouraged to confine their eating, including snacking, to just one place. They are also asked to use a distinctive table setting, including an unusual, colored place mat and napkin, and to make their eating a pure experience involving no other activity. In addition, they are asked to do such exercises as count each mouthful of food, put utensils back on the plate every third mouthful until that mouthful is thoroughly chewed and swallowed. Among patients so treated, 53 percent have lost more than twenty pounds and 13 percent more than forty pounds, results better than for those receiving conventional group psychotherapy and among the best ever reported in the medical literature.

THE CONCEPT OF NOT JUST TOO MUCH FOOD
BUT TOO MUCH OUT OF FOOD

We have touched briefly on the roles in obesity of the lack of fiber in the diet and of excess sugar.

Both deserve consideration in greater depth.

For one thing, obesity appears to be a modern phenomenon. In the late seventeenth century, agricultural and technological changes were opening up a new age of elegance for the upper classes. An agricultural revolution was beginning to provide, at least for them, more food, with striking increases in meat, milk, and butter. From the recently founded West Indies colonies, sugar was being imported for use in coffee, chocolate, and tea, and then in cakes and puddings.

A new milling system now began to produce flour of varied qualities. In all, some of the bran was sifted out. And the palest flour, with the least bran left in, was most expensive, most prized—a status symbol. At first, white flour and, from it, white instead of whole-meal bread, were strictly for the upper classes. Later in the eighteenth and nineteenth centuries, the highly refined flour and the products of it became available to the lower classes.

The feeding habits of the gentry in other sophisticated Western nations changed much in parallel with those of the gentry in Britain in the eighteenth century—and gross obesity appeared in all.

Much more recently, obesity has made its appearance in Africa, becoming increasingly common where it was rare before, as the feeding habits of Western nations have been adopted.

Was it the tampering with food that led to obesity? Why not the change in living patterns, the increasingly sedentary existence, the decline in physical activity?

But the view that lack of exercise is responsible for obesity, common though it is, seems quite vulnerable to some investigators. One of these investigators, Surgeon-Captain T. L. Cleave, former director of medical research at the Institute of Naval Medicine in Britain, points out that nature "certainly never inflicts on any organism the penalty of obesity for 'laziness.'

"Even in cases of *imposed* lack of exercise," he emphasizes, "obesity does not occur as long as the food is not tampered with. A visit to any zoo will show this clearly. Here will be seen the two opposite poles of creation —a large animal like a tiger, accustomed to hunt its prey over many square miles of jungle, and now confined to a space measured in cubic feet; and a small bird, like a finch, accustomed to fly about many acres of countryside, and now confined to a space measured in cubic inches. In each case the natural exercise has been enormously curtailed. Yet, just because each of these creatures continues to take its food in its natural form, in the one case raw meat and bones, and in the other case unaltered seeds, the weight remains the same and obesity does not occur."

The *sole* cause of obesity, Cleave is convinced, lies in the consumption of refined carbohydrates, and neither a large appetite nor a dislike of exercise is a cause, although, to be sure, once obesity is present, restraint of appetite or enforcement of exercise will reduce it.

Cleave was among the very first to focus on refined carbohydrates— both starches and sugars from which fiber has been removed—as the cause of obesity. Today, a growing body of scientists, taking a fresh view of the obesity problem, are tracing it to the use of refined carbohydrates that, in effect, pervert the appetite and appetite control.

Carbohydrates make up a large part of the modern diet, typically providing 50 percent of the calories. And they are, very largely, refined carbohydrates, from which much or even all the fiber has been removed.

Why should fiber removal have any great consequences in terms of obesity?

For one thing, fiber removal changes the physical state of the food, and that, in turn, alters the demands the food makes upon the digestive tract.

Fiber is the skeleton providing strength and cohesion for plants, and it is exactly because plants have such strength and cohesion that animals, including man, have to grind them with their teeth and break them up to extract the nutrients.

As long as they are fiber rich, foods have to be chewed. But with fiber removed, chewing is no longer needed. And a critical fact is that refined foods, with little or no fiber, are much easier and quicker to ingest. In one study, volunteers took forty-five minutes to eat a loaf of whole-meal bread; they took only thirty-two minutes to eat an equivalent loaf of white bread simply because the whole-meal bread took more chewing.

As for sugar, when extracted from the beet or cane, it is a material you can drink—whereas to get sugar from the original cane or beet requires much chewing, as does getting sugar from a normal source such as fruit.

Moreover, fiber has a space-filling effect. It is nonnutritive, is not absorbed, does not supply calories; and so less energy (or potential pounds) is available than if the same amount of fiber-depleted food is consumed.

Fiber, in addition, provides a third obstacle to obesity—by promoting satiety. We have seen that chewing a food tends to make it more appetite-satisfying. The chewing stimulates secretion of both saliva and gastric juices. The saliva and juices, along with the food, help to fill the stomach and promote satiety. The eating of fiber-depleted food calls for less chewing, less saliva, less juices, less stomach distention, and less satiety.

"If man restricted himself to unrefined foods," says Dr. Kenneth Heaton of Bristol University, England, "he would not suffer obesity except in rare and special circumstances. He is obese because the foods he eats are artificially easy to ingest and unsatisfying. He is not overeating. He is eating foods with an artificially high energy to satiety ratio. It is not his appetite center that is at fault and producing an abnormal demand for satiety. It is the foods that are at fault because they have been changed so that an abnormally large amount is needed for normal satiety."

Heaton often demonstrates his point with a can of Coke and four medium-sized eating apples. The one can contains 38 grams of sucrose, the equivalent of 10 sugar lumps or 4 1/2 to 5 teaspoonfuls of sugar. The four apples contain the same amount. "And I simply ask," says Heaton, "which of those will be easiest and quickest to take and which will satisfy you most? Isn't the answer obvious? Anyone who has eaten one apple knows that to eat four would leave you feeling stuffed, whereas with a can of Coke you can just quench your thirst and go on half an hour later to have a meal."

In one study in Cape Town, fifty-one office workers were instructed to cut out sugar-containing foods but to try and maintain their weight by eating more of other foods. They did not succeed in the weight maintenance. After five months, weights averaged three pounds less than when they started and some in the group involuntarily lost more than five pounds.

In San Francisco, a group of men already on a cholesterol-lowering diet undertook to reduce the carbohydrate content of the diet by eliminating all sugar. Although the altered diet was designed so it provided the same number of calories as the original cholesterol-lowering one, the men's weight fell by an average of four pounds in six months.

In both these studies, it was only refined sugar that was excluded. It is likely that if other refined carbohydrates had been left out and replaced with unrefined, there would have been greater weight loss.

Many recent studies have shown that out of a typical modern refined diet, 93.2 percent of the available energy in the foods can be absorbed. That is high. Other studies have shown that if the diet is altered to contain brown instead of white bread, plus fruit and vegetables, the figure goes down to 91.1 percent. And on whole-meal bread, high in fiber, almost completely unrefined, the absorption rate is cut further to 88 to 89 percent.

Some investigators believe that it is the latter rate—88 to 89 percent absorption of energy in the diet—that is the natural, inherited, evolutionary rate needed to keep body weight at a natural level.

Calories, of course, do count. It is not, however, just calories but the kind that count most. And if the calories are in foods with bulk from fiber, with high satiety value and with less of them being absorbed, it may not even be necessary to do any calorie counting to lose weight.

After his first studies of refined versus unrefined carbohydrates, Dr. Heaton altered his own personal diet to exclude refined sugar, white flour, and refined carbohydrates as completely as he could. He did it on general health grounds, with no interest in or any need at all for losing weight. He was not overweight at all. Much to his surprise, he lost weight, some fifteen pounds. His wife, also a physician, altering her diet along with his, also unexpectedly lost weight, ten pounds. There were no restrictions at all on caloric intake. Both husband and wife ate as much as they wanted and still do. All they do is use whole-meal bread and avoid artificially sweet-ened foods. And associates of Dr. Heaton at the university and the Bristol Royal Infirmary have similarly lost weight with the same diet changes and without calorie counting.

(For suggestions on cutting down refined carbohydrates and increas-ing the unrefined, high-in-fiber carbohydrates in your diet, see chapter 7.)

12

If your gut rumbles, it may or may not be singing a significant tune...and more on that most common problem of intestinal gas

IT WAS not destined to make any popular Hit Parade but a special tape recording released to the medical profession not long ago contained an array of gut rumblings that was meant to focus physicians' attention on the value of listening to intestinal sounds in patients.

Although many physicians have forgotten it, Dr. LeRoy H. Stahlgren, professor of surgery at the Temple University School of Medicine, Philadelphia, who made the recording, reminded them that a very old technique—using a stethoscope applied to the abdomen—can be invaluable in diagnosing many gastrointestinal malfunctions.

All bowels rumble and the father of medicine, Hippocrates, long ago employed the descriptive, onomatopoetic term borborygmus for the sounds. They arise from the peristaltic contractions of the intestinal wall and from the movement of gas and liquid within the intestinal channel, or lumen.

Quite normally, there are soft, gurgling sounds that wax and wane in concert with the rhythmic contractions of intestinal loops. The loudness of the sounds indicates the force with which the intestines are contracting while the frequency of the sounds indicates the rate of contractions. Various disorders can cause changes in the loudness and contraction rates as well as the pitch or tonal quality.

When there is an obstruction—as, for example, when a peptic ulcer blocks the opening leading from the stomach to the duodenum and small intestine—there will be increased contractions and loud, high-pitched sounds much like those of splashing water in a partially filled container. With an obstruction in the colon, there will be explosive staccato pops. With gastroenteritis (see Part Two), however, although intestinal activity increases and the sounds are more frequent, there is no substantial heightening of the pitch of the sounds.

In a person complaining of gas, there will be rushing, crackling noises, louder and more turbulent than normal. The sounds are hurried but pitch is not appreciably modified.

Dr. Stahlgren's message to fellow physicians is that the stethoscope can provide an "auditory window" through which intestinal function can be monitored and that it ought to be included as part of every examination of patients with abdominal disorders.

"THE WHIRLWINDS"

If rumblings of gas in the gut accompany some organic intestinal conditions, they also can be—and all too commonly are—present without them.

Discomfort from intestinal gas is an old story—and a modern one. The estimable Benjamin Franklin, in a moment of pique with a restless gut, exclaimed: "What comfort can the vortices of Descartes give to a man who has whirlwinds in his bowels!"

Too much gas causing abdominal pain and bloating is the most common gastrointestinal complaint in medical practice. And gas distress can sometimes produce symptoms alarmingly similar to and often mistaken for those of organic diseases.

The formidable powers of gas are demonstrated in the extreme in pasture bloat, a condition that occurs in cattle that have gorged on legumes (cattlemen call it "green dynamite"). The rumen (first stomach) of cattle is a fermentation vat capable of producing copious amounts of gas, and all the more so when handed "green dynamite." Cattle, exactly like bipeds, release some gas by belching but in pasture bloat the gas is trapped in a frothy mass of foam and cannot be belched up.

The consequences are dire: the rumen distends, enormous internal pressures build up, and at the climax death comes quickly to the prostrated animal unless its rumen is punctured with an instrument.

Fortunately, gas distress in humans is far less catastrophic, although under exceptional circumstances it is possible for a healthy stomach to suffer a "blowout" from overdistention. Some years ago, University of Oregon researchers reported three instances of stomach rupture in patients who received an excess of oxygen by the nasal route. The Oregon physicians estimate that the greatest amount of food or gas the human stomach can hold without rupturing is four quarts, a volume ordinarily beyond attainment by even the most borborygmic trencherman.

But the ability of gas distress to mimic symptoms of serious organic diseases can be alarming. It can produce pain in the lower left chest and at times may be referred to the left side of the neck, shoulder, or arm—which may be confused with angina pectoris, the chest pain associated with coronary heart disease.

It can produce discomfort much like that of gallbladder disease. More than one gallbladder has been unnecessarily removed as the result of symptoms caused by flatulence, not gallbladder disease.

Many vital organs are located in areas where gas pressures may be exerted. Which is why skilled diagnosis is necessary rather than any leaping to unwarranted conclusions. It is sometimes necessary to prove to an understandably worried patient that despite thoughts about the direst of diseases, his or her problem is all a matter of gas.

The most frequent consequences of gas distress, however, are not those that fill one with morbid thoughts of disease, but which cause private distress, pain, bloating, rumbling, excessive belching and flatulence, and sometimes public embarrassment in social situations.

WHERE DOES GAS COME FROM?

Gas in the gastrointestinal tract is normal and inevitable. As we have seen, we all swallow some air with food and drink; belching can follow but does only when you are in an upright position or lying on your left side. In these positions, the gas is near the cardia, or upper opening of the stomach, and when the sphincter muscle there relaxes, belching can take place.

Air that is not belched quickly descends the gut to be expelled at a rate of about half a quart a day, either as part of defecation or independently. The air can reach the upper part of the colon within six to to fifteen minutes and may be expelled within as short a time as half an hour.

Analyses of gas removed from the upper gastrointestinal tract and the lower tract have shown great variations from person to person. In general, gas removed from the stomach has a composition similar to exhaled air. It is full of nitrogen, of course, since air is four-fifths nitrogen and nitrogen remains inert in the GI tract. It is low in oxygen and high in carbon dioxide. Flatus contains very low oxygen and high carbon dioxide levels, but beyond this the composition is quite variable. Odor is contributed by mere traces of a great variety of gases derived from the bacterial fermentation processes that go on in the colon.

Also air-entrapping habits such as gum chewing, smoking, talking, and gulping can inflate one's pneumatic pressures.

Some people are accomplished, though usually unknowing, air swallowers. They suffer from what is known medically as aerophagia, literally, "air eating." We have seen that carbonated drinks, often taken to trigger a burp, may merely increase the unconscious air swallowing, and that some people swallow large amounts of air because they eat too fast; some, because they are emotionally upset. Some gastroenterologists tend to label aerophagia as a nervous habit by which, as one puts it, the individual "just scratches himself with air."

Some gas sufferers may be on a special diet that includes low-caloric liquids, which are offered as complete meals in themselves. Frequently they produce the symptoms of excess gas.

A certain amount of gas also accumulates by diffusion from the bloodstream into the intestinal tract. And some—not as much as many people suppose but up to about 30 percent—comes from bacterial fermentation and food ingredients.

There are such marked differences in individual reactions to foods that it is impossible to name one that produces gas in all people all the time. But many people know that, for them, certain foods cause gas or "don't set well."

In one study, when five hundred patients were questioned about foods that caused gaseous distress, onions were named the worst gas producers, cooked cabbage next, and, in descending order, raw apples, radishes, baked beans, cucumbers, milk, melons, cauliflower, chocolate, coffee, lettuce, peanuts, and eggs.

REMEDIES

Anyone who is a chronic sufferer from gas for which there is no organic cause can make something of a dent on the problem by not gulping food and drink, by avoiding gum chewing if that is a habit, and by making some conscious effort not to gulp air.

A trial of eliminating some foods, such as those mentioned, could be worthwhile. And there are others that may be worth an elimination trial: soufflés, beaten omelets, cake, fresh bread, and meringues contain more gas than other foods; and malted milk, effervescent drinks, and whipped egg white contribute more gas than fluid to the stomach.

For milder forms of flatulence, local application of heat by electric pad, hot water bottle, or a warm bath may provide some relief.

For acute pain and abdominal distention, relief may sometimes be obtained by massage, or a pint-sized lukewarm tap-water enema.

Several positions may provide relief by encouraging the expulsion of gas. Not long ago a nurse, after undergoing surgery and the agonies of gas retention (a common problem after surgery), set out to determine what positions might be effective. She has come up with several that help postsurgical patients and might do the same for nonsurgical gas sufferers.

One is called the "telephoning teen-ager" position. It involves simply lying, stomach down, on a bed, with legs bent at the knees and held up at a comfortable 90-degree angle, and with arms, bent at the elbows, turned toward each other and stretched out ahead and supporting the head held higher than the rest of the body. It is, claims the nurse, a restful position and effective if the gas problem is not too severe—and sometimes also circling the lower legs provides mild abdominal muscle exercise, which aids peristalsis and the expulsion of flatus.

Another position, the "headstand," may be useful for stubborn flatulence. By reversing the gravitational field, it serves to "roll back" any fecal obstruction and allows the gas to rise freely. It is acceptable, says the nurse, to prop one's feet against a wall or support the body in a corner while standing on your head. The position has to be maintained only briefly; it should not be maintained for great lengths of time since the flow of blood to the head may cause flushing, headache, and other discomforts. After a brief headstand, you return immediately to a comfortable reclining position, and with the gas now at the rectum expel it easily.

A slightly less strenuous variation, called the "modified headstand," is achieved by bending over the edge of a bed or a padded table so the body forms a right angle, flexed at the hips, with the hands on the floor and the legs supported on the flat surface. While not "pure" in form, observes the nurse, this is acceptable for the aged or infirm.

AND OTHER REMEDIES

In recent years, simethicone, an inert chemical compound, has been used as a help for the gaseous. Simethicone, which is available in a number of preparations, is designed to keep sticky materials from adhering to each other and to disrupt bubble surfaces so that trapped gas can merge more readily into a large free bubble that could be more easily vented—in industry or in humans. The silicone material is of a type used in industry to defoam liquid products. (One ounce is enough to defoam 250,000 pounds of molasses.) Production of wine, yeast, ice cream, varnishes, and many other materials may be impeded by excessive foam formation, a phenomenon that may be somewhat comparable to gas-filled bubbles that may collect in the human intestinal tract.

As for some of the old remedies, we seem to have lost them by the wayside. In the opinion of some leading gastroenterologists, they were more effective than any in common use today.

One of these was asafetida, a gum resinous substance, which used to be remarkably effective as a carminative—an agent for removing gases from the GI tract—when taken by mouth in the form of a pill.

"But unfortunately," says one of the country's top gastroenterologists, Dr. Eddy D. Palmer, "asafetida is no longer manufactured in this country. This is a great pity."

Plain charcoal is helpful in a large majority of cases, Dr. Palmer reports, although unfortunately charcoal for medicinal purposes is not always easy to find. However, with a little effort by an interested pharmacist it can be obtained in tablet form.

Dr. Palmer has some other relatively simple recommendations. "History tells us," he notes, "that every society since New Testament days has found that buttermilk preparations are very helpful for gas problems and for colon function in general. One useful move is for the gassy patient to add large amounts of buttermilk (at least a quart a day) to his diet. If he cannot stand buttermilk, the commercial Lactobacillus preparations [available in drugstores under such trade names as Bacid, DoFUS, and Lactinex] are the next best, although not really a good substitute for the real thing."

A NEW INSIGHT INTO THE GAS PROBLEM

Some gastroenterologists have long recognized that there seems to be a great deal of individual variation from patient to patient in tolerance to gas; that the patient having the most trouble is not necessarily the one who has the most gas; and in some patients, a small amount of gas can cause a great deal of misery.

A study reported in 1975 throws new light on the gas problem.

At the University of Minnesota, three investigators—Drs. Robert B. Lasser, John H. Bond, and Michael D. Levitt—used a special technique to study the volume, production rate, and transit of intestinal gas in sixteen patients with bloating and nonorganic abdominal pain. These were matched with eight healthy volunteers.

The investigators infused gas through a tube down the throat, stomach, and duodenum into the jejunum portion of the small intestine, then later removed all the gas from both the stomach and rectum.

They established that the volume and composition of the gas was similar in the patients and the healthy volunteers, as were the production rates of various normal gases in the intestine.

But there were striking differences in the symptoms induced by infusing the gas as well as its transit. Thirteen of the sixteen patients developed severe abdominal pain and distention but only one of the healthy volunteers had the same complaints.

Moreover, in those complaining of pain, a considerable amount of the gas was found to have been sent back upward from the intestine into the stomach. And the transit time of gas through the GI tract—and out—was on the average about forty minutes, almost twice as long for the pain group as for the others.

Putting all the facts together, the study indicates that gaseous patients do not have any particularly increased volume of gas and, while they may often be more sensitive than others to the presence of gas in the gut, their primary problem is slow transit and disordered intestinal motility.

The best answer to the problem for them could well be not trying to get the gas out but rather treating the irritable gastrointestinal tract for its slow transit and faulty motility.

And with the evidence (see chapter 7) that lack of fiber in the diet has much to do with slow transit time of intestinal contents and even irritation of the colon, the replacement of fiber could turn out to be, although no definitive studies have thus far been done to establish this, a considerable aid for the flatulent.

PART TWO

The Unhappy World and Righting It

IT IS A WONDERFUL world, the human digestive tract, and a full appreciation of its normal workings can do much to keep it functioning well.

But disturbances do occur. They account for a solid one-sixth of all major illnesses of all types in this country and an even greater proportion of minor but annoying discomforts.

Here are the most important—in terms of commonness or seriousness —of the disorders of the gastrointestinal system, arranged alphabetically: Acute Gastroenteritis, Anal Itching, Appendicitis, Cancer, Constipation, Diarrhea, Diverticular Disease, Gallstones, Gastritis, Hemorrhoids, Hernia, Hiatus Hernia, Indigestion, Intestinal Obstruction, Irritable Colon, Liver Diseases, Malabsorption—Celiac Disease, Pancreatitis, Peptic Ulcer, Pernicious Anemia, Pyloric Stenosis, Regional Enteritis, Ulcerative Colitis, Worm-induced Diseases.

In each case, you will find discussed the nature of the problem, the symptoms, the causes, and the methods of diagnosis, where available, and treatment (including home treatment where possible). Where applicable, surgical treatments are indicated: the various operative procedures available, when they may be essential and when not, how long they take, how much hospitalization is necessary, how long for recovery, what to expect immediately after surgery and during recuperation, and chances for success.

This is meant to be a practical section, helpful in several ways:

Some relatively minor disturbances may be readily correctable at home when you are aware of what causes may be at work and what to do about them.

More serious problems require medical attention, and it is very much worth knowing as much as possible about those problems, how to be alert to them, and what can and should be done for them. Better informed, you are likely to seek help more readily and to get greater benefit from that help. When medical help is required, the less mystery, the less anxiety about it, the more likely will there be success—and quicker success—in treatment.

You will find various medications mentioned here in connection with medical treatment. In addition, Part Three presents a fuller discussion of medications used in the treatment of GI problems—and, as well, of medications used for other purposes but which may sometimes have side effects that involve the GI tract.

It would be well to read through these two sections rather than wait for some disturbance to arise. It is not at all inconceivable that understanding in advance could serve as a preventative.

ACUTE GASTROENTERITIS

Acute gastroenteritis—acute inflammation of the lining of the stomach and intestine—can be caused by a virus ("intestinal grippe"), overindulgence in alcohol, food allergy, food poisoning, various drugs (such as salicylates or aspirinlike compounds, quinacrine, colchicine), heavy metals (arsenic, lead, mercury, cadmium), and infectious diseases (typhoid fever and cholera).

The inflammation develops suddenly, and while the nature and severity of the symptoms depend on the severity of the irritating factor, how much of the gastrointestinal tract is affected, and the general health and resistance of the individual, commonly there is some degree of malaise, loss of appetite, nausea, vomiting, cramps, gut rumbling, and diarrhea. Prostration may occur. In severe cases, blood and mucus may appear in the stools. If the gastroenteritis is infectious in origin, fever often develops.

Treatment. Often, symptoms subside within forty-eight hours. During that time, bed rest is advisable and usually nothing is permitted by mouth as long as nausea and vomiting are present; when they stop, light fluids such as tea and strained broth, bouillon with added salt, and cereal can be taken. And when these are tolerated, other foods such as eggs, gelatin, and simple puddings may be added.

If vomiting persists, fluids may be given by vein to counter dehydration. The vomiting may be controlled by a sedative such as sodium phenobarbital alone or with scopolamine, or by injections of an antiemetic or antivomiting agent such as dimenhydrinate or chlorpromazine. If diarrhea persists, one or another of such agents as paregoric, diphenoxylate with atropine, or a combination of bismuth, belladonna, and kaolin may be used.

In severe cases, medical tests, including stool examination, instrument examination of the lower bowel, and blood counts, may be required to determine whether something more, such as ulcerative colitis, may be involved.

FOOD INFECTION GASTROENTERITIS

In most cases, the bacteria responsible belong to the Salmonella family. Responsible for some outbreaks are other organisms, including *Clostridium perfringens, E. coli, Bacillus cereus*, and streptococci.

Symptoms develop from six to forty-eight hours after contaminated food is eaten. They include headache, chills, fever, muscle aches, nausea, vomiting, cramps, diarrhea, and prostration. In severe cases, both stools and vomitus may contain blood.

Usually, the illness is over in twenty-four to forty-eight hours and sometimes it can be mild enough so that the patient goes about his usual activities during its course.

Treatment is the same as for acute gastroenteritis, above. In severe cases, an antibiotic such as tetracycline, ampicillin, or streptomycin may be used.

STAPHYLOCOCCUS TOXIN GASTROENTERITIS

This sometimes violent upset, one of the most common from food poisoning, is caused by a toxic material produced by staph bacteria growing in such foods as milk, cream-filled pastries, custards, and processed meat and fish. Improperly supervised food handlers are largely responsible for its spread.

Symptoms usually develop within two to four hours after the contaminated food is eaten; they include nausea, vomiting, cramps, diarrhea, and sometimes headache and fever.

The attack is brief, commonly lasting only three to six hours, and recovery is complete. Treatment, if needed, is the same as for acute gastroenteritis. In very severe cases, fluid infusion into a vein to replace lost fluid and electrolytes often produces dramatic relief.

BOTULISM

This acute intoxication, or poisoning, is almost always caused by improperly preserved food in which a bacillus, C. botulinum, grows and produces a toxin.

Symptoms may appear anywhere from four hours to eight days after the food is eaten. They begin with fatigue and lassitude, which are followed after a short time by visual disturbances. Vomiting and diarrhea occur in only about one-third the cases. The visual disturbances are followed by muscle weakening and difficulty in swallowing. Medical advice should be sought as early as possible.

The death rate is high, 65 percent, with most deaths occurring between the second and ninth days, usually from breathing paralysis or pneumonia. For survivors, recovery is slow and there may be weakness of the eye muscles for months, but no permanent aftereffects.

Hospitalization is essential. Botulism antiserum is administered. For relief of anxiety and sedation, a drug such as chloral hydrate may be used. Saliva has to be sucked out of the mouth when the patient cannot swallow and it may be necessary to use intravenous feeding for several days. A respirator is used if there is a threat to breathing.

NONBACTERIAL FOOD POISONING

Some plants and animals contain naturally occurring poisons.

Some species of mushroom contain a poison which, within a few minutes to two hours after being eaten, produces cramps, diarrhea, confusion, sweating, collapse, and sometimes convulsions; still others contain a poison that also causes liver damage, jaundice, low blood pressure, racing pulse, and subnormal temperature. In half the cases mushroom poisoning may be fatal. Medical advice should be obtained immediately for this and the following food poisonings.

Other poison-bearing foods include immature and sprouting potatoes that may contain a toxic compound—solanine—that within a few hours can produce nausea, vomiting, cramps, diarrhea, throat constriction, dilation of the pupils, and prostration. Virtually all victims recover.

Some clams and mussels, especially on the Pacific coast, may from June to October ingest an organism that produces a toxin that is not destroyed by cooking. The toxin causes symptoms very rapidly, within five to thirty minutes, including nausea, vomiting, cramps, muscle weakness, and paralysis. Sometimes death may occur because of breathing failure.

Ergot poisoning results from the eating of grain, particularly rye that is contaminated with a fungus. The symptoms may include chest pain, heartbeat disturbances, weakness, headache, itching, painful cramps in the extremities, gangrene of the toes or fingers, and epilepticlike convulsions.

Fava bean poisoning (favism), which may occur in people sensitive to the bean, produces dizziness, vomiting, diarrhea, severe prostration, and anemia.

In treatment for nonbacterial food poisoning, bed rest is essential. The stomach may be washed out. Meperidine may be given for pain, and fluids may be injected to combat dehydration.

For mushroom poisoning, atropine may be used to combat nervous-system overstimulation. Various drugs may be used for this and other types of poisoning, including drugs to relieve blood-vessel spasm when that is present and an anticonvulsive agent for convulsions.

ANAL ITCHING (PRURITUS ANI)

Of all body areas, the region around the anus is one of the most susceptible to the development of a chronic itch-scratch cycle. That is because the skin in this area is almost always moist and exposed to some fecal matter retained in the anal folds.

Any of many factors can trigger the cycle in which itching leads to scratching—which in turn leads to more itching and then more scratching. Poor anal hygiene or minor injury produced by defecation, or irritating soaps and clothing can do it. So can a local anorectal disease such as hemorrhoids, of course. Infectious and parasitic agents including intestinal parasites such as the pinworm may do it. So, too, allergic conditions and some disorders such as jaundice and diabetes, which are associated with itching.

The itching is usually worse at night and aggravated by heat and by scratching. The affected area is red, with scaly, oozing, or moist excorations.

Treatment. If a definite cause can be established and treated, chances of cure are excellent. But more often than not, no such specific cause can be pinned down. Then the patient has to be urged to stop scratching and to keep the skin of the area dry and clean. Thorough drying should be done with cotton or tissue, and talc or dusting powder should be applied often. In severe, persistent cases, a corticosteroid or cortisonelike drug in a silicone cream may be prescribed for use two or three times a day, which usually provides relief. Physicians warn, however, against the use of anesthetic or other ointments that may cause more trouble by macerating the skin.

APPENDICITIS

The vermiform (wormlike) appendix, an approximately four-inch-long appendage at the juncture of the large and small intestines, serves no known use. Appendicitis, an inflammation of the appendix, occurs most often in children aged six to twelve but may occur at any time in life.

The symptoms usually are nausea, loss of appetite, and abdominal pain. Constipation is common but about 10 percent of patients have diarrhea. Typically, the pain appears first and, at the outset, is localized in the umbilical or navel area of the abdomen. After several hours, it shifts to the lower right abdomen over the appendix and may be continuous, dull or severe, accentuated by coughing, sneezing, or movement. Because the appendix in some people is located in an unusual position, the pain in such cases may localize elsewhere, even on the left side of the abdomen. There may be mild fever, up to 102, in adults, sometimes high fever in young children.

Appendicitis is not always a simple matter to diagnose. Other conditions such as gallbladder disease, kidney infection, pancreas inflammation, pelvic inflammatory disease in women, and even spastic colon may sometimes produce symptoms similar to those of appendicitis and these conditions may have to be ruled out—on the basis of a patient's history and by examination—before appendicitis can be diagnosed. Among aids to diagnosis are a laboratory test showing an increased white blood cell count and tenderness over the appendix elicited when pressure is applied there.

Appendicitis occurs when the appendix becomes obstructed by fecal material, a foreign body, or kinking. Bacteria then multiply and produce inflammation. An infected, inflamed appendix, filled with bacteria and pus, may enlarge to half a dozen or more times its usual size.

Because appendicitis, although common in Western industrialized countries, is rare in Africans on a high fiber diet, there is increasing suspicion (see chapter 7) that our highly refined, low fiber diet may account for our high incidence. The belief is that a low fiber diet, leading to constipation and increased pressures in the colon, may also produce increased pressures in the appendix that could damage the lining of the appendix, paving the way for ready bacterial invasion and multiplication.

Treatment. Fatalities from appendicitis and its complications could be almost completely eliminated if victims avoided attempts at self-treatment and delays in seeking medical help. Any abdominal pain lasting three or four hours properly calls for medical attention. Applications of local heat should be avoided since they may obscure symptoms and may also encourage rupture. Cathartics and enemas also are to be strictly avoided because both intensify intestinal contractions and pressure that may extend into the appendix and lead to rupture.

Early surgical removal is usually recommended in all cases of appendicitis, even those in which the disease cannot be definitely established but is strongly suspected. It is safer to operate than to risk gangrene, rupture, and peritonitis—a widespread infection throughout the abdominal cavity following the bursting of a severely inflamed appendix. Peritonitis often can be controlled with antibiotics but there is some risk of fatality.

Surgery. Surgery for uncomplicated appendicitis is relatively simple and highly successful. Through a two- to five-inch-long incision in the lower right part of the abdomen, the appendix can be lifted up and its base tied, after which the appendage is cut away, and the incision closed. The operation, done under general or spinal anesthesia, may take as little as ten minutes. When there are complications, an hour or two may be needed.

After an operation for uncomplicated appendicitis, the patient is often out of bed the next day, although there is some discomfort from the incision for two or three days. Often, the patient can go home in five or six days; the wound is completely healed in seven to ten days, after which your doctor may advise complete resumption of all activities. A normal diet is usually resumed within a few days after the operation.

When there is a complication, such as rupture with or without peritonitis, the hospital stay may be lengthened to two weeks to a month, with the use of special measures, including antibiotic treatment and intravenous medications.

CANCER

STOMACH CANCER

Fortunately, even if for unknown reasons, cancer of the stomach has been declining in incidence in the United States in recent years. It is largely concentrated at ages over sixty and affects men twice as often as women.

Symptoms include upper abdominal discomfort, which sometimes but not always is worse after eating; pain, sometimes irregular, over the pit of the stomach; appetite loss; weight loss; vomiting; and anemia. The symptoms may occur singly or in various combinations.

Diagnosis is aided by X-ray films of the stomach. Another important help is gastroscopy in which, under local anesthesia, a lighted tube is passed via the mouth into the stomach for examination of a growth and removal of a small piece (biopsy) for microscopic examination.

Surgery. Immediate surgery is essential when stomach cancer is diagnosed and may even be strongly advisable in cases where there is doubt.

Depending upon the extent of the cancer, a major portion of the stomach or all of it may have to be removed along with lymph nodes and adjacent membranes and fatty tissue. If the entire stomach is to be removed, a connection may be made between the esophagus and the duodenum (the first part of the intestine) so that food passes directly from one to the other.

The operation, carried out under general anesthesia, may require from two to five hours or more depending upon the extent of the surgery. For several days afterward, there will be moderate pain and feedings will be by vein. The incision—which can run either across the upper part of the abdomen or from breastbone to about the navel in the center or to one side—heals in about two weeks, about the length of the hospital stay. After complete stomach removal, small, frequent meals rather than large ones are needed.

Overall, the five-year survival rate after stomach cancer surgery has been 11 percent for men, 14 percent for women. However, when surgery is done early, with the cancer still confined to the stomach, the rate has been 37 percent for men and 43 percent for women. Also, there is increasing hope now that with earlier recognition and treatment and with newer experimental methods of treatment the survival rates may be improved.

INTESTINAL CANCER

Cancer of the small bowel is rare. But the colon, or large bowel, is a major site for malignancy. Cancer of the colon (and of the rectum) accounts for about one-eighth of all malignancies in the United States and much of the Western world. Because it is relatively uncommon in Africa and elsewhere in the world not yet given to eating Western diets, attention is increasingly centered on the possibility that the refined foods and lack of dietary fiber characteristic of Western diets may be responsible for colorectal cancer; also, that it might be sharply reduced with a return of fiber to the diet.

Cancer of the colon may manifest itself by blood in the stool, by cramps, by a change in bowel habits (either from few stools to many or from many to few). In some cases, anemia, weakness, and weight loss develop.

About three-fourths of colonic cancers occur low enough in the colon so that they can be seen with the sigmoidoscope, an instrument that can be inserted through the rectum for a distance of about ten inches. An important new diagnostic development is the colonoscope, a slender, flexible instrument that can be inserted much further, allowing visual examination of the whole length of the colon.

Other aids to diagnosis are examinations of stool samples for the presence of occult—or hidden—blood, and X-ray films taken after a barium enema.

Surgery. When cancer of the colon is diagnosed, surgery is the only definitive treatment.

Surgery also may be considered when benign growths, called polyps or adenomas, are found in the colon. The growths, which extend from the mucous membrane lining and may be attached by long stalks, occur in about 10 percent of the population, may appear at any age, cause few if any symptoms, and are often discovered during periodic medical checkups. Because some of these growths have a tendency to become malignant over a period of time, their removal is advised by many doctors. And their removal is relatively simple: An instrument can be inserted either through the sigmoidoscope or the colonoscope and a polyp can be snared or burned off.

For a cancer of the colon, surgery involves removing the malignancy along with the section of colon containing it and, to be safe, some more of the colon on each side; also the mesentery, or suspending membrane, in the area since the mesentery can provide a pathway through which cancer cells from the original site may spread. The two remaining ends of the colon are then stitched together securely.

Prior to surgery, during several days of hospitalization, intensive antibiotic or other drug treatment is used to sterilize the colon, anemia is treated, and the patient strengthened. After the operation, which is carried out under general or spinal anesthesia and may require up to five hours, there may be several days of discomfort. Healing of the incision over the tumor site, usually from five to eight inches long, takes about two weeks. Bowel function usually returns within the first week, sometimes in a few days, although feeding will be by vein for two to four days. Hospitalization usually lasts about two weeks.

After surgery for cancer of the colon, the five-year overall survival rate for women has been 47 percent and for men 42 percent. But the rates increase when the disease is not widespread: 74 percent for women and 70 percent for men.

RECTAL CANCER

Rectal bleeding is often due to other causes but it can be an important symptom of rectal cancer; so, too, any change in bowel habit. The cancer is readily diagnosable since most rectal growths are within reach of the physician's examining finger. Diagnosis is confirmed by microscopic examination of a small piece of the tissue.

Surgery. Complete removal of the malignancy is essential. The rectum is six inches long. If the cancer is no more than three or more inches inside the rectum and away from the anal opening, it may be cut out and enough healthy rectum may remain to preserve sphincter muscle function. Most rectal cancers, however, are nearer to the anal opening so that much of the rectum must be removed, making it impossible to preserve sphincter function.

When the sphincter can be preserved, surgery is done through an incision in the abdomen. A portion of the rectum, the growth, and a section of colon just ahead of the growth are removed. The ends of the colon and rectum are then sutured together.

When much or all of the rectum must be removed, another operation, called abdominoperineal resection, is used. In addition to the incision in the abdomen, another is made in the perineum, an area between the legs. The rectum is cut out and the space left in the perineum is closed. It is then necessary to bring the end of the colon to a circular opening usually in the lower left abdomen to form a colostomy, or abdominal anus.

Surgery for rectal cancer is done under general or spinal anesthesia and may take from two to five hours or longer. The bowel is sterilized beforehand. After the operation, there is discomfort for several days. Feedings may be given by vein. Bowel function returns gradually over a period of about four or five days, both in the cases where colon and rectum can be rejoined and where a colostomy is required.

Often, the patient is out of bed in one to three days, goes home in about two weeks, resumes a normal diet after a few weeks, as well as normal activities.

The overall five-year survival rate for women is 45 percent, for men, 39 percent. For cancers treated in early stages, the rate is 68 percent for women and 63 percent for men.

A new experimental procedure that may be used when a rectal cancer cannot be treated with standard surgical techniques involves inserting an instrument through the rectum to freeze the growth with extreme cold. Early results are promising but, because of the newness of the procedure, long-term results in quantity are not yet available.

LIVER CANCER

Cancer may sometimes develop in the liver itself. The liver, too, because of its key position in blood circulation, is also the most common organ in which cancerous cells from elsewhere in the body may be deposited.

More often than not, liver cancer is fatal because the malignancy is spread throughout the liver and cannot be removed. Sometimes, however, the cancer is confined to one of the two lobes of the liver and removal of that lobe may lead to cure.

Malignancy may cause the liver to become tender and enlarged. Even with extensive involvement, liver function may remain normal for a time but blood enzyme tests may reveal the presence of the cancer. In some cases, jaundice and abdominal fluids may develop.

Surgery to remove a liver tumor is done under general anesthesia through an incision in the upper right abdomen and may require from 1 ½ to 4 hours. When there is success a normal life-style is possible.

CANCER OF THE PANCREAS

An initial symptom of cancer of the pancreas is abdominal pain that commonly radiates to the back. Jaundice, appetite and weight loss, and nausea and vomiting are common. Blood and urine and other laboratory tests and X-ray films may suggest the presence of cancer.

Surgery. About three times as many malignancies occur in the head of the pancreas as in the body and tail.

When the cancer is entirely in the tail, removal of that part of the gland and the spleen, which joins the pancreas at the tip, often may provide cure.

When the malignancy is in the head where it may press upon the bile duct and produce jaundice and when it has grown so much that it cannot be removed entirely, a short circuit operation may be used. The gallbladder is disconnected from the bile duct and connected to the duodenum or stomach so that bile can flow unimpeded, bypassing the pancreas-obstructed bile duct, thus relieving jaundice and severe itching.

Sometimes the short-circuit operation is done first to allow the patient's condition to improve enough for a very extensive procedure that may be lifesaving. In other cases, the extensive, quite heroic, procedure may be used to begin with. The entire portion of the pancreas containing the growth, sometimes even the entire pancreas, is removed, along with all the duodenum to which the cancerous pancreas has adhered. The stomach is then attached to the lower end of the duodenum or to the next portion of the small intestine, the jejunum, and the common bile duct is also attached to one site or the other.

The extensive procedure, performed under general anesthesia through an abdominal incision, may require as long as six hours and carries a high risk, with an operative mortality rate of about 15 percent. But it does hold some hope for cure if the growth has not spread beyond the pancreas.

With removal of much or all of the pancreas, however, diabetes can develop, but this can be controlled with diet and medication. Digestive disturbances can be avoided, too, with use of juice substitutes for the pancreatic juices.

CONSTIPATION

Constipation—the difficult or infrequent passage of stools—is an exceedingly common problem, leading to a huge business in laxatives, cathartics, and other "bowel openers" that are not without their hazards and do nothing to correct the problem at the source.

Constipation can arise from many causes, some of them organic. A debilitating infection, a thyroid or adrenal gland disorder, or an intestinal obstruction, as we have seen, can interfere with bowel movement, which will not return to normal until the organic problem is corrected.

And in the late stages of pregnancy, constipation may result from pressure of the fetus on the large bowel.

But by far the vast majority of cases of constipation—simple constipation as it is called medically—stem from two causes.

One is failure to respond to the urge to evacuate the bowel. Sometimes, especially when traveling, it may be impossible to respond promptly. If this situation persists, it can lead to constipation. A good way, then, to relieve it, along with eating properly and drinking plenty of fluids, is to engage in regular daily physical activity such as walking. A good long walk when you reach your destination is very much in order after a particularly inactive period riding in a car, boat, plane, or train all day.

The other basic problem is faulty diet.

An old wives' tale has it that roughage in the diet is important. Sometimes old wives' tales turn out to be true, well confirmed by scientific studies. This one about roughage falls in that category, except that roughage, as your grandmother or great-grandmother may have termed it, is not really roughage at all. Our highly refined diet today is clearly at fault in constipation. As a means of curing constipation caused by faulty diet, there is nothing better than resorting to an increase of fiber in the diet, as per the suggestions in chapter 7.

Although you may get some relief from a mild laxative (see Part Three), the frequent use of laxatives can be the cause of constipation rather than its cure.

DIARRHEA

Diarrhea—the repeated passage of unformed, watery stools—may be a symptom of many disorders. It occurs with regional enteritis, malabsorption, and gastroenteritis. Sometimes, disease of the liver or malfunctioning of the adrenal or thyroid gland may be responsible. A common cause of chronic diarrhea is the irritable colon syndrome. And diarrhea sometimes can be a response to treatment with antibiotics or to excessive use of laxatives.

In all types of diarrhea there is rapid loss of water and electrolytes, which are essential substances. And chronic diarrhea is likely to lead to anemia and malnutrition.

Treatment. The occasional mild case of diarrhea of short duration can be treated with a bland diet, increased intake of water and other liquids, and use of kaolin-pectin compounds to relieve the symptoms. Paregoric (camphorated tincture of opium) and other medications on prescription are sometimes used to decrease peristaltic contractions and relieve cramps.

In more severe and chronic cases, since diarrhea is a symptom rather than a disease, extensive diagnostic procedures and laboratory tests may be needed to determine the underlying cause. In the meantime, symptomatic treatment must be started to relieve the dehydration, nutritional deficiencies, and disturbances of acid-base balance produced by the loss of water, food elements, and electrolytes in the stools. Liquids and semisolids may be given by mouth at frequent intervals if they can be tolerated. In cases in which the diarrhea is accompanied by vomiting, fluids may be given by vein. Paregoric or other antidiarrheal drugs are often prescribed in small doses to be taken after each stool. The use of soap and warm water to cleanse the anal region after each bowel movement will help reduce local irritation and discomfort.

DIVERTICULAR DISEASE

A diverticulum—from the Latin *divertere*, meaning to turn aside—is a blind pouch, or sac, formed by protrusion of the mucous membrane lining of the intestine into the muscular wall of the intestine. Most often, this happens in the colon, particularly the sigmoid section of the colon. There can be scores, even hundreds, of such small pouches.

Diverticulosis, the presence of many such diverticula, occurs in more than one-third of all Americans and English over the age of forty and the incidence rises far higher in the fifties, sixties, and later. It is the commonest problem of the large bowel.

Diverticulosis is, in the beginning, always benign, producing no difficulties; and it may remain so. But not infrequently the pouches trap and hold fecal material, inflammation develops, and diverticulitis results.

Diverticulitis has sometimes been called "left-sided appendicitis" because the pain it produces seems like the mirror image of the right-sided lower abdominal pain of appendicitis.

The pain is severe, occurring in attacks that may last minutes to hours to days. It may come on at any time without relationship to eating or activities. It may be associated with fever, usually with a degree of constipation, and sometimes with complete cessation of bowel movements for the duration of the attack. Sometimes, constipation and diarrhea may alternate.

The diagnosis can best be established by X-ray examination of the intestine after a barium enema. The film discloses the pouches and sometimes a little barium outside the bowel can be seen on the film, indicating that a pouch has ruptured.

What causes the development of diverticula? It is the high pressures generated in the colon in the effort to move along the small, hard stools characteristic of patients with diverticula, who commonly have long histories of constipation. The pressures, acting on the lining of the intestine, push it through to form the sacs in the weakest areas of the intestinal wall.

Treatment. Acute diverticulitis is treated with bed rest, feedings limited to clear fluids such as soups and broths, and antibiotics such as tetracycline or ampicillin. After several days, this usually leads to improvement in the inflammation. If pain is severe, a drug such as meperidine may be used for relief.

Then, in most cases, an attempt at further medical treatment is made to see if surgery can be avoided. Antibiotic treatment may be extended over a period of two or three weeks before being tapered off.

As an acute attack subsides, a very soft diet may replace the liquid diet. And about six weeks after the attack, more and more physicians now place patients on a high fiber diet. Even in patients with severe diverticular disease who might otherwise be candidates for surgery, a high fiber diet often can prevent the need for operation.

Surgery. There are conditions, however, under which surgery may be advisable. In some cases, there may be considerable obstruction in the colon as a late result of abscess formation caused by diverticular disease. In some cases, an inflamed pouch may burst, spill intestinal contents into the abdominal cavity and produce peritonitis. Surgery is essential, too, if there is a suspicion that cancer is present. Although in most cases, X-ray studies can distinguish between diverticulitis and cancer, it is sometimes difficult to exclude the possibility of cancer, particularly when diverticulitis is accompanied by complications, such as a bursting pouch.

Usually, the operation involves cutting out the diseased section of colon and bringing the healthy sections together and stitching them securely.

If that is not possible because there is so much inflammation that the surgeon cannot do a good job in removing the diseased part of the bowel, the operation may have to be carried out in stages.

First, a loop of disease-free intestine is moved onto the abdomen outside the body and an opening is made in the loop so that, temporarily, stools will come out through the opening, called a colostomy, rather than go on through the diseased portion of the bowel and then to the rectum. With the fecal stream thus diverted, the diseased portion of the colon gets a rest and has a chance to calm down.

In a second operation, the diseased section is removed and the healthy portions joined together. Because the colostomy remains in place and the stool is still being rerouted, the joined portions of intestine have a chance to heal, and usually do so readily.

Finally, in a third operation, the colostomy is eliminated. The opening in the loop is closed, the loop returned to within the abdomen, and the abdominal incision is closed so that stools again take the normal route.

General anesthesia is usually used and the length of operation may vary from an hour to four hours or more depending upon what procedure has to be used. Usually the patient is up within one to three days after surgery. If several procedures are needed, a hospital stay of about ten days may be required for each, with an interval of several weeks between operations.

Although diverticulitis surgery is major, the chances for recovery exceed 95 out of 100.

There may be recurrences but it is increasingly recognized now that a high fiber diet may minimize that likelihood considerably, and possibly even eliminate it, by eliminating the constipation and the pressures within the colon that brought on the disease originally.

GALLSTONES

Because of gallstones, about one-third of a million gallbladders are removed each year in the United States. In American women, gallbladder removal is a more common operation than appendectomy. In England, over 40 percent of women and 20 percent of men develop gallstones by their seventies. The stones also affect younger people.

The gallbladder, as we have seen, is a storage sac for bile coming from the liver, holding an ounce or two and discharging it as needed for use in the duodenum in helping in the digestion of fats.

Gallstones form in some people out of the fluid content of the gallbladder. Commonly they contain cholesterol, which precipitates out of the bile to make small crystals that grow into stones.

Often gallstones are "silent," producing no symptoms. Many people with the stones, however, experience upper abdominal discomfort, bloating, belching, and inability to tolerate fried foods and various vegetables.

It is when complications develop that the pain becomes severe. In an attack of acute cholecystitis, as it is called, a gallstone gets stuck in the neck of the gallbaldder or in a duct, producing obstruction and inflammation. The gallbladder becomes distended and swollen and inflammation can occur even without bacteria because of the obstruction. But the bacteria are usually there to help the inflammation along.

The pain of acute cholecystitis is very severe, knifelike. It occurs in the upper right part of the abdomen and may spread to the back or right shoulder. In some cases, jaundice, or yellow discoloration of the skin, may develop as bile pigments, unable to flow because of the stone obstruction, back up into the bloodstream.

In making a diagnosis, other possibilities have to be considered, including heart attack, pneumonia, perforated duodenal ulcer, acute pancreatitis, and appendicitis. The diagnosis can be established with X-ray films taken after a dye is administered in the form of pills by mouth or by injection into a vein. The film sometimes may show the stone itself or, also indicative of stone formation, the gallbladder may fail to fill with the dye and then does not appear at all on the film.

Despite the prevalence of gallstones, their natural history has not been well studied and the reason for their formation is not clear. But some investigators recently have found a clue in studies showing that gallstones are not a universal phenomenon. Despite their frequency in Western countries, they are rare in Africa and other areas not yet highly industrialized and converted to Western diets. Some early studies, particularly in England, suggest that a refined diet may be responsible and that on a high fiber diet the liver secretes bile that has less cholesterol in it, and is therefore less likely to lead to the settling out of cholesterol crystals and gallstone formation.

Treatment. Once gallstones develop, there is no established medical treatment although a large-scale study is now under way in this country seeking to determine whether a material—chenodeoxycholic acid—can be used safely to dissolve gallstones over an extended period of time; in early, preliminary, small-scale studies it has shown some promise in doing so. Chenodeoxycholic acid is not now commonly available.

Sometimes acute cholecystitis may subside if the stone either drops back into the gallbladder or manages to get through both the cystic duct and the common bile duct into the intestine. Even so, if there should be repeated attacks of acute cholecystitis and the stones eventually get through in each case, the repetitions may lead to chronic cholecystitis in which the gallbladder shrinks and becomes scarred, often producing abdominal discomfort, bloating, and flatulence.

During an acute attack, bed rest and administration of fluids by vein may be advised. Pain-relieving agents may be used. Antibiotics may be given to treat or prevent infectious complications. Abdominal distention may be relieved by means of a tube passed down into the stomach via the nose, allowing the gas to escape. For chronic cholecystitis, if X rays fail to indicate the presence of stones, a low fat diet may be prescribed and antispasmodic drugs may be helpful.

Surgery. Surgery may be advised when during an acute cholecystitis attack the diagnosis is quickly established—within forty-eight to seventy-two hours. If the diagnosis is established later than that, operation may be postponed for about six weeks until the inflammation subsides.

Surgery is considered advisable and even essential for a patient who has recurrent attacks, or when stone-caused jaundice is present, or when the patient is bothered with chronic indigestion, nausea, and flatulence known to be caused by the gallbladder problem. Some physicians and surgeons consider it sensible to remove the gallbladder when even silent stones are detected since they may cause trouble later.

In the operation, called cholecystectomy, the entire gallbladder and the stones it contains are removed through an incision below the ribs and to the right of the navel. During the procedure, X-ray films of the main bile duct are taken after a solution is introduced, and if any stones are present there, the duct is opened and cleaned out.

Cholecystectomy usually is completed in an hour or less, and although the incision causes enough discomfort for several days so that pain-relieving medication is usually needed, the patient is out of bed the next day. Often, after surgery, a rubber tube is inserted through a small incision to drain the operative site of excessive fluids or other materials; it is removed after several days. The hospital stay averages eight to fourteen days.

Cholecystectomy is major surgery but in the hands of a competent surgeon, the odds are greatly in favor of success. In about 80 percent of cases, all digestive disturbances due to gallbladder disease are eliminated. In others, occasionally some minor discomfort may occur as the result of spasm of the common bile duct, which usually can be relieved with antispasmodic medication.

Since the gallbladder is not an essential organ, only a storage depot, and its functions can be taken over by the bile ducts, its absence is of no consequence.

GASTRITIS

Gastritis is an inflammation, either acute or chronic, of the mucous membrane lining of the stomach.

The acute form, sudden and sometimes violent in onset and usually lasting only briefly, is a common disorder. It may be the result of acute alcoholism, drugs such as aspirin, hot spicy foods, foods (notably milk, eggs, fish) to which an individual may be allergic, bacteria or toxins in food poisoning, or an acute viral illness. Acute gastritis also may be caused by swallowing strong acids or alkalis, iodine, potassium permanganate, or other corrosive materials.

The symptoms may include loss of appetite, general malaise, sensations of fullness, nausea, headache, vertigo or dizziness, and vomiting.

In acute corrosive gastritis, the symptoms and signs will depend upon the kind and the amount of the corrosive material swallowed. The lips, tongue, mouth, and throat may be corroded; usually the esophagus, or gullet, is inflamed and painful and there is difficulty in swallowing. Often the abdomen is tender and rigid; blood may be vomited and may appear in the stools; and the pulse may race.

For acute corrosive gastritis, hospitalization and immediate treatment are needed. The corrosive agent must be removed by a stomach tube, emetic, drugs, or neutralized by antidotes. Transfusion of blood or plasma may be needed. And a drug such as meperidine may be required to relieve severe pain.

For the common form of acute gastritis, fortunately, the mucous membrane lining of the stomach is replaced every thirty-six hours so the problem is usually a brief one unless the precipitating cause is still present to continue doing what it did originally: produce inflammation and erosion and sometimes small hemorrhages in the mucous lining.

When the cause of the gastritis is eliminated, symptoms usually disappear within forty-eight hours. So it is important to remove the offending agent whatever it may be—aspirin, alcohol, a specific food or set of foods.

Special diets are not needed; there is no evidence that they are helpful. Often, nausea and vomiting may prevent eating anyway. The drug prochlorperazine may be used to control the nausea and vomiting. Antacids may help to relieve pain, which, if severe, may be relieved by meperidine.

Chronic gastritis is another matter. Its cause is not clearly established, although it may be associated with chronic use of aspirin as well as pernicious anemia, diabetes, and thyroid or other gland disorders.

The symptoms may be much like those of ordinary indigestion, including discomfort upon eating, mild nausea, and burning sensations in the upper abdominal region overlying the stomach. Any long-continued symptoms of seeming indigestion should call for a physician's advice.

There is no specific treatment for chronic gastritis. If chronic aspirin use is involved, it should, of course, be discontinued. Any associated disease requires treatment. Bland diets have not been found to be helpful but any foods that appear to contribute to symptoms should be avoided. Antacids are helpful for some patients.

HEMORRHOIDS (PILES)

Hemorrhoids, also commonly called piles, are stretched veins under the mucous membrane lining of the anal and rectal area. They are called internal when they occur in the wall of the rectum above the sphincter muscle; those below the muscle, in the anal canal, are called external. Both internal and external hemorrhoids may be present.

They are an astonishingly common affliction. According to some estimates, 50 percent of people over fifty have them and more than one-fourth of persons between twenty-five and fifty are afflicted. Even teenagers and younger children occasionally suffer from them.

One indication of hemorrhoids is bleeding from the rectum. Another is a protruding swelling, which can be felt or seen in or near the anus. Sneezing or coughing may cause the swelling to protrude even further.

Pain is the main symptom. Four of every five people with hemorrhoids suffer some pain during a bowel movement. Almost one of every five experiences general pain in the rectal area.

If bleeding is profuse or prolonged, anemia may develop, and such symptoms as pallor, listlessness, and dizziness may be experienced.

There are several possible causes of hemorrhoids. During defecation, the veins, like other structures in the anorectal area, are stretched. After passage of the stool, they return to a normal, relaxed state. If the veins are weak, they may remain permanently stretched.

Hemorrhoids may develop in the later months of pregnancy, when great pressure from the unusual weight of the abdomen adds to the strain on blood vessels. But such hemorrhoids usually disappear rapidly after childbirth.

The main cause of hemorrhoids is straining at stool, which produces increased pressures that dilate the veins about the rectum. The straining is the result of constipation, which in turn is the result of intake of the typical Western low fiber, refined carbohydrate diet.

Treatment. In the case of external hemorrhoids, no special treatment may be necessary. Usually, they clear up within a few days. Anesthetic ointments and hot baths can be used to relieve pain or itching in the meantime. If, however, the hemorrhoids become large, they may be removed by surgery.

Internal hemorrhoids, if slight, need only conservative measures. Anesthetic ointments or suppositories may be used to alleviate pain and itching. Hot baths may also provide relief. If the hemorrhoids do not respond to such measures, they may be treated with injections of irritating solutions that scar and obliterate them. (External hemorrhoids have been found to be unsuitable for injection treatment.)

Much can be done, as many hemorrhoid victims have been discovering, to relieve existing hemorrhoids and to prevent recurrences simply by resorting to a high fiber diet.

Surgery. The standard operation for hemorrhoid removal, called hemorrhoidectomy, is simple enough for the surgeon and is not considered major surgery. Under spinal, caudal, or general anesthesia, the hemorrhoids are tied off close to their origin, dissected out from surrounding structures, and removed, with the whole procedure taking no more than half an hour.

But for as long as five days afterward, the patient may experience considerable pain, with bowel movements especially painful. For relief, local anesthetics may be applied and sitz baths—sitting in warm water—may be used. Usually, the rectal area becomes entirely painless in ten to fourteen days and all normal activities can be resumed.

Once removed, hemorrhoids cannot recur and surgery provides permanent cure for more than 90 percent of patients. Sometimes, however, other veins may enlarge for the same reason the first ones did.

New surgical techniques for hemorrhoid removal are now in increasing use. One is cryosurgery, surgery performed by application of extreme cold. It involves touching the hemorrhoid with a special probe that very quickly freezes it. There is only a slight discharge for a few days and healing is good. Cryosurgery can be performed in a doctor's office with only moderate pain.

Another technique, called rubber-band ligation, is often used now for internal hemorrhoids. The procedure is essentially painless and can be done in a doctor's office. With a special instrument, the doctor places a special latex band over the neck of a hemorrhoid. The band ties off the hemorrhoid so that it receives no blood, dies, and sloughs off, usually within three to nine days. The ligated hemorrhoid may produce a sensation of fullness for a time. When the hemorrhoid drops off, there may be some brief spotting of blood. And itching may be aggravated for a time when the hemorrhoid drops off.

HERNIA

With the exception of tonsillectomies, hernia repair operations are the most common, with about 500,000 done annually in the United States alone.

A hernia develops when internal organs protrude through the abdominal wall.

Around the abdominal organs lies the peritoneum, a thin but tough membrane. Necessarily, the peritoneum has a number of passageways through it: for the femoral arteries that supply blood to the legs; for the umbilical cord that nourishes the fetus in the womb; for the spermatic cords that carry sperm cells from the testes; and other openings.

At any of these passageways, muscles and connective tissue supporting the peritoneum may weaken and, with the weakening, anything that adds to stress or strain on the abdomen—a sudden muscle pull, heavy lifting, attacks of coughing, straining because of constipation, marked gain in weight, pregnancy—may lead to a hernia.

A common term for hernia is rupture but the word rupture is misleading, because it suggests tearing and nothing is torn in a hernia. Instead, the peritoneum pushes out through the weakened area, forming a sac with a lump under the skin, and the sac may contain a fold of the peritoneum called the omentum or a portion of the intestine or both.

Hernias can occur at any age and sometimes do in babies as well as in women, but are more common in men.

INGUINAL HERNIA

This hernia in the groin is the most common type, accounting for two-thirds or more of all hernias. It occurs much more often in men than in women.

In a male fetus, the testes remain in the abdomen until about a month prior to birth when they descend to the outside through inguinal canals. The canals are then occupied by the spermatic cords, which are designed to carry sperm from the testes up through the abdominal wall to the prostate gland and seminal vesicles.

Normally, a tight seal of tissue forms around the spermatic cords in the canal. But in some men the seal is lacking; in some others, it is relatively weak and may give way under stress. Pressure of the contents of the abdomen may then lead to a hernia.

To begin with, the hernia may be hardly noticeable, appearing as a soft lump under the skin, no larger than a marble, and there may be no pain. As time passes, the size of the lump may increase.

Often, protruding abdominal contents slip out of the abdomen and into the hernia sac in the course of a day of activity and then slip back into normal position when the patient lies down; if they do not slip back, they can usually be pushed gently back by the patient, especially in the early stages of a hernia.

A truss or abdominal support may be used to hold the abdominal contents back but this may not be satisfactory and, of course, it never cures the condition.

As a hernia progresses and bulges out, the opening behind it often tends to close, forming a narrow neck. If this neck is pinched tight enough to cut off the blood supply, a dangerous condition develops. The hernia swells and becomes strangulated. Unless blood supply is restored promptly, intestinal gangrene can develop and may cause death.

If a hernia suddenly enlarges, will not go back into place, and there is pain and nausea, the hernia is strangulated, although in occasional cases, especially in older patients, there may be no pain or even tenderness when strangulation occurs.

Surgery. This can be curative for an uncomplicated but disturbing hernia and lifesaving for a strangulated one. It involves tying the neck of the sac and cutting away the sac itself after the pushed-out loops of intestine are returned to the abdomen. Muscle and fibrous tissue are overlapped to provide support, and if such support may not be fully adequate, a wire or plastic mesh may be sutured in for additional support. The mesh is strong but flexible enough so its presence afterward is not noticed.

Hernia repair may be carried out under general, spinal, or even local anesthesia, and when the hernia is uncomplicated the surgery may be finished in less than an hour. While some discomfort ensues for a few days, it is usually not severe enough to require potent pain-killers. The patient is commonly up the day afterward, home a few days later, the wound healed in about ten days, and normal strength in the abdominal wall achieved in about six weeks, at which point activities usually need not be limited. Hernias can recur but the improved surgical techniques now provide a permanent cure rate of 90 percent.

FEMORAL HERNIA

Although women develop inguinal hernias less often than men because of a tighter bond in their inguinal canals, they are subject more often than men to femoral hernias.

In a femoral hernia, a loop of intestine protrudes into the femoral canal, a tubular passageway that carries nerves and blood vessels to the thigh. The hernia occurs high up in the thigh, and often can be felt about an inch or so below the groin.

Surgery. The curative procedure is essentially the same as for an inguinal hernia, with the incision, about three inches long, made in the groin or upper thigh, the intestinal loop replaced in the abdomen. After the same six-week period for the strengthening of the repair, activities usually can be unlimited.

UMBILICAL HERNIA

This is a protrusion of abdominal contents through the abdominal wall at the umbilicus, or navel.

During the development of the fetus in the womb, the intestines grow more rapidly than the abdominal cavity. For a time, part of the intestines of the unborn child usually lies outside the abdomen in a sac within the umbilical cord. Normally, by the time of birth, the intestines return to the abdomen and the abdominal wall closes. Occasionally, however, the abdominal wall does not close solidly and a loop of intestine covered with skin protrudes so that the navel of the child appears to be inflated. The defect is more likely to occur in premature infants and in girls rather than boys.

The defect in the abdominal wall usually closes by itself. Coughing, crying, and straining temporarily enlarge the sac but the hernia never bursts and digestion is not affected. The hernia may be strapped with adhesive tape or a truss may be used.

Surgery. If an umbilical hernia has not repaired itself by the time a child is one to two years old, surgical repair can be carried out. Especially for a girl infant, repair may be advisable since the hernia may enlarge later during pregnancy and require repair after childbirth.

In the repair procedure, which may be done under general, spinal, or local anesthetic, the navel is lifted, the sac removed, the muscles brought together firmly, and the navel repositioned. Usually, in infants, no limitations are needed after the operation but in adults there may be some limitation of activity for about six weeks until the repair is fully strengthened.

INCISIONAL HERNIA

This is a protrusion, after an operation, at the site of the surgical incision, resulting from improper healing or excessive strain on the healing tissue caused by excessive muscular effort—such as in lifting or severe coughing or by obesity, which creates additional pressure on the weakened area.

A swelling about or through the incision may become apparent and there may be a hard lump that sometimes goes away when the patient lies down. Depending upon the site of the incision, part of the intestine, stomach, or liver may be present in the hernia.

Surgery. The incision is opened, the sac removed, the muscle layers overlapped, and a plastic mesh may be inserted for additional support, after which the incision is stitched securely. Usually, the patient is up the next day, pain is mild, and hospitalization is required for about a week.

One-day hernia repair. In a newer procedure—based on recent research findings and coming into increasing use—hospitalization is brief.

The patient enters the hospital the night before for routine blood and other tests, and surgical repair is carried out the next morning after only a local anesthetic injection in the abdomen.

Half an hour after the operation starts, the first line of stitches is in place and the patient, who has been conscious throughout, is asked to cough to test the strength of the stitches. If more stitches are indicated, they are put in, and a few minutes later the patient gets off the operating table on his own, dons robe and slippers, and not only walks back to his room but is under instructions to keep walking all day. He spends the next day walking about the hospital, and the morning after, following another check by the surgeon, goes home. The abbreviated hospital stay is followed by a return to work a few days later.

The procedure was developed after studies showed that with the use of strong sutures, such as those made of Teflon and Dacron, a closed surgical wound, immediately after surgery, has 70 percent of normal tissue strength and may be as strong then as sixty days later. And that with a patient under local anesthesia, fully conscious though experiencing no discomfort, the strength of the repair can be tested and if not satisfactory can be supplemented. A success rate of better than 95 percent has been reported. Some surgeons, however, still prefer the older techniques and being able to keep an eye on patients for several days after surgery in order to be certain that there are no postoperative complications.

HIATUS HERNIA

Also known as hiatal hernia and diaphragmatic hernia, this is one of the most prevalent gastrointestinal defects, occurring in almost half the population in the Western world.

Hiatus comes from the Latin, *hiare*, to yawn, and a hernia is a rupture that permits an organ to protrude through it. In hiatus hernia, there is a defect in the diaphragm, the muscle separating chest from abdominal cavity, at the point where the esophagus, or gullet, passes through to join the stomach.

As noted earlier, through the defect—an enlargement of the normal opening in the diaphragm—part of the stomach may enter the chest cavity, either intermittently or constantly.

A hiatus hernia can be so minor—and frequently is—that it produces no symptoms at all during one's lifetime. On the other hand, it can give rise to a good deal of discomfort when it permits esophageal reflux, an abnormal return flow of gastric juices from the stomach to the esophagus. Reflux can produce such symptoms as heartburn and burning pain in back of the breastbone. The pain may be confused with the anginal chest pain associated with coronary heart disease or with peptic ulcer or gallbladder ailments. The symptoms of hiatus hernia are usually worse after eating, and when lifting or stooping.

What causes the defect? In a few cases, it may be present at birth, the result of a slightly faulty development of the diaphragm. Or it may be caused by injury to the diaphragm, sometimes in connection with a rib fracture.

But such relatively rare causes do not explain the huge incidence of hiatus hernia in the Western world and, as investigators have been discovering recently, its rarity elsewhere, such as in Africa, among populations not exposed to Western ways of eating.

And there is growing belief now that hiatus hernia is one end result of the lack of dietary fiber in Western diets and, alternately, the massive consumption of refined carbohydrates.

It is now clear that fiber-depleted diets are the major cause of constipation and of the exaggerated bowel contractions needed to propel through the bowel the small hard fecal content associated with low residue foods and the straining at stool that goes with constipation. The straining raises pressures within the abdomen. Such pressures, many investigators are coming to believe, could well exert tremendous force upward, enough over a period of years to push up the stomach, widening the normal gap in the diaphragm and producing the hernia.

Hiatus hernia is diagnosed by X-ray studies. After the radio-opaque material barium is swallowed, any protrusion of the stomach through the diaphragm can be seen on X-ray film. The esophagus also may be examined through an esophagoscope, a lighted instrument, inserted through the mouth under local anesthesia. This determines whether the gullet has become inflamed because of reflux of juices from the stomach.

Treatment. No medical treatment may be required in the absence of symptoms. Patients with symptoms may benefit from eating five or six small meals a day instead of three big ones, not eating anything just before lying down, avoiding stooping over, and giving up wearing tight belts and other tight items of clothing. Elevating the head of the bed a few inches on blocks may be helpful. Antacids may help neutralize stomach acids and cool off the burning esophagus.

Such measures are often useful. A high fiber diet is a growing means of speeding relief and perhaps promoting healing of the defect by helping to eliminate raised pressures. Some investigators consider that such a diet, if used before hiatus hernia develops, may well prevent the development.

Surgery. Surgery for hiatus hernia is not commonly needed. It may be used when the above medical measures fail and symptoms are intolerable.

Surgical techniques vary somewhat in detail but all are directed at returning the stomach to its normal position below the diaphragm and repairing the hernia so the stomach no longer will slide upward.

After the operation, which is performed under general anesthesia, there is moderate discomfort for a few days. Wound healing usually requires one to two weeks. Often patients are able to leave the hospital within ten days and can return to normal activities after a few weeks.

In most cases, surgical repair is successful in eliminating symptoms permanently. But in 10 to 20 percent of cases, there are recurrences that may have to be treated again.

INDIGESTION

It is often referred to loosely as dyspepsia, upset stomach, nervous indigestion, acid indigestion, acute indigestion, gas around the heart, or just plain indigestion.

Few, if any, of us escape an occasional experience with it.

Sometimes, it produces a sense of discomfort in the midriff; sometimes, nausea, heartburn, upper abdominal pain, or a sense of fullness, a feeling of abdominal distention, gas and belching—singly or in combination.

Indigestion can be caused by organic disease in the gastrointestinal tract or even by disease originating elsewhere. Among possible triggers for it are gallbladder disease, liver disease, a kidney stone, peptic ulcer, an intestinal obstruction, and appendicitis. Or it can be the result of food poisoning, intolerance for milk or another food, or a nutritional deficiency.

But the common causes, responsible for the vast majority of cases, are eating too much or too rapidly, inadequate chewing, eating during emotional upsets, and swallowing large amounts of air. Other factors are excessive smoking, constipation, eating poorly canned foods, foods with high fat content, and in some cases radishes, cucumbers, beans, cabbage, turnips, and onions. Also such seasonings as pepper, garlic, and chili may cause indigestion.

When food is not thoroughly chewed, the stomach may secrete more acid to aid in digesting it. This, in combination with excessive air that may enter the stomach with hurried chewing and swallowing, may irritate the stomach lining.

Most dyspeptic symptoms result from altered stomach motor activity. Normally stomach motility—its desirable churning activity—is stimulated when the stomach is moderately distended with food. But marked distention—as from overeating—inhibits the activity and may produce a sensation of fullness and nausea.

Food with a high concentration of fat, or food fried in fat, also inhibits stomach activity and prolongs the time before the stomach empties its contents into the small intestine. An excess of fatty food may have the same effects as overeating.

Hunger and the prospect of appetizing food produce increased stomach motor activity. On the other hand, fear, shock, depression and other emotional upsets—also pain, anywhere, or physical fatigue—tend to slow down the stomach activity.

Alcohol and coffee may overly increase stomach activity but smoking decreases it, thus delaying stomach emptying.

Constipation may contribute to indigestion as it distends the rectum, causing consciousness and anxiety about what is going on in the gastrointestinal tract.

Treatment. In a case of mild stomach upset, symptoms may disappear if nothing more is done than to refrain from eating for a few hours. Indigestion sometimes can be relieved by loosening any tight-fitting clothes and by lying down on the right side so that gravity can help the stomach move its contents along into the duodenum.

To avoid stomach upsets, eat a normal balanced diet, without haste and in a relaxing environment, in moderate amounts, avoiding smoking before a meal.

If you experience mild upsets with some frequency, it can be helpful to keep a record of what you eat to see if you can find a pattern between eating certain foods and experiencing the upsets. You can then cut down or eliminate those foods that seem to be causing the problem. If you do not succeed in eliminating the upsets, you will have, at least, some useful information for a physician. If you do succeed, you can at a later time challenge your stomach again by trying once more the food you eliminated, and if the symptoms reappear, you are sure of the cause. If the stomach does not react, you know the cause lies elsewhere.

(If constipation is in the picture, see the section on constipation.)

Many victims consider antacids valuable for providing some measure of relief. The preparations are sold for heartburn, sour stomach, and acid indigestion. Antacids recommended by physicians are usually of the type that are not absorbed from the gut into the bloodstream, as is sodium bicarbonate (baking soda). They discourage the use of sodium bicarbonate except for perhaps very occasional indigestion; it is quick-acting but its antacid effect is short-lived and its frequent or excessive use may produce increased blood alkalinity. Also, the sodium it contains may not be desirable for people with hypertension or a heart problem. (Increased blood alkalinity, or alkalosis, may, ironically, produce the same symptoms—abdominal discomfort or pain, nausea and vomiting—for which bicarb may be used to excess and, in advanced stages, may cause fever, muscle spasms, and other serious consequences.)

When stomach upset is severe or when the episodes are very frequent or almost chronic, certainly medical advice is needed.

Chronic heartburn, for example, sometimes may be the result of poor functioning of the esophageal sphincter muscle at the entrance to the stomach, a prime purpose of which is to prevent backward flow of food from the stomach. In such cases, a drug, bethanechol, which previously has been used after gastrointestinal surgery to stimulate the intestinal tract to contract normally, may be prescribed. Often it is helpful.

Heartburn and other symptoms of indigestion in some cases are the result of hiatal hernia, and this will require treatment, sometimes surgical, if the upsets are to be avoided rather than merely relieved somewhat with antacids or other preparations.

When chronic nervousness and tenseness are contributing to the episodes of indigestion, they may be allayed with small doses of phenobarbital or a tranquilizer.

And the possibility that more or less chronic indigestion may be related to an organic disease, in or out of the gastrointestinal tract, will need to be taken into account by a family physician and perhaps by a consultant gastroenterologist or other specialist.

INTESTINAL OBSTRUCTION

Intestinal obstruction, which interferes with the normal passage of intestinal contents, may be either partial or complete and may occur in either the small or large bowel.

Symptoms vary with the degree of obstruction and the site.

Complete obstruction of the small intestine produces severe on and off cramplike pain around the navel area, with vomiting soon following. The higher up in the small bowel the obstruction, the sooner the vomiting occurs. At first the vomiting and the pain appear together. Later, the vomiting occurs irregularly and may include fecal matter. If the obstruction is high up, there is little distention of the abdomen; if low in the small bowel, the distention is conspicuous.

When the obstruction is partial, the symptoms are similar but less severe and cramps may be followed by diarrhea.

With complete obstruction of the colon, the development of symptoms is often insidious. The abdomen becomes distended, but slowly. Vomiting is infrequent. Pain is likely to be less severe than with small bowel obstruction.

If the obstruction of the colon is partial, on-off abdominal cramps and constipation develop, and the constipation in some cases may alternate with diarrhea.

One cause of obstruction is adhesion. Normally, the bowel is coiled within the abdomen somewhat like a hose, and the intestinal loops with their smooth and moist surfaces move easily over each other. As the result of infection or injury, sometimes stemming from an old operation, an area of surface may become dry and scarlike tissue may develop. That area then may adhere to other tissue, including another intestinal loop. This is an adhesion. There may then be twisting and knotting, leading to obstruction.

Or the small bowel may become obstructed when a loop of it gets caught in an inguinal (groin) hernia.

Adhesions and hernias are the most common causes of mechanical obstruction.

A less common cause is volvulus, a condition in which the mesentery, the tissue that attaches the intestine to the back wall of the abdomen and thus supports it, becomes twisted so that one or more folds of the intestine are turned abnormally, producing obstruction. Volvulus tends to occur more in the elderly than in younger people.

Intussusception, another less common cause, mostly affects children under the age of three. In this condition, one part of the small intestine, the ileum, telescopes into the colon and obstruction results.

Important aids in diagnosis are plain X-ray films of the abdomen that can show dilated loops of intestine indicative of obstruction. X-ray films taken after a barium enema may be used to point to obstruction in the colon.

Treatment. The aim of medical treatment is to support the patient and overcome the obstruction as soon as possible. Fluids will be administered by vein and drugs used to relieve pain.

If the obstruction is incomplete, a long intestinal tube may be used to try to remove it. Sometimes this works. If not, surgery is undertaken without delay, which is essential when obstruction is complete. Failure to act promptly to relieve obstruction can lead to a dangerous toxic state, rupture of the distended intestine followed by peritonitis, or strangulation, in which blood supply to the area is cut off leading to development of gangrene within a few hours.

Surgery. When small bowel obstruction is the result of adhesions, simple cutting of the adhesions may be all that is required.

When blood circulation to an obstructed bowel segment has been impaired, the surgeon first relieves the obstruction and then watches to determine if, with obstruction overcome, circulation is restored to normal. If the circulation is restored, nothing further is required. But if circulation has been permanently damaged because of prolonged strangulation, the affected bowel segment must be removed and the healthy segments above and below are then stitched together.

In the case of obstruction because of hernia, the bowel segment is freed from the hernia sac. If strangulation has occurred, the affected segment must be removed and the healthy portions joined up. The hernia then is repaired.

In volvulus, the affected intestinal loop can be straightened and attached to the abdominal cavity or it can be removed. The likelihood of volvulus recurrence is great. Attachment reduces it somewhat. But if the patient is strong enough, the loop may be removed and the remaining sections joined, reducing still further the likelihood of recurrence. When volvulus has led to strangulation, the affected intestinal section must be removed.

In a child with intussusception, a telescoped loop of intestine sometimes may slip free of its own accord. Most often, it does not but if operation is not long delayed, the loop can be readily freed and placed in normal position. With delay, gangrene may develop in the loop, necessitating its removal and the joining of healthy sections.

In some cases of colon obstruction, a colostomy may be required. An opening is made in the colon ahead of the obstructed area and the opening is then brought out onto the abdomen, outside the body. A special pouch is placed over it to receive stools. The colostomy permits passage of feces and gas, improves nutrition, and the patient's general condition. Several weeks later, the diseased section of colon can be removed more safely. After several more weeks, during which the intestinal repair has a chance to heal, the colostomy is closed and bowel movements are again passed in normal fashion via the rectum.

A general or spinal anesthetic may be used for operations to overcome obstruction. Length of operation may vary from less than an hour for a temporary colostomy to four hours for procedures involving removal of bowel segments.

Recovery time, too, varies depending upon the procedure. After the simple cutting of an adhesion, the patient may be out of bed the next day; in other cases, after several days. Hospital stay may range from ten days or less to four weeks or more, depending upon the type of procedure and whether it is accomplished at one time or in two or three stages several weeks apart. The incision usually heals within two weeks and normal life often can be resumed in four to six weeks.

The success rate overall for intestinal obstruction surgery is remarkably high—91 percent—considering that there is often delay on the part of the patient in seeking help, and sometimes physician delay after that. It is expected to go even higher because of the increasing conviction of physicians that surgery should be considered even "on suspicion" of intestinal obstruction.

IRRITABLE COLON

This is a very common disorder, also known by such names as spastic colon and mucous colitis, although the latter is erroneous since colitis means inflammation of the colon and the irritable or spastic colon is not inflamed.

However, symptoms are variable. Abdominal distress, which is common, may take the form of abdominal distention; cramps may mimic those of appendicitis when they occur on the right side (but they may occur on the left); and there may be sharp, knifelike pains or deep dull pain. Often, discomfort is relieved after a bowel movement or the passage of gas.

Not only is it usual for patients with irritable colon to suffer from constipation but, in many cases, constipation and diarrhea alternate. Also, excess mucus may appear in the stool but no blood unless hemorrhoids are also present, which they commonly are in constipated people.

Many patients complain of lack of appetite in the morning, nausea, heartburn, or excessive belching, and there may also be complaints of weakness, palpitation, headaches, sleeping trouble, faintness, and excessive perspiration.

What causes irritable colon? Many explanations have been proposed. Emotional stress or anxiety has been considered to be a prime factor. Many physicians have found that patients with the problem often are tense, anxious, and given to emotional ups and downs. There is often a history of overwork, inadequate sleep, hurried and irregular meals, and abuse of laxatives.

The activities of the colon are under nervous system control. There are nerve impulses that stimulate activity; others that inhibit it; and, with a fine balance between the two types of impulses, gastrointestinal contents pass smoothly through the colon.

In the irritable colon, the balance is disturbed. In addition to regular contractions required to propel the contents along, there are irregular nonpropulsive contractions. Constipation occurs when the propulsive movements are inhibited, and water absorption in the colon is increased, leaving the feces dry and hard. Diarrhea results when the propulsive movements are excessive and there is little chance for water absorption. Abdominal discomfort and pain result from spasm of the colon and gas distention of the bowel.

Treatment. Treatment has often included efforts to explain the problem to the patient and encouragement to avoid stressful conditions as much as possible. Mild sedatives and tranquilizers often have been used. Drugs such as belladonna tincture and atropine relieve symptoms, although they do so only in doses that produce a dry mouth and some interference with vision. Patients whose symptoms seem to be exacerbated either by very hot or very cold drinks or coffee, alcohol, and tobacco have been urged to avoid them. And some physicians have recommended a bland diet—meat, fish, eggs, cooked fruit, cooked vegetables—and, generally, avoidance of raw fruit and vegetables.

Some patients have been helped by some or many of these measures but, on the whole, the results of treatment of irritable colon have been less than dramatic.

Some new hope has recently entered the picture with the findings in England and in the United States that the irritable bowel syndrome or collection of symptoms may not be the result of a bowel that is irritable but rather of a bowel that is irritated—with the irritation, contrary to previous opinion, coming not from "irritating roughage" in the diet but rather for lack of adequate dietary fiber. Early studies have found many patients with irritable colon responding quite remarkably to the addition of fiber in the diet. There is some possibility of a regular high fiber diet having preventive value.

LIVER DISEASES

The liver is the most versatile and among the most vital organs of the body. A diseased liver becomes a serious handicap to health.

Viruses are sometimes enemies of the liver; also, toxic materials such as alcohol, carbon tetrachloride, and other solvents; occasionally, even otherwise valuable medications—including the powerful antibiotic Chloromycetin, the potent tranquilizer Thorazine, and the antiinflammatory Butazolidin—may cause liver trouble. Also, bacteria, amoebas, and larger parasites such as worms sometimes attack the liver, as do cancers.

Severe liver disease may manifest itself by jaundice, which indicates either that most liver cells are not functioning properly or that bile flow is blocked by a gallstone.

Acute liver disease, such as viral hepatitis, commonly is accompanied by exhaustion, nausea, loss of appetite, and tenderness over the liver itself. Often there is some pain around the liver area.

Among signs of chronic liver disease are a characteristic redness of the palms of the hand and a red streaking on the skin.

There may be swelling of the abdomen by fluid (ascites). This is caused by back pressure on veins produced by a scarred, damaged liver. Because of such pressure, enlarged veins in the esophagus and stomach may bleed (varices), hemorrhoids may develop, and ankles and legs may swell with fluid.

Many tests are available to aid in the diagnosis of liver diseases. Tests for several enzymes in the blood—alkaline phosphatase, transaminase, lactic dehydrogenase—are valuable because diseased liver cells increase enzyme production, leak enzymes or die and discharge enzymes into the blood.

Because the liver plays a key role in the metabolism of carbohydrates, proteins, fats, bile pigments, bile acid, and drugs, liver disease may lead to upsets in one or more of these metabolic functions. Therefore, various tests of these functions are useful in determining the state of the liver.

Liver biopsy may be used. While the patient is under local anesthesia a five-inch-long needle may be inserted between the ribs or through the front of the abdomen into the liver. Then with a tiny instrument that is moved through the needle, and a little beyond the tip, a small section of liver can be taken for study.

VIRAL LIVER DISEASE

Viral hepatitis is a common acute infectious disease of the liver.

It can be caused by a virus that enters the system via the mouth, having been spread by fecal contamination, in which case the disease is called infectious hepatitis, or hepatitis A. It tends to occur in epidemics—in crowded places such as military camps and mental hospitals.

Another form, serum hepatitis, is caused by a similar virus found in blood and tissue rather than feces. It is spread by contaminated blood transfusions or when people, usually drug addicts, use the same contaminated needle and syringe. Serum hepatitis is also known as hepatitis B.

Viral hepatitis symptoms are much like those of flu and commonly begin with lassitude, weakness, loss of appetite, nausea, abdominal discomforts, fever, and headache. Jaundice may or may not develop. When it does it lasts about two weeks and may be accompanied by dark urine, gray stools, and mild body itching.

Actually, for every person made sick by viral hepatitis, there may be several others who have it in such mild form that the disease is never diagnosed.

Treatment. Once strict bed rest and a rigid low fat, high carbohydrate diet were considered essential in treatment. Now diet and activity are adjusted to the individual patient and his condition. Alcohol is discouraged. In severe cases, cortisonelike drugs may sometimes be used to counter the inflammatory response to the virus.

It is often possible to protect people in the family and others in close contact with a patient with infectious hepatitis by injection of immune serum globulin.

Generally, complete recovery is the rule. About 85 percent of patients recover uneventfully after six to eight weeks. Others recover after a prolonged course of the disease, which may last a year or after a number of relapses. Extended corticosteroid therapy may be needed in some cases of chronic hepatitis.

TOXIC HEPATITIS

Among the drugs and chemicals that can cause liver inflammation are carbon tetrachloride, insecticides, industrial solvents, and various metallic compounds, including those containing arsenic, gold, mercury, and iron, and they can have a direct toxic effect on the liver and on other organs as well, including kidney, brain, or bone marrow. Nausea, vomiting, jaundice, stupor, and coma may follow exposure to large amounts of such chemicals.

Some drugs such as isonazid and halothane anesthetics may in certain sensitive people produce a condition much like that of acute viral hepatitis. Other drugs—such as more potent tranquilizers (phenothiazines) and sulfa drugs—may cause damage to liver cells and jaundice in the sensitive.

Whatever is causing trouble must be removed and treatment is then much the same as for viral hepatitis, with recovery the rule.

CIRRHOSIS

Cirrhosis is a chronic disease in which the liver becomes hardened and overgrown with scar tissue and its functions impaired. Leading causes are alcoholism and malnutrition (especially deficiency of B vitamins). Less often, cirrhosis may be a result of infectious or other types of acute liver disease, or syphilis.

In the early stages, there may be no symptoms. Even then, however, some signs may be obvious. Among them are redness of the palms, swelling of the legs with fluid, and clubbing of the fingers.

As liver function begins to fail, other symptoms appear. They include loss of appetite, nausea, vomiting, weight loss, malaise, weakness, abdominal discomfort, loss of libido, and in women failure of menses.

Cirrhosis is treated with reasonable rest, strict avoidance of alcohol, a nutritious diet moderately high in protein, with vitamin supplements prescribed for any specific deficiencies.

Fluid swelling of the abdomen often can be controlled by restricting salt and fluid intake. If this is not enough, diuretic drugs to increase fluid outflow may be used.

The damage of cirrhosis cannot be reversed. It can be slowed; occasionally it can be stopped from progressing.

Surgery. A complication that may develop with cirrhosis occurs when blood flow through the veins of the liver is impeded. The back pressure that then follows may cause the formation of internal varicose veins in the stomach or esophagus as well as elsewhere. Those in the esophagus, called esophageal varices, can be the source of repeated hemorrhages.

A shunt operation may sometimes help. In the operation, the portal or entrance vein to the liver is connected elsewhere—to the inferior vena cava, the major vein, which empties directly into the heart and returns to it blood from the lower part of the body. The aim is to cut down on the amount of blood that must go through the obstructed vein system of the liver and to allow more blood to bypass the liver. In that way the backup of blood and the back pressure are reduced and hemorrhages from the esophageal varices may be stopped.

The operation, done under general anesthesia through an incision in the upper right abdomen, may take two to six hours, and two weeks or more of hospitalization may be required. The surgery is delicate and, because a severely diseased liver may reduce the chances for successful healing afterward, not all patients with the problem can be operated on with a reasonable hope of success. If liver tests show extensive damage that cannot be mitigated before operation by a period of intensive in-hospital treatment, surgery may be inadvisable.

About half the patients who are considered reasonably suitable candidates for surgery may benefit from it. The cirrhosis itself, of course, is not cured, but with continuing medical treatment return to work may be possible, depending on the patient's general condition.

MALABSORPTION—CELIAC DISEASE

Celiac disease, a form of malabsorption, is a comparatively uncommon disorder of the digestive tract, which tends to appear in families, and involves a special sensitivity to the gluten of wheat and rye. The sensitivity, or intolerance, leads to changes in the lining of the small bowel, which cause impaired absorption. Both the symptoms and the lining changes disappear when wheat and rye cereals are avoided—only to reappear if they are ingested again.

The symptoms may start insidiously, often at the age of six to eighteen months. They may appear from age twenty to fifty, or sometimes after appearing and disappearing at younger ages reappear at later ages.

When full blown, the disease is characterized by flatulence and large, foul-smelling, bulky, frothy, and pale-colored stools containing much fat. There may be recurrent attacks of diarrhea, sometimes with accompanying stomach cramps. The diarrhea may alternate with constipation. The abdomen may be swollen. A child with severe celiac disease left untreated may become weak, undernourished, and anemic; his growth may be stunted; and he may be irritable.

The outlook for patients with celiac disease is excellent. Treatment involves a well-balanced but gluten-free diet, high in calories and normal in fat. All cereal grains except rice and corn are excluded.

It is essential to read all food labels carefully in order to eliminate completely products containing wheat, rye, barley, and oat proteins. Rice, corn, soy, and wheat starch flour may be used as substitutes.

At the beginning, it may be necessary to use supplements to make up for malabsorption-caused deficiencies of iron, folic acid, B vitamins, calcium, and vitamins A, D, and K.

With a gluten-free diet, there will be full recovery, although that may take a year or more. If the diet is disregarded, there may be relapses.

Tropical sprue is another form of malabsorption. It occurs in the Caribbean area, the Indian subcontinent, and Southeast Asia. It does not occur in temperate zones except among people who previously lived in the tropics. The primary cause, recent research suggests, is infection rather than diet.

In the beginning, tropical sprue produces diarrhea and appetite and weight loss. Later, because of changes in the lining of the small bowel, malabsorption leads to anemia and many of the same symptoms as celiac disease.

Treatment, which involves a balanced diet high in protein and normal in fat, usually produces weight gain and correction of nutritional deficiencies. An antibiotic such as tetracycline or oxytetracycline is mandatory as well. And supplements with iron and vitamins and other nutrients may be required as in celiac disease. After about six months, it may be possible to discontinue treatment.

Whipple's disease is still another form of malabsorption. It occurs mostly in men aged thirty to sixty, and while the symptoms are similar to those of celiac disease and sprue, there are unique additional symptoms: fever, arthritis of the knees, wrists, and back, cough, abdominal pain, and chest pain.

With adequate treatment, the outlook is excellent. Best results have been produced by intensive antibiotic therapy, beginning with injections of an antibiotic such as procaine penicillin for ten days to two weeks followed by use for ten to twelve months of an oral antibiotic such as tetracycline.

PANCREATITIS

Pancreatitis—inflammation of the pancreas—can be acute or chronic.

In acute pancreatitis, severe abdominal pain is the outstanding symptom. It is usually steady and boring, centered in the epigastrium, the region of the upper abdomen overlying the stomach, and radiating to the back and chest. Sitting up provides partial relief. Nausea and vomiting are common. Constipation or diarrhea may occur; constipation is more usual. A fever of 100 to 102 usually appears within the first few days.

The causes are still not completely understood. In about 40 percent of cases, gallstones are also present; in another 40 percent, alcoholism appears to be a factor; in 10 percent, pancreatitis appears to develop after an injury, penetrating peptic ulcer, mumps, elevated blood fat levels, use of some drugs such as cortisonelike agents, or pregnancy. No cause is apparent in the remaining 10 percent.

In acute pancreatitis, pancreatic enzymes that ordinarily go into the duodenum to aid in digestion may be released into the pancreas itself and may digest some of the pancreas tissue and blood vessels. Therefore, in treatment, no food is given by mouth, only by vein, and acid may be sucked out with a tube introduced through the nose into the stomach. Both measures—by keeping food and acid out of the duodenum—help to inhibit pancreas secretion. A drug such as atropine or propantheline may be used to help further reduce pancreas secretion. For pain, meperidine may be used, and antibiotics to counteract the inflammation.

Chronic pancreatitis, which may follow acute attacks or develop insidiously, is more common in men than in women. It is often associated with chronic alcoholism or gallstones. In the course of the disease, stones may form in the pancreatic duct and scar tissue in the gland.

Pain may be constant or intermittent, mild or severe. It usually begins in the epigastrium and may radiate to the back and left shoulder. Fever and slight jaundice may develop during a flareup of chronic pancreatitis. About one-fifth of patients develop mild diabetes.

Treatment. Medical treatment may be helpful, although there is no specific therapy. Alcohol is banned. A high carbohydrate, low fat diet along with vitamin B supplements is used. Pancreatin, a preparation containing pancreatic juice compounds, may be used in some cases in which malabsorption of fats has developed as a complication. A patient may need treatment for diabetes and iron-deficiency anemia as well. Pain-relieving drugs are used, narcotics often being necessary when the pain is severe.

Surgery. Surgery for acute pancreatitis is rarely needed. When cysts develop because of the inflammation, they may enlarge until they reach grapefruit size and press on surrounding structures. Surgery then can relieve the pain, gaseous distention, and appetite and weight loss caused by the cyst.

Usually carried out after inflammation has subsided, the operation for a cyst is done under general anesthesia through a four- or five-inch-long incision in the upper abdomen. The cyst may be removable but the usual procedure is to open it and stitch the edges to the stomach, small intestine, or abdominal wall, and after some weeks the cyst shrivels and disappears or remains only as a scarred, harmless remnant. The operation takes one to two hours. The wound may take several weeks or longer to heal completely, and there is discomfort for several days, although the patient is often out of bed within two or three days and returns to normal activities after complete healing of the wound.

When gallbladder disease is present, surgery for that is usually indicated.

In chronic pancreatitis, surgery may be used to relieve severe pain. One operation, called subtotal pancreatomy, involves emptying any stones out of the pancreatic duct, and the removal of a small portion, about an inch, of the tail of the pancreas, after which the remainder of the tail is attached to a loop of intestine. Alternatively, the pancreas may be split lengthwise along the duct and the split surface then attached to the small bowel. With either procedure, previously dammed up pancreatic juice can flow freely into the intestine, improving digestion and relieving pressure-caused pain.

Performed under general anesthesia, pancreatic surgery takes up to two or three hours and uses a four- to five-inch-long incision in the upper abdomen. The patient may be out of bed in one to three days, although there will be some discomfort at first. The incision usually is healed in two weeks, at which point the patient may go home from the hospital, resuming normal activities about two months later.

PEPTIC ULCER

Nearly 10 percent of all Americans suffer from a peptic ulcer at some time in their lives. It is the most common organic gastrointestinal disease in the United States, and not too uncommonly affects children as well as adults.

A peptic ulcer, which may range in size from a just discernible sore to a crater an inch or more wide and half an inch deep, may occur in the stomach. This makes it a gastric ulcer. Far more commonly, it occurs in the duodenum, which, of course, makes it a duodenal ulcer.

The typical symptom of ulcer is pain in the upper abdomen, which comes on one to four hours after eating and is relieved by foods or antacids. Burning or gnawing in character, the pain comes and goes for about half an hour, often appearing in the middle of the night.

Commonly, for some weeks or months before the typical ulcer pain appears, there may be frequent heartburn and belching. There may also be general abdominal malaise, diarrhea, nausea, and vomiting.

On the basis of such symptoms, a physician can make a tentative diagnosis of peptic ulcer. He may become a little more certain if the patient is male and if the blood group is type O. (Ulcers are more frequent in men than in women and in those with type O blood than in those with other types.)

The diagnosis is confirmed by X-ray and fluoroscopic studies of the stomach and duodenum after a swallow of barium. In some cases, a scope, or lighted tube, may be inserted to allow observation of the ulcerated area.

What causes peptic ulcer? The stomach secretes hydrochloric acid to aid digestion. Even when the stomach is empty, there is a normal, intermittent flow of the acid and a much greater flow with a meal. ("Peptic" comes from the Greek *peptein*—to digest.)

The acid, strong enough to dissolve even iron, does not dissolve the stomach itself because of the protective effect of the mucus secreted by the mucus glands. There is also mucus protection in the duodenum and, in addition, bile from the liver and gallbladder to neutralize the acid.

An ulcer may develop if there is an excess secretion of acid by the stomach or an alteration of the mucus coating.

Some ulcer patients have been found to have two to four times as many acid-secreting cells as normal. The large number, it is believed, could be the result of hereditary influences. Or extra cell formation may occur because nerve impulses through the vagus nerve are excessive, calling for increased acid secretions, which may trigger development of more cells.

The overactivity of the vagus nerve leading to excessive acid secretion sometimes may be the result of a disease elsewhere, such as diabetes or chronic lung disease, which stimulates the vagus. Acid production also may be increased by alcohol, smoking, nervousness, tension, rage, or fear.

The mucosa, or stomach-lining cells, may be affected by alcohol and by drugs such as aspirin and cortisonelike agents. And there is a current theory that sometimes the stomach mucosa may be injured by upstream regurgitation of bile from the duodenum.

There are still many mysteries surrounding peptic ulcer. One of the puzzles is why ulcer symptoms hit their peak in autumn and spring, and bleeding from an ulcer is most frequent between September and January.

Another puzzle is new: Physicians have been noting a sharp decrease in the number of duodenal ulcer cases. As late as 1960, they affected one out of every ten American men; now they affect less than one in twenty.

Duodenal ulcers virtually were unknown in Europe prior to 1900. In England there were only about seventy known cases during the entire nineteenth century. But they started increasing about the time of World War I and by World War II ranked as an extraordinarily common disease, affecting one in ten men and a lesser but still considerable number of women in this country and abroad.

Nobody knows why the problem suddenly started to decline. Certainly stress, which is often blamed for increased acid secretion, has not decreased. In England during World War II, the number of cases of perforated ulcers—so bad that the acid had eaten completely through the lining of the stomach or duodenum—increased in the cities where the Germans were bombing; when the Germans shifted the bombing sites, perforated ulcers increased in the new locations.

Treatment. Medical treatment is effective for most patients with peptic ulcer. The basic principles of treatment include rest—physical and mental—and overcoming excessive acid secretion activity in order to allow healing.

For gastric ulcer, many physicians consider two to three weeks of bed rest essential, preferably in the hospital. Stomach ulcers require very close watching. It used to be thought that they led to stomach cancer, which is not true. But what looks like a stomach ulcer may sometimes be a cancer that has produced an area of ulceration. So, in the case of gastric ulcer, after two to three weeks of bed rest and treatment, the ulcer may be examined again by X ray. If healing or marked improvement has not occurred by then, malignancy may have to be suspected and surgery considered.

For duodenal ulcer, hospitalization for one to two weeks may sometimes be desirable, especially if there is considerable pain, but often acute symptoms can be brought under control by seven to ten days of rest at home.

Although special diets were once considered essential, there is no evidence that they are particularly beneficial, and many physicians now believe that the patient can eat what he likes. Others prescribe small hourly feedings of skim milk during the painful acute phase.

Frequent feedings usually can prevent the buildup of excess acidity, although in some cases antacids after and between meals and feedings may be needed. An antacid often used is a combination of aluminum hydroxide and magnesium trisilicate, which is less likely to lead to constipation than is aluminum hydroxide alone.

Stomach-emptying time may often be rapid with peptic ulcer. To slow it down and hold food in the stomach longer—for its acid-countering effect and also to reduce stomach acid secretion—any one of a number of drugs may be used. They include methscopolamine, tricyclamol, propantheline, and belladonna tincture.

When treatment is effective, it usually takes two to six weeks for an ulcer to heal, and the healing may be checked by X rays that show the disappearance of the crater.

Surgery. Despite medical treatment, some ulcers refuse to heal or tend to recur. In such cases, surgery may be considered. It may also be necessary if ulcer complications develop.

One complication is perforation. The ulcer penetrates all the way through the wall of the stomach or duodenum so that stomach secretions and contents may spill into the abdominal cavity. Then there is usually agonizing abdominal pain. Commonly, breathing becomes shallow, beads of sweat appear on the forehead, and the abdomen over the ulcer becomes boardlike. Later, peritonitis—inflammation of the membrane lining the walls of the abdominal and pelvic cavities—may develop. Perforation requires immediate surgery.

Hemorrhage is another complication. The bleeding develops when a nearby blood vessel is eroded, its wall eaten way. The bleeding may manifest itself through the vomiting of bloody or dark brown stomach contents or the passage of black tarry stools. In other cases, the bleeding may not show itself and the only symptoms may be weakness, dizziness, and sometimes fainting.

Medical measures, including blood or plasma transfusions or venous infusions of dextrose and saline and liquid feedings, may control the bleeding. If the bleeding continues, however, surgery is necessary.

Still another complication is obstruction. An ulcer sometimes may lead to spasm, scarring, or inflammatory swelling at the outlet of the stomach or in the duodenum, causing partial or complete blockage. Symptoms may include vomiting of food from previous meals and foul, gaseous belching.

If obstruction is due to spasm or swelling, usually medical measures will relieve it, at least partially, within ninety-six hours and entirely after about a week. But when obstruction cannot be relieved by medical treatment, surgery is advisable.

Several operations have been developed for unyielding peptic ulcer or its complications. The choice in a particular case will depend upon many factors, such as the site and size of the ulcer, the degree of hyperacidity, which, if any, complications are present, and the surgeon's own preference based on his experience and success rate with one or another procedure.

Partial gastrectomy. Most of the acid-secreting cells of the stomach are in the lower portion, and in this operation the lower half—or a little more —of the stomach is removed along with an inch or two of the first part of the duodenum. The remainder of the stomach is then stitched to the small bowel at a point beyond the duodenum.

Food then moves from the stomach to the small bowel, bypassing the duodenum. Excessive acid is thus reduced in the stomach and acid entering the small bowel no longer affects the sensitive duodenum. The duodenum still works in aid of digestion, receiving as always the important enzymes from the pancreas and bile from the liver, passing both along to the rest of the small bowel.

For a period of a few months after partial gastrectomy, with half or more of the stomach removed, smaller meals are eaten until the stomach distends enough to allow virtually normal meals.

Gastroenterostomy. When an ulcer has healed but has left scar tissue that blocks the lower opening of the stomach into the duodenum, a simpler procedure than gastrectomy may be used. In gastroenterostomy, the stomach is joined to the small bowel, using a new opening so that food can pass through into the duodenum.

Vagotomy and pyloroplasty. The vagus nerve, which stimulates stomach secretion and motility, is cut. After the nerve interruption, with secretion and motility reduced, an ulcer that previously would not heal may do so.

With impulses from the vagus nerve no longer reaching it, the pylorus muscle at the stomach outlet into the duodenum tends to tighten so that food passage is slowed. To counter this, when vagotomy is performed, another procedure, pyloroplasty, is also used to enlarge the outlet.

In some cases, vagotomy may also be used in combination with partial gastrectomy or gastroenterostomy.

Surgery for perforation. Perforation of an ulcer calls for immediate surgery and because the patient often is quite ill surgery may be limited to the immediate problem. The perforated area is stitched closed and escaped fluid and pus are sucked out of the abdominal cavity.

In some patients, vagotomy and partial gastrectomy may be performed at the same time. Otherwise, these procedures may be carried out later.

The ulcer surgery success rate is high. Ninety-eight percent of patients come through the operations well. Symptoms are relieved completely in at least 80 percent of cases and in the remainder the symptoms usually are mild and transient.

Operating time, depending upon the procedure or combination of procedures used, may run from two to four or five hours. General anesthesia is used. If there is time, a patient may be hospitalized a day or two before the operation to allow the intestinal tract to be rested and emptied.

After surgery, for several days there is abdominal discomfort, usually mild. For the first two or three days, food is withheld and nourishment provided by vein. Many surgeons now believe in having the patient up and out of bed at least for a brief period the day after the operation. The surgical wound heals in one to two weeks and many patients leave the hospital after about ten days.

There will be a scar, usually not greatly disfiguring. Depending upon the type of incision used, it may run across the upper part of the abdomen, or from about the breastbone down to about the navel or a little beyond, either in the midline of the abdomen or to the left or right side of the midline.

In some cases, a "stomach-dumping" syndrome—with symptoms such as weakness, sweating, nausea, and warmth after eating—may develop after gastrectomy. The syndrome may appear because there is a tendency for the stomach, after operation, to empty food more rapidly into the intestine than usual. The symptoms, which usually come on after eating, last about half an hour and usually can be minimized or prevented by frequent small rather than three large meals. Drugs, called anticholinergics, which reduce nerve impulses, may be used if necessary and are often helpful. The dumping problem usually disappears after several months.

Once fully recovered from successful ulcer surgery, a patient is left with no limitations and is likely to be able to lead a more normal life than before.

PERNICIOUS ANEMIA

Anemia can stem from, among other things, deficiencies of various materials essential for the formation of red blood cells or of the hemoglobin in the cells that carries vital oxygen to all body tissues. There are iron-deficiency anemias and anemias due to shortages of various vitamins—vitamin C, folic acid, and others.

But one anemia is the result not of a shortage of a vitamin, B_{12} , in the diet but rather of the shortage of a vital material that normally is produced in the stomach and without which vitamin B_{12} cannot be absorbed.

This is pernicious anemia, so named (pernicious meaning deadly) because not much more than fifty years ago it almost invariably was fatal, its cause and mechanisms entirely unknown.

Pernicious anemia occurs most often in white people after the age of fifty, although it is not limited to whites and can occur at younger ages as well. There is some tendency for it to run in families but a family history of the problem does not mean that it must inevitably develop nor is lack of a family history any assurance of immunity.

Its onset is usually insidious. Commonly, the general symptoms of anemia—such as weakness, shortness of breath, and palpitation—do not occur until the disease has been present for some time.

Often, the first indications may be soreness of the tongue and pins-and-needles sensations of the hands and feet, and, in the beginning, these symptoms may be quite mild.

Varying from one patient to another, gastrointestinal symptoms may appear earlier or later and may include loss of appetite, nausea, vomiting, diarrhea, and attacks of abdominal pain. Weight loss is common.

Often, the mucous membrane lining of the mouth becomes pale or sometimes greenish yellow. The tongue is in a state of chronic inflammation with irregular, fiery red patches resembling a burn near the tip.

Commonly, a sensation of burning, itching, or stinging in the mouth is present, and there may be complaints of tenderness or paroxysmal pain on food intake or on drinking fluids, both hot and cold.

Frequently, the skin develops a lemon yellow tint.

In almost half the patients with pernicious anemia, central nervous system symptoms develop. The earliest may be persistent numbness and tingling of hands and feet. Abnormalities of reflexes develop and, with progress of the disease, a victim becomes unsteady in walking, especially in the dark, with weakness and stiffness of the extremities. Disturbances of bladder and bowel control may develop.

Memory may be affected. In some cases, there may be euphoria, or exaggerated feelings of well-being. Clouding of mental awareness may occur. In advanced cases, even psychotic behavior may develop.

It is important that the nervous system changes of pernicious anemia be recognized early for what they are, especially when they appear before any usual symptoms of anemia, such as weakness and pallor. For if treated early, the changes can be reversed completely; if neglected and treated late, complete reversal may not be possible.

The cause of all this is a permanent deficiency of a material called intrinsic factor, which is produced in the stomach and is normally present in gastric juice.

Why intrinsic factor deficiency develops is not yet clearly established. But there is increasing evidence now that an autoimmune mechanism is involved, which means that the body's immune, or defense, system goes awry. That system produces antibodies that are designed to attack invading disease organisms. In autoimmune disease, the system strangely, harmfully, produces antibodies to the body's own tissues. And recently in as many as 90 percent of patients with pernicious anemia, antibodies either against the intrinsic factor or the stomach cells that produce the factor have been detected.

Vitamin B_{12} is an astonishing vitamin. It is essential for the formation of red blood cells, for normal growth, and for the maintenance of healthy nerve cells. Yet, remarkably little of it is needed. An amount in the diet as small as just one microgram a day is enough—a millionth of a gram—and a gram, in turn, is one twenty-eighth of an ounce.

But vitamin B_{12}, coming in through the diet, cannot be absorbed effectively without intrinsic factor. It is the intrinsic factor that helps get the vitamin through the gastrointestinal lining and into the bloodstream.

Pernicious anemia can be diagnosed with the aid of laboratory tests. A sample of blood often shows a slight decrease in hemoglobin, the red cell pigment, and an increase in the size of red blood cells. A sample of bone marrow, obtained by simple needle puncture, shows distinctive changes.

An excellent diagnostic test is the Schilling test, which involves administering by mouth a small amount of radioactive vitamin B_{12} and then measuring the amount of it excreted in the urine. The test provides a clear indication of whether the vitamin is being properly absorbed.

Pernicious anemia sometimes may be diagnosed by therapeutic trial. An oral dose of vitamin B_{12} is given daily for a week. If the anemia fails to respond but subsequently does improve on the same oral dose plus intrinsic factor, the test indicates that the anemia is pernicious.

Because patients with pernicious anemia have somewhat more of a tendency than others to develop stomach cancer, although this is not by any means inevitable, gastrointestinal X rays should be taken for every patient with the diagnosis.

Sometimes the X rays may disclose other causes of pernicious-like anemia. One of these is sprue, also called celiac disease (see Malabsorption), a chronic intestinal disorder caused by intolerance to gluten in some foods that leads to impaired absorption and can be treated by diet.

Something else may have to be considered before a final diagnosis of pernicious anemia is reached. Theoretically, without eating meat and even without eating eggs or dairy products, it is possible to get all essential nutrients except one—B_{12}. Tiny though the needed amount of B_{12} is, it is virtually impossible to get it on a strict vegetarian diet. It is worth noting that George Bernard Shaw, who was a vegetarian, was under strict orders from his doctor to take liver extract, what Shaw called "those chemicals."

Treatment. Until B_{12} itself was discovered and isolated and then produced—only about thirty years ago—liver extract was used in treating pernicious anemia. It was not known then but the vital material in liver extract that combated pernicious anemia—the extract was given by injection —was vitamin B_{12}.

Today, the treatment of pernicious anemia begins with injections of fifty to one hundred micrograms of B_{12} every one to seven days for two to four months in order to overcome the deficiency, correct abnormalities in the blood and elsewhere that have resulted from the deficiency, and create an adequate body vitamin B_{12} reserve.

Thereafter, permanent maintenance therapy is needed. Vitamin B_{12} by mouth may be used for maintenance therapy but is not recommended for initial treatment. Large doses of the vitamin may be taken once a day or still larger doses once a week. Many physicians prefer a monthly injection —so that there is no room for patient forgetfulness.

With treatment, anemia can be relieved completely, blood returned to normal, and nervous system manifestations can be prevented, arrested, or lessened.

PYLORIC STENOSIS (INFANT STOMACH OUTLET OBSTRUCTION)

Within a few weeks after birth, some infants begin to vomit; mild at first, it becomes increasingly forceful until curdled milk shoots out from the mouth.

Such projectile vomiting is an important clue to pyloric stenosis. In this condition, the sphincter muscle at the stomach outlet, the pylorus, which normally opens to permit food to leave the stomach and enter the duodenum, swells and stiffens, losing its ability to contract and relax normally. Stomach-emptying is impeded, so that the infant vomits and, if allowed to continue to do so long, will suffer from dehydration and marked weight loss.

Pyloric stenosis occurs in about one in every seven hundred babies and is about three times as frequent in boys as in girls. The cause is unknown.

Often the tight sphincter muscle can be felt as a lump in the upper right abdomen, and X-ray study can confirm the diagnosis.

Some infants respond to antispasmodic drugs, which act to relax the sphincter muscle. Such medication may be tried and, if the infant responds, there may be no need for surgery.

Surgery. When an infant fails to respond to medical treatment, relatively simply surgery can be used to correct pyloric stenosis.

Under light gas anesthesia, a small incision, about two inches long, is made in the upper right abdomen and, without need for opening the stomach, the surgeon can slit the fibers of the sphincter muscle, then close the abdomen, with the total procedure sometimes taking less than half an hour.

The fibers are simply left slit. Later they will grow and reunite and the sphincter will function normally.

Within twelve to twenty-four hours after the operation, the infant retains feedings. No special nursing is required, the incision is usually healed within seven to ten days, and the child may be home from the hospital in less than a week.

REGIONAL ENTERITIS

Regional enteritis—which is also known as ileitis and Crohn's disease—is an inflammatory disease that usually affects the lower part of the ileum, the last portion of the small intestine, but may sometimes involve other parts of the gastrointestinal tract, including the colon.

Its cause is unknown. It affects men and women in equal proportions, and most commonly begins between the ages of twenty and thirty but may occur at other ages.

One frequent symptom is midabdominal cramping pain with several loose stools a day. Mild fever and appetite and weight loss are common. In some cases, there may be recurrent episodes of severe intestinal colic, abdominal distention, and vomiting caused by partial intestinal obstruction. In other cases, there may be pain much like that of acute appendicitis.

For unknown reasons, part of the ileum becomes swollen, red, and hard. The lining becomes ulcerated. Abscesses may form. A diseased section of the ileum may adhere to another loop of the ileum. Fistulas—abnormal tubelike connections between ileum loops—may appear.

X-ray studies, including films taken after a barium enema, are needed to clearly demonstrate the disease and allow a definite diagnosis to be made.

It sometimes happens that complete recovery follows a single attack of regional enteritis. But in most cases the disease is on-again-off-again, involving repeated acute attacks and remissions in between.

Treatment. There is no specific therapy for the disease. During acute attacks, bed rest is often advised. A high calorie but low-residue diet with supplemental multiple vitamins is often used. In acute stages, a corticosteroid, or cortisonelike drug, such as prednisone, often helps by reducing fever, improving appetite, decreasing the number of stools, and increasing intestinal absorption of nutrients. Other medication, including Azulfidine, small doses of phenobarbital several times a day, and, when abscesses or infected fistulas are present, antibiotics, may be used.

Surgery. Surgery is often necessary under a number of circumstances: when intestinal obstruction, fistulas, or abscesses develop; if massive bleeding should occur; when medical treatment fails to help at all; or if the possibility of acute appendicitis cannot be ruled out without operation.

Either one of two procedures may be used. Diseased areas may be removed and the remaining healthy portion of the ileum connected to the colon. The removal is well tolerated since there is ileum to spare. (One well-known ileitis sufferer who did well after ileitis surgery was President Dwight D. Eisenhower.) In an alternative procedure, the diseased areas are not removed but are bypassed by connecting a healthy loop of ileum to the colon.

Either procedure is carried out, under general or spinal anesthesia, through an incision to one side of the navel and extending several inches above and below the navel. The operation may require from one to three hours. Feeding for several days thereafter is by vein. Depending upon how ill and run down the patient has been, he may remain in bed for several days or be up the day following surgery. Similarly, depending upon the condition of the patient before operation and how quickly he regains strength afterward, hospitalization may range from two weeks to two or three months.

Surgery for ileitis is not curative. It usually relieves symptoms and controls complications. In many cases, no further problems are experienced. But in about 30 percent of patients, recurrences are experienced after some years, requiring further treatment. In patients over fifty, the recurrence rate is less than in younger patients.

Cancer as a complication now is increasingly recognized.

ULCERATIVE COLITIS

Ulcerative colitis is a chronic, inflammatory, and ulcerative disease of the colon. Its cause is unknown, and it may occur at any age but most often affects young adults of twenty to forty years.

The disease manifests itself as a series of attacks of bloody diarrhea with absence of symptoms in between. The onset of an attack may be sudden and acute but more often is slow and insidious, beginning with mild cramps, increased urge to defecate, and some bloody mucus in the stools. Loss of appetite, some malaise, and mild fever in the evening also occur.

As the disease becomes more extensive and severe, stools become looser and ten to twelve bowel movements may occur in a day, often with severe cramps, from which there is no respite at night. Fever too is often high, appetite loss is severe, nausea and vomiting occur, and anemia develops.

A tentative diagnosis is usually possible from a patient's history and from stool examination. And the diagnosis can be confirmed by inspection with a lighted instrument of the lower colon and rectum and by X-ray studies showing changes in the lining of the colon and rectum.

Various theories have been offered to try to explain the disease. One holds that it has an infectious origin; another that it is allergic in nature; while still another holds that emotional factors play a major role.

About one in five patients recovers completely after a single attack and never has trouble again. But more typically, there are recurrent attacks.

Treatment. There is no specific therapy for the disease and the major objectives of medical treatment are to give the bowel as much rest and the patient as much support as possible.

Bed rest—more likely in the hospital—is usually prescribed during an acute episode along with a high fluid intake (although milk may be banned by physicians who believe the disease to be of allergic origin) and a high protein and high caloric diet. When a patient is unable to eat or drink, vitamins, minerals, and other nutrients may be given by injection.

Anemia is treated with iron or if severe by blood transfusion. Sedatives are employed and, if pain is severe, analgesics such as meperidine or anileridine. Drugs such as opium tincture and belladonna tincture may be used to lessen cramps and stool frequency. Antibacterial drugs also may be used to combat inflammation.

Cortisonelike drugs such as prednisone and hydrocortisone are key agents in treatment. They do not cure but they do bring about remissions in as many as 85 percent of patients, sometimes with dramatic speed. The drugs are given by mouth and also by enema.

Surgery. Surgical treatment may be indicated for any one of several reasons: when medical measures are of virtually no use; if the disease advances relentlessly; if there should be either massive bleeding or obstruction of the colon; when there is suspicion that a malignancy may be present.

The operation, called proctocolectomy, is a drastic one but it can be lifesaving. Both the colon and rectum are removed. The last part of the small intestine, no longer emptying into the colon, is diverted into a permanent opening in the abdomen through which stools are passed.

After the operation, which is carried out under general or spinal anesthesia, the patient may be out of bed within one to three days and for the first several days takes nourishment by vein only. He may leave the hospital after four to six weeks or sometimes longer, during which he is taught how to function with and care for the new bowel opening, called an ileostomy, which begins to function within a few hours after surgery.

Formidable as the operation seems, and even though it is used often for very sick patients otherwise in danger of losing their lives, the success rate is better than 90 percent. There is no interference with digestion from loss of the colon since digestion takes place in the small bowel. And after a time, the small bowel even takes over the colon's normal job of absorbing water. A specially fitted appliance used by the patient with an ileostomy is unobtrusive and odor-sealing. Although, understandably enough, he may face some emotional problems after the operation and need emotional support—which is increasingly available now from special therapists in hospital clinics and from ileostomy clubs formed by patients themselves—he can expect, after the initial period of adjustment, to be able to live as long as others who have not had ulcerative colitis and to function well in all aspects of living.

Newer surgical techniques may no longer require wearing an external appliance.

WORM-INDUCED DISEASES

Many types of intestinal parasitic worms can cause disease.

TRICHINOSIS

This parasitic disease, one of the better known and worldwide in distribution, is caused by infection with the roundworm *T. spiralis* as a result of eating raw or inadequately cooked or processed pork or pork products.

Many patients remain free of symptoms. Symptoms when they occur may begin with swelling of the upper eyelids about the eleventh day after infection. This may be followed by bleeding in the eye, pain, and sensitivity to light. Diarrhea, nausea, vomiting and other gastrointestinal symptoms, and slight fever may precede or accompany the eye symptoms. Muscle soreness and pain, hives, thirst, profuse sweating, chills, weakness, and prostration may follow.

The outlook is good in most cases. Trichinosis seldom leads to any permanent disability. Purgatives and deworming preparations are ineffective. Treatment is aimed at relieving symptoms and supporting the patient until the parasites become enclosed in sacs, or cysts, where they may do no more harm. Muscle pains can be relieved by bed rest and aspirin or codeine. A cortisonelike drug such as prednisone used for about ten days may relieve other symptoms.

SCHISTOSOMIASIS

This parasitic disease results from bathing or wading in (or other contact with) water infested with flukes of the genus *Schistosoma* that penetrate the skin and mature in one to three months into adult worms that invade the intestines or bladder. The flukes are carried by freshwater snails.

Schistosomiasis is rare in the United States except in Puerto Ricans living here. It is most common in Africa, the Middle East, parts of the West Indies, the northern part of South America, Japan, China, the Philippines, and the Celebes.

The disease may first cause fever and hives. Later, there may be dysentery with unusually fluid stools, cramps, and spasms of involuntary straining to evacuate. Sometimes, there may be symptoms like those of cirrhosis of the liver.

Bed rest is necessary. Among the most effective medications are tartar emetic and stibophen, which are given by injection. Doses have to be adjusted carefully since the drugs, while valuable, can produce side effects, including upper abdominal pain, heart-rate changes, dizziness, nausea and vomiting, and pain in the joints and muscles.

VISCERAL LARVA MIGRANS

This is an infection with nematode larvae, which are normal intestinal parasites of pet dogs and cats. The disease usually appears as a relatively benign one in two- to four-year-old children but may occur in older people.

Commonly, the source of infection is soil or a child's open sandbox contaminated by pet feces containing parasite eggs, which the child may then transfer to his mouth while playing. The eggs hatch in the human intestine and the larvae can penetrate the intestinal wall and get into the circulation. The larvae may remain alive for months, producing damage as they move about.

They may cause liver enlargement, fever, lung inflammation, and coughing.

The disease is self-limited. No specific treatment is available but the cortisonelike drug prednisone helps control symptoms. If there is no reinfection, the disease disappears after six to eighteen months.

As a preventive measure against infection or reinfection, infected pet dogs and cats should be dewormed regularly by a veterinarian and children's sandboxes should be covered when not being used.

OTHER INTESTINAL PARASITIC INFECTIONS
COMMON IN THE UNITED STATES

The giant intestinal roundworm enters as an egg through the mouth—via contaminated vegetables. The most common symptoms of roundworm infection are colicky pains and diarrhea. Diagnosis can be made when immature eggs or worms are found in stools. Effective medication includes piperazine, thiabendazole, bephenium hydroxynaphthoate, and hexylresorcinol.

Hookworm may enter through the mouth but more commonly does so through the skin, usually the feet. The source of infection is fecal contamination of soil. The worm can produce darkening of the stool with blood pigments, anemia, heart insufficiency, and retarded growth. The diagnosis is clear when immature eggs are found in the stool. Effective medication: tetrachloroethylene, hexylresorcinol, bephenium hydroxynaphthoate, and thiabendazole.

Threadworm, found in the southern United States, enters through the skin, usually the feet, and the source is fecal contamination of soil. It causes pain in the pit of the stomach (the pain may radiate) and diarrhea. Diagnosis is certain when larvae are found in the stool. Effective medication: thiabendazole.

Whipworm, found in the Gulf Coast region, enters as an egg through the mouth, and the source is fecal contamination of soil. It produces diarrhea, nausea, anemia, and retarded growth. It may sometimes produce acute appendicitis in children. Diagnosis can be made when immature eggs are found in the stool. Effective medication: hexylresorcinol enemas and thiabendazole.

Pinworm or seat worm enters in the form of an egg via the mouth, the source being a contaminated environment. It produces itching around the anal area and the infection often involves the whole family. The diagnosis is clear when eggs are found in anal swabs or adult worms appear. Effective medication: piperazine, pyrvinium pamoate, and thiabendazole.

Dwarf tapeworms, common in children in the southern part of the United States, enter the mouth as eggs from a contaminated environment, and produce diarrhea, abdominal discomfort, dizziness, and inanition, a physical condition like that resulting from starvation. Diagnosis is certain when eggs are found in the stool. Effective medication: quinacrine hydrochloride.

Beef tapeworm enters in larva form from poorly cooked or raw infected beef. It produces abdominal distress and appendicitis-like symptoms. Diagnosis can be made when eggs are found in the stool. Effective medication: quinacrine hydrochloride.

Fish tapeworm enters in larva form from infected freshwater fish and may cause pernicious anemia or bowel obstruction. Diagnosis can be made when immature eggs are found in the stool. Effective medication: quinacrine hydrochloride and aspidium oleoresin.

Amebic dysentery is caused by the protozoan *Entamoeba hystolytica*, which enters via the mouth from feces-contaminated water, food, and the environment. It can cause attacks of diarrhea over a prolonged period and may produce complications such as liver abscess and lung abscess. Diagnosis can be definite when the organism is found in one form or another in the stool. Effective medication includes emetine hydrochloride, tetracycline, metronidazole, and chloroquine phosphate.

Giardia is a protozoan parasite that enters as a cyst through the mouth. Source: human feces. It produces mucous diarrhea, abdominal pain, and weight loss. Diagnosis can be certain when the organism is found in cyst or vegetative stage in the stool. Effective medication: quinacrine hydrochloride and metronidazole.

PART THREE

Gut Medicines

THE HISTORY OF modern medicines is full of remarkable successes. But it also includes disasters. Huge benefits have followed the discovery of such agents as antibiotics and other antibacterials that combat infections, cortisone and similar compounds that counter inflammation, sedatives and tranquilizers that calm people and often may help to calm diseases.

But there have been tragedies caused by indiscriminate use and abuse of these and many other agents. No drug yet developed is foolproof, 100 percent effective for all with a particular problem, or free of undesirable effects. Just as virtually every food may produce unpleasant effects for at least a few people very sensitive to it, so may virtually every drug.

If a drug is good for treatment, it is so because it does something. But no drug is 100 percent specific, hitting only the bull's-eye, so to speak. In the course of combating the problem for which it is being used, it may produce other effects and these have to be reckoned with.

Consider, for example, the cramps, diarrhea, sore mouth, and rectal itch that may occur after use of some antibiotics. The symptoms develop because an antibiotic may sometimes upset the natural germ balance in the gut; many harmless bacteria are always present there; some, in fact, are essential to digestion; some produce vitamins. Sometimes that friendly bacterial population that a potent antibiotic decimates has been keeping under control other harmful organisms resident in the digestive tract. Killed off in such large numbers, friendly bacteria offer less competition to the harmful residents, which can multiply, resulting in superinfection—a new and different infection from the one being treated.

Use of potent modern medical preparations, not only antibiotics but many others, involves a calculated risk. Ideally, a physician using them should do so after careful consideration and an informed decision that the good to be gained outweighs any risks along the way. And ideally he should use them with caution, he and his patients alerted to the earliest indications of any trouble, any potentially serious side effects, so that they can be overcome by change of dosage or medication, adding other medication, or, when necessary, discontinuance of treatment.

That is no less true for medications obtained without prescription. Generally, they are less potent but not entirely free of risk.

Consider laxatives, for example. According to a recent report by Johns Hopkins Hospital researchers in the Archives of Neurology, a number sold over the counter in this country can cause mercury poisoning. The report described the death of two women who used such laxatives daily for many years. Before their deaths from complications of mercury poisoning, the women exhibited such typical mercury poisoning symptoms as tremor, loss of intellect, hearing loss, and kidney failure. One of the women who died at age sixty-three had taken two laxative tablets daily, each containing 120 milligrams of mercurous chloride, better known as calomel, for many years. The other, aged fifty-six at death, had taken a similar daily dose for a known period of six years. Calomel, once a popular laxative that was considered safe, is no longer recommended. But several laxative products containing it are still marketed and their labels state that they contain the mercury compound.

About the same time as the report on the two women appeared, so did another about a forty-two-year-old woman. According to X-ray films and other studies, she appeared to have chronic ulcerative colitis and cancer of the colon. Her colon was removed because of the presumed cancer. But after thorough study of the removed portion of colon in the pathology laboratory and a good deal of added detective work on the woman's history, physicians arrived at a true diagnosis. It was not cancer at all and, if it had been known, she could have avoided the surgery. Earlier the patient had said she had been taking two stimulant laxatives daily for four years, but her husband, when questioned later, disclosed she had been taking the laxatives habitually for eighteen years. Her real problem, instead of cancer or ulcerative colitis, was a cathartic colon, a colon battered by laxative abuse.

No drug—bar none—prescribed or not prescribed—can be abused without possible penalty.

Unfortunately, drugs are probably used the most freely for problems affecting the gut.

When really needed, they can be helpful. But they should be used only then—with respect and care and with an understanding of some of the basic facts about their actions and possible liabilities.

ANALGESICS

Analgesics—drugs that relieve pain without causing loss of consciousness—fall into two groups: the potent and potentially addicting and the mild and nonaddicting.

The nonaddicting may act by raising the threshold of pain perception; some also seem to act locally to reduce pain arising in joints and muscles. They are effective mainly for mild to moderate degrees of pain and act without causing significant sedation.

The addicting not only raise the threshold of pain perception; they also suppress the natural tendency to react to severe pain with alarm and apprehension. They often cause drowsiness and euphoria and may produce tolerance and physical dependence or addiction.

The commonly used nonaddicting analgesics include many available without prescription, including the salicylates such as aspirin, salicylamide, and sodium salicylate; aniline or coal tar derivatives such as acetanilide, phenacetin, and acetaminophen; and a pyrazolone group of compounds such as antipyrine, aminopyrine, dypyrone, oxyphenbutazone, and phenylbutazone, available on prescription.

In addition to raising the threshold of pain perception, nonaddicting analgesics also relieve fever and have other actions. The salicylates, for example, often relieve joint tenderness, redness, and swelling. Oxyphenbutazone and phenylbutazone have less pain and fever relieving activity than the salicylates but are more potent in antirheumatic activity. The aniline or coal tar derivatives have pain and fever relieving but not antiinflammatory activity.

Most of the nonaddicting analgesics cause relatively few undesirable effects when taken in doses ordinarily used for relieving minor pain. Still, in some very sensitive people, they may cause allergic reactions, sometimes severe, even in small doses.

The salicylates in a small percentage of people cause stomach irritation and some bleeding, and the addition of a small amount of an antacid buffer does not significantly counteract these gastric reactions. For patients so affected, a physician may suggest use of an analgesic such as acetaminophen.

Large doses of salicylates, such as aspirin, used for acute rheumatic conditions sometimes may cause salicylism, manifested by ringing in the ears, headache, dizziness, and mental confusion.

Phenylbutazone and oxyphenbutazone may produce potentially serious blood disturbances in a small but significant number of susceptible patients, and when they are used, a patient should be under close medical supervision.

Some people are given to taking excessive amounts of nonaddicting analgesics over prolonged periods. The abuse of headache remedies containing acetanilide or phenacetin has sometimes led to severe toxicity, manifested by blueness, labored breathing, headache, dizziness, and sometimes collapse. And kidney damage has been reported after prolonged use of large daily doses of analgesic products containing phenacetin.

The potent, potentially addicting analgesics, available only on prescription, include the natural alkaloids of opium such as morphine and codeine; semisynthetic derivatives of morphine and codeine such as heroin, hydromorphone, and oxymorphone; and a variety of synthetic analgesics that resemble morphine in many of their actions, and include meperidine, alphaprodine, anileridine, piminodine, levorphanol, methadone, and phenazocine.

Such potent compounds should be used only for managing pain that is not readily relieved by nonaddicting agents.

Morphine must be given by injection for reliable action. Some synthetic drugs, such as meperidine, methadone, and levorphanol, are effective by mouth but more so by injection. Use at the same time of a phenothiazine-type tranquilizer often allows control of pain with relatively small doses of morphinelike analgesics because the tranquilizer reduces emotional reaction to pain.

Some of the potent analgesics such as morphine, hydromorphone, methadone, and codeine are also valuable as antitussives or cough suppressants.

Despite their pain-relieving value, the potent analgesics have disadvantages. One is addiction liability.

The most potentially dangerous side effect of the drugs is depression of breathing, which occurs most often in elderly, debilitated patients and in those suffering from lung diseases.

Reduced doses of the drugs should be used for patients who are also receiving tranquilizers, barbiturates, or other drugs that tend to increase breathing depression.

The potent analgesics also tend to produce drowsiness and clouding of the mental processes, which may be desirable for some sick patients but not for ambulatory ones.

Other side effects may include feelings of light-headedness, dizziness, warmth, itching, nausea, and vomiting. To minimize these effects patients usually need to be confined to bed after taking a potent analgesic.

Morphine almost invariably produces constipation, but some other agents such as meperidine produce this to a lesser degree.

ANOREXIANTS (APPETITE REDUCERS)

Anorexiants are drugs sometimes prescribed to help allay the sensations of hunger for people who are trying to overcome obesity.

They include the amphetamines such as amphetamine sulfate, dextroamphetamine, and methamphetamine and some other compounds known as sympathomimetic amines such as benaphetamine, chlorphentermine, diethylpropion, phenmetrazine, and phentermine, which also act on the nervous system.

Although the drugs have the effect of allaying hunger—the effect appears to be related to stimulation of the central nervous system—the exact mechanism of these appetite suppressants is not clear.

And although they do tend to lessen the distress of a strict adherence to a diet—especially in the early stages—many if not most physicians believe they should be used only as short-term crutches, if at all.

They may sometimes have undesirable effects, including nervousness, restlessness, sleeplessness, and gastrointestinal disturbances such as nausea, constipation, abdominal pain, and diarrhea.

Tolerance to them also may develop so that a dose that was once effective no longer is. However, an increase in dosage may lead not only to increased restlessness and insomnia but to toxic psychoses, with hallucinations and delusions.

In some people, a serious depression may follow intensive use of anorexiants in crash dieting.

These drugs generally should not be used by anyone with high blood pressure, heart or blood vessel disease, or hyperthyroidism.

ANTACIDS

Antacids act to reduce acidity in the stomach and are commonly used for heartburn and digestive upsets as well as for peptic ulcer. Because they neutralize some of the secreted acid but do not inhibit the activity of the acid-secreting cells of the stomach, their effects are temporary.

Nor is there definitive evidence that antacids speed the rate of healing of duodenal ulcers or prevent recurrence; however, they do appear to speed the rate of healing of stomach ulcers.

One major factor to be considered in selecting an antacid is cost; except for calcium carbonate, antacids are quite expensive. Palatability is a matter of individual preference; some manufacturers make their products in several flavors. Liquid preparations are generally more effective than tablets, but for convenience tablets win here. Yet many tablets contain aluminum hydroxide, which loses much of its acid-buffering effectiveness in the drying process involved in making tablets. Other important factors, of course, are efficacy and side effects. All of the following are available without prescription.

Sodium bicarbonate. This compound is highly soluble and reacts almost instantly with hydrochloric acid to neutralize it. But it is not recommended for long-term use because it tends to increase blood alkalinity, which may produce shallow or irregular breathing, prickling or burning sensations in the fingers, toes, or lips, muscle cramps, and, in severe cases, convulsions. The sodium it contains also may not be advisable for people with high blood pressure or a heart problem.

Calcium carbonate. This is the cheapest antacid available and, according to the latest studies, as effective as any. Because it is insoluble, it is emptied from the stomach at a slower rate than sodium bicarbonate, which prolongs its antacid action. Calcium may cause increased acid secretion rebound, and some physicians oppose its use.

The disadvantages of calcium carbonate powder include its inconvenience, chalky taste, and slight tendency to produce constipation. These disadvantages are eliminated when calcium carbonate is prepared as a tablet, or as a liquid containing small amounts of magnesium antacid, which, unfortunately, have a tendency to produce diarrhea.

Because some of the calcium from calcium carbonate is absorbed and may produce an undesirable elevation of blood calcium levels, tests of blood calcium levels are recommended. The excessive blood levels usually are temporary, rarely persistent.

Aluminum hydroxide. Different preparations of aluminum hydroxide vary considerably in acid-neutralizing activity. Tablets are less effective than liquids. The preparations often contain significant amounts of sodium and should not be used by people on a sodium-restricted diet.

The advantages of aluminum hydroxide are its relative palatability and lack of toxic effects. The most common undesirable effect is constipation, which can be countered with use of a magnesium antacid or a preparation that combines aluminum hydroxide with a magnesium compound.

Because aluminum compounds can interfere with the effectiveness of the tetracycline antibiotics and with the absorption of anticholinergics, iron, barbiturates, warfarin, quinine, and quinidine, they should not be used simultaneously with these drugs.

Magnesium antacids. Magnesium hydroxide, or milk of magnesia, although mainly used as a laxative, is a relatively effective antacid. It does, however, have a tendency to produce diarrhea as do other magnesium compounds, such as magnesium carbonate, magnesium oxide, magnesium phosphate, and magnesium trisilicate. Magnesium compounds therefore are usually combined with calcium or aluminum compounds to avoid diarrhea.

Some magnesium is absorbed and is excreted harmlessly by the kidneys, but undesirable magnesium retention may occur in patients with chronic kidney disease.

A new type of drug, known as an H_2 antihistamine, promises to be a major development in the treatment of peptic ulcers.

ANTHELMINTICS (MEDICATIONS FOR WORMS)

Usually, common intestinal worms—tapeworms, pinworms, and others—can be removed with reasonable certainty by anthelmintics, prescription drugs that are designed to destroy worms.

Because the drugs are relatively specific, the particular type of worm involved usually must be identified if the right type of drug is to be prescribed.

These drugs are potent and some can cause undesirable effects. But proper use can minimize them. A physician in prescribing an anthelmintic will take care to inform a patient about expected side effects as well as proper methods of use.

For example, tetrachloroethylene in some cases may cause nausea and even symptoms of inebriation. Because alcohol will potentiate these effects it should be avoided. A patient receiving the drug should rest for several hours afterward.

Hexylresorcinol, when taken orally, may produce burns in the mouth if the tablets are chewed. When administered by enema, it may produce burns of the perineum—the region between the anus and vaginal orifice or scrotum—if the area is not properly prepared by application of an oily material such as mineral oil.

Quinacrine may produce yellowing of the skin. Piperazine preparations sometimes may produce nausea, vomiting, headaches, cramps, diarrhea, dizziness, tremors, muscular weakness, or skin rash; all are transitory and disappear when the medication is discontinued. Pyrvinium pamoate may in some cases cause nausea, vomiting, and diarrhea, but is usually well tolerated.

If your physician may have overlooked giving you full information about an anthelmintic, it is wise to request it. That way you will know which side effects, if they appear, are permissible, even if unpleasant, and which are cause for checking immediately with your physician to determine whether treatment should be stopped.

ANTIBACTERIALS

Antibacterials—agents that check the growth of bacteria—include antibiotics and sulfa drugs. There are dozens of them, some more effective than others against individual types of disease organisms.

Penicillin, the first widely used antibiotic, was accidentally discovered in 1929 by Sir Alexander Fleming when bacteria in a laboratory dish were killed by mold spores floating in the air. Antibiotics are chemical compounds produced by and obtained from some living cells, especially bacteria, yeasts, and molds, and the compounds are antagonistic to some other forms of life. Some are biocidal: they kill; others are biostatic: they check growth and multiplication.

Penicillin came into use during World War II and prevented many deaths from wound infections and disease. But while it was effective against some organisms it was not against others. A worldwide search in soil and other natural sources yielded new antibiotics such as chlortetracycline, chloramphenicol, and oxytetracycline, called broad-spectrum antibiotics because they are effective against a broader range of bacteria. Many antibiotics are now produced synthetically. And sulfa drugs, also called sulfonamides, are effective against certain bacteria and are available in many forms.

Antibacterials are powerful substances but, unless properly prescribed, can be harmful. If an antibacterial not effective against a specific organism causing a disease is used, time is wasted, the disease progresses, and there may be some risk of fatality. It is also possible for disease organisms to develop resistance to an antibacterial when the drug is used incorrectly, and the value of the drug against the disease is then destroyed.

Antibacterials on occasion can also produce side effects because of direct toxic effects or because an individual happens to be extra sensitive. Quite a few people are highly sensitive to penicillin, for example, and should make this fact known to a new physician. Reactions during treatment do not always make it mandatory to stop treatment, especially if the drug is the only effective and available one, but the type and severity of reaction and the possibility of influencing it by proper measures must be weighed against the gravity of the infection.

Undesirable effects can take many forms. Skin eruptions may occur with any of the drugs. Fever may develop as a reaction.

Most common with the broad-spectrum antibiotics are dryness, burning, soreness and itching of mouth and tongue, and gastrointestinal complications such as nausea, vomiting, and diarrhea.

Sometimes, jaundice may develop. Other possible side effects include urinary obstruction, breathing difficulty, blood disturbances that may be life-threatening, neuritis, abnormal burning or tingling sensations.

An antibacterial effective for a particular patient at a particular time and with a particular infection should be chosen, adequate doses should be used, and the infection brought under control as quickly as possible. There should be no resort to old leftover antibiotics, which not only may be of no value for the particular infection at hand but even if they could be of value may have lost potency during storage or may have been so chemically changed that they may cause harm.

The physician's prescription should be followed rigidly—in terms of the dose to take, when to take it, and for how long. Symptoms may pass but an infection may not be wiped out with inadequate dosage or with too early cessation of treatment, and the infection, when it then recurs, may no longer be readily controllable.

Any untoward effects should be noted by a patient and reported immediately to the physician so that he can do whatever is needed to counter the effects by modifying dosage, changing the drug, or using additional medications.

ANTICHOLINERGIC (ANTISPASMODIC) AGENTS

The antispasmodic, or anticholinergic, agents are among the most widely prescribed drugs for relief of gastrointestinal symptoms. They are frequently used for peptic ulcer, pancreatitis, gastrointestinal inflammations, and nonorganic bowel disorders involving excessive or abnormal gut motility.

Anticholinergics act to block the effects of acetylcholine (a natural body chemical involved in the transmission of nerve impulses), and cause a decrease in bowel motility and stomach and pancreas secretions.

Unfortunately, anticholinergics are not selective in their action and they have effects elsewhere than in the gut. When given in large enough doses to effectively reduce bowel motility and secretions, they may cause blurring of vision, dryness of the mouth, difficulty in urination, increased pressure within the eyes, headache, dizziness, palpitation, racing pulse, nausea, heartburn, skin rash, flushing or excessive dryness of the skin, and constipation.

When given by mouth in an amount just below the dose that may produce such undesirable effects, anticholinergics do cut in half the basal acid secretion in the stomach. But they do not reduce acid secretion stimulated by food. So while there may be some reduction in total acid secretion, it is not as much as physicians would like to see.

Patients with irritable colon syndrome probably have received larger amounts—and greater varieties—of anticholinergics than patients with any other single disorder. But the response, even when the drugs have been given in large doses, has been disappointing.

Atropine and tincture of belladonna are the time-honored anticholinergics, and belladonna is still considered by many physicians to be one of the most effective and satisfactory of the preparations available. Individual response varies considerably and it is important that the dose be adjusted to a particular patient's requirements. Often, the starting dose of tincture of belladonna is five to ten drops four times a day, with perhaps fifteen to twenty drops at night. But some patients may have relief of ulcer pain and have side effects, for example, with as little as five drops two or three times a day. Atropine sulfate is available in tablet form; 0.5 milligram is equal to ten drops of tincture of belladonna.

In addition, a large number of newer anticholinergic agents have been synthesized in efforts to find drugs that are effective while producing fewer adverse effects than atropine and belladonna. But side effects still do occur in effective doses.

Among available anticholinergics are adiphenine, amprotropine, dibutoline, diphemanil, glycopyrrolate, homatropine methylbromide, isopropamide, methantheline, methscopolamine bromide, propantheline, and tridihexethyl. There are still others.

However, many physicians regard anticholinergics as merely adjunctive therapy. They may be useful in duodenal ulcer patients who are not responding to other measures; a larger dose at bedtime may relieve nocturnal symptoms and prolong antacid activity. One of these drugs though may be an exception. Some reports indicate that glycopyrrolate seems to speed initial healing and reduce the recurrence rate in patients with gastric ulcers.

Anticholinergics are contraindicated for patients with glaucoma or prostate enlargement; also in those with bleeding or obstructing ulcers and —because they reduce the pressure of the lower esophageal sphincter—in patients with reflux, heartburn, and hiatus hernia.

ANTIDIARRHEALS

Paregoric in teaspoonful doses after each bowel movement is an old-time remedy for diarrhea. It is a mixture of powdered opium, anise oil, benzoic acid, camphor, and glycerin in diluted alcohol. The opium reduces excessive peristaltic contractions.

In addition, various substances that absorb or bind are available without prescription. They include kaolin, a clay, pectin from fruit rinds, and aluminum hydroxide gel, and come in combination preparations. These materials absorb bacteria and toxins and carry them along for excretion. In bacterial toxins have been formed in the intestine, kaolin or pectin further helps prevent absorption by forming a film on the intestinal wall.

Bismuth subcarbonate is another inert chemical not absorbed from the digestive tract that has an absorptive and protective action.

Some preparations combine paregoric or powdered opium with kaolin and pectin and some add bismuth subcarbonate as well.

Another often prescribed preparation combines atropine sulfate and diphenoxylate hydrochloride, a compound related to the narcotic meperidine, and has a strong inhibiting effect on bowel contractions. It is not an innocuous preparation and has to be used with caution.

Other agents, including antibiotics such as colistin sulfate, may be used when the diarrhea is the result of bacterial infection.

Also available (without prescription) are preparations containing cultures of *Lactobacillus acidophilus* and *bulgaricus*, or *acidophilus* alone, designed to help restore the normal intestinal bacterial populations after upsets caused by antibiotic therapy—and in so doing the *Lactobacillus* preparations combat diarrhea.

ANTIEMETICS (ANTINAUSEA AND ANTIVOMITING DRUGS)

Many drugs are available to control nausea and vomiting associated with gastrointestinal disturbances and motion sickness.

They fall into two basic classes, both requiring a prescription.

One group consists of drugs known as phenothiazines, which also serve as major tranquilizers useful in the treatment of mental illnesses. The phenothiazine compounds include chlorpromazine, fluphenazine, perphenazine, promethazine, thiethylperazine, trifluoperazine, and triflupromazine.

The second group, nonphenothiazine compounds, includes buclizine, cyclizine, dimenhydrinate, diphenhydramine, hydroxyzine, meclizine, and trimethobenzamide.

Because the nonphenothiazine antiemetics are considered safer, they are often used when relatively long-term treatment may be needed—as in women with nausea and vomiting in early pregnancy; also in patients with cancer or other diseases who must have prolonged treatment with anti-cancer drugs that may induce nausea and vomiting.

In situations in which vomiting is severe and potentially hazardous but is likely to be of short duration, the nonphenothiazine compounds are generally considered not to act as quickly as the phenothiazines and the latter may be used.

The most common untoward effect of the two classes of antiemetic drugs is drowsiness, and so they should be used with caution by people who need to be constantly alert in operating machinery, especially vehicles. But the incidence and degree of sedation are least when such non-phenothiazine agents as cyclizine and trimethobenzamide are taken in small doses to prevent motion sickness.

Because phenothiazines have an additive or potentiating effect on the action of other drugs that depress the central nervous system, they need to be used with special care in people under the influence of alcohol, barbiturates, or potent analgesics.

CORTICOSTEROIDS

Corticosteroids are compounds that are naturally secreted by the adrenal glands. Synthetic chemicals that are capable of producing essentially similar effects are available by prescription.

These include cortisone, hydrocortisone, prednisone, prednisolone, and many others, which have antiinflammatory action.

The drugs are used in a wide variety of conditions: allergic states, arthritic problems, severe skin disorders, inflammatory eye conditions, and kidney disorders. They are also sometimes used in gastrointestinal problems such as chronic ulcerative colitis.

The drugs can have side effects, which may vary somewhat from one drug to another, from one person to another, depending on dosage and length of use.

Corticosteroids affect the body's metabolism of carbohydrates, fats, protein, and water: They may sometimes produce a diabetes-like state, or deplete body protein and lead to some muscle-wasting, or redistribute fat so that it may be decreased in the extremities and increased in the face and abdominal regions. In high doses a corticosteroid sometimes may lead to sodium and water retention and edema. And in some cases a corticosteroid appears to favor the development of a peptic ulcer.

Properly administered by a knowledgeable physician, corticosteroids, when needed, can be valuable and their undesirable effects commonly avoided or overcome by careful adjustment of dosage, by dietary modifications, and by other medications.

During treatment, there should always be close attention to the appearance of any undesirable effects, such as weight gain, edema, signs of infection, psychiatric disturbances, back pain, abdominal pain, or gastrointestinal bleeding. When a patient is properly informed by a physician and impressed with the importance of early reporting of any such undesirable effects, they can usually be managed effectively without harm.

DIURETICS

These valuable prescription drugs are used in many conditions that share in common the retention, in the body, of excessive sodium and water. The drugs act to increase their excretion. They are often employed particularly in treating high blood pressure and congestive heart failure.

Many diuretics belong to a class of compounds known as thiazides, including chlorothiazide, benzthiazide, cyclothiazide, hydrochlorothiazide, and hydroflumethiazide. Others, similar acting, but not thiazides, include chlorthalidone and quinethazone.

Diuretics sometimes may lead to the excretion of too much sodium, and resulting weakness. In rare cases, they may precipitate an attack of gout. Or sometimes the gastrointestinal tract may be affected, leading to nausea and vomiting.

Undesirable reactions, if they occur, very often can be overcome by a change in dosage, by a switch to another diuretic, or by combining two or more diuretics.

The physician is likely to inform his patient—if not, he should be asked—about possible side effects and when these require immediate consultation to consider a change in treatment.

LAXATIVES

Laxatives and drugs that affect fecal consistency facilitate bowel evacuation.

Just as years ago there was a common practice of bleeding people to "purge" them of various illnesses, so even in the early part of this century in the United States a common weekly ritual was the Saturday night taking of a laxative for the expected "desirable" result on Sunday, a nonworking day, a "thorough cleansing."

Even today, while many people resort to laxatives for constipation problems that often could be cured very simply by a high fiber diet, there are others who use the drugs even when they have no constipation problem. They do so in the carryover belief that somehow a regular "purification" is good for headaches, skin condition, and even for "dusting cobwebs from the brain."

Laxatives may be valuable in avoiding excessive straining in people with hernias and for some other specific problems on occasion—such as for avoiding potentially dangerous rises in blood pressure during defecation in patients with high blood pressure or with heart or artery disease.

But regular use can lead to complete loss of the spontaneous bowel rhythm needed for normal evacuation—in effect, laxatives become habit-forming.

Most of the following laxatives are available without prescription.

Irritant stimulant laxatives. These are laxatives with a stimulating effect on peristalsis. Although they are dependable, a dosage good for one person may be too stimulating and irritating for another, having effects several times in a day or for several days.

Cascara sagrada is one of the milder ones. It usually produces a soft or formed stool in six to eight hours with little colic.

Phenolphthalein, an ingredient in many proprietary laxatives, stimulates the colon vigorously, producing a stool within eight to ten hours. Phenolphthalein can be a particularly dangerous drug if abused because it has prolonged effects and can also produce skin rashes, tendencies to hemorrhages, fainting, and labored breathing.

Castor oil gives off a highly irritating material, ricinoleic acid, which stimulates peristaltic activity in the small intestine. The intestinal contents are propelled so rapidly through the colon that normal absorption of fluid does not take place and a fluid stool is produced within a few hours. Physicians restrict its use to preparation for X-ray examinations and proctoscopy.

Bisacodyl induces defecation by stimulating the colon. It is most commonly used by physicians postoperatively and in obstetric patients; also in preparing patients for X-ray examinations and proctoscopy.

Bulk-forming agents. These are laxatives that absorb water from the intestinal contents, producing increased stool bulk. The bulk then stimulates peristaltic activity. Bulk-forming agents include psyllium methyl-cellulose and sodium carboxymethylcellulose preparations. They are mild, produce formed stools without colic, and must be taken with plenty of water. There have been rare reported cases of bowel obstruction and per-foration from their use.

Bulk-forming products are not really laxatives since they act to aid evacuation simply on the basis of the slippery bulk they provide when taken with water.

Saline cathartics. These agents—magnesium hydroxide or milk of magnesia, magnesium citrate, sodium phosphate, and potassium and sodi-um tartrate—cause diffusion of fluid from the intestinal lining. The result-ing large volume of fluid then stimulates peristalsis in the small intestine and liquid stools are produced within several hours. Sometimes saline ca-thartics are used in the treatment of certain drug and food poisonings, par-asitic infections, and in cleansing in preparation for X-ray studies and proc-toscopy.

Lubricant. Mineral oil, which is not absorbed by the colon, is a lubri-cant that when mixed with the intestinal contents softens them and pro-vides an oily coat that facilitates evacuation.

But one problem with mineral oil is its tendency to drip from the rec-tum, causing embarrassment. It may also produce anal irritation. Also, it should be used only for short periods since it cuts down absorption of some nutrients, particularly the fat-soluble vitamins.

Wetting agents. These are compounds—such as dioctyl sodium sul-fosuccinate and polaxalkol—that tend to soften the stool and facilitate elimination. Some stimulant laxative preparations contain dioctyl sodium sulfosuccinate. Wetting agents are generally well tolerated but do not act rapidly, and several days may elapse before their effect is apparent.

TRANQUILIZERS

Tranquilizers are compounds that calm or quiet. They differ from sed-atives, which include barbiturates and chloral hydrate. Sedatives act as depressants of the nervous system and diminish the response to certain stimuli. They often bring about a lessening of anxiety and may also cause the patient to become drowsy. Alcohol, for example, is well known for its effect in relieving emotional tension by a depressant action; it is essentially a sedative.

Tranquilizers seem to have a more direct effect in lessening anxiety. Although they may cause some drowsiness, the body still reacts to stimuli. A person who has taken a tranquilizer is easily aroused from his drowsiness while one who has taken a sedative is not.

Tranquilizers fall into two classes: major and minor, both requiring prescriptions.

The minor, used to suppress the less severe manifestations of anxiety and tension, include such compounds as meprobamate, chlordiazepoxide, diazepam, hydroxyzine, and buclizine. They are sometimes used for psychosomatic conditions, illnesses that may involve an emotional cause. Such illnesses are peptic ulcer, regional enteritis, and ulcerative colitis.

Adverse reactions sometimes occur with the minor tranquilizers. Drowsiness is the most common. Dizziness and headache occur occasionally. And in some people who happen to be particularly sensitive to the drugs, there may be chills, fever, rash, nausea, vomiting, dryness of the mouth, and gastrointestinal discomfort.

The major tranquilizers differ from the minor in that they may reduce psychotic symptoms in some patients. They include compounds known as phenothiazines. Like other valuable drugs, the major tranquilizers sometimes can produce adverse effects—including tremors, blurring of vision, circulatory disturbances, racing pulse, urinary hesitancy, dry mouth, and constipation. The compounds may also be habit-forming.

A selected bibliography

PART ONE

CHAPTER 1

Williams, R. J. *You Are Extraordinary*. New York: Random House, 1969.

"A Study of Health Practices and Opinions." National Analysts, Inc., 1972, National Technical Information Service, Springfield, Virginia 22151.

CHAPTER 2

Franklin, M. A., and Skoryna, S. C. "Studies on Natural Gastric Flora." *Canadian Medical Association Journal* 105:380.

Staas, W. E., and DeNault, P. M. "Bowel Control." *American Family Physician* 7(1):90.

"The Aging Gastrointestinal Tract." Editorial, *West Virginia Medical Journal* 71 (3):67.

Grollman. *The Human Body*. New York: Macmillan, 1969.

Miller, B. F., and Galton, Lawrence. *The Family Book of Preventive Medicine*. New York: Simon & Schuster, 1971.

CHAPTER 3

Dodd, G. D., Singleton, E. B., and Brogdon, B. G. "The Gut Reaction to

Civilization." Medical X-ray Forum No. 29, American College of Radiology.

Coats, G. et al. "Measurement of the Rate of Stomach Emptying." *Canadian Medical Association Journal* 108:180.

Nourse, A. *The Body*. Life Science Library, revised 1970 edition.

Eckstein, G. *The Body Has a Head*. New York: Harper & Row, 1970.

Clendening, L. *The Human Body*. New York: Alfred A. Knopf, 1973.

CHAPTER 4

Mayer, J., and Thomas, D. W. "Regulation of Food Intake and Obesity." *Science* 156:328.

Skalka, P. "Does Your Favorite Drink Actually Quench Your Thirst?" *Today's Health*, July 1974, p. 45.

"What Makes Your Mouth Water." Research Capsules, No. 30, 1975, National Institute of Dental Research.

Azimov, I. *The Human Body*. Boston: Houghton Mifflin, 1963.

CHAPTER 5

Pyke, M. *Food Science and Technology*. London: John Murray, 1964.

Chaney, M. S., and Ross, M. L. *Nutrition*. 8th Edition. Boston: Houghton Mifflin, 1971.

CHAPTER 6

Williams, R. J. *Nutrition Against Disease*. New York: Pitman, 1971.

Pyke, M. *Food Science and Technology*. London: John Murray, 1964.

Chaney, M. S., and Ross, M. L. *Nutrition*. 8th Edition. Boston: Houghton Mifflin, 1971.

"Proposed Fortification Policy for Cereal-Grain Products." Food and Nutrition Board, 1974, National Research Council, Washington, D.C. 20418.

Merck Manual. 12th Edition, Merck, Sharp & Dohme/Research Laboratories, 1972.

DiCyan, E., and Hessman. *Without Prescription*. New York: Simon & Schuster, 1972.

DiCyan, E. *Vitamins in Your Life*. New York: Simon & Schuster, 1974.

Ellis, J. M., and Presley, J. *Vitamin B6: The Doctor's Report*. New York: Harper & Row, 1973.

Galton, L. *The Disguised Disease: Anemia.* New York: Crown Publishers, 1975.

Schroeder, H. A. *The Trace Elements and Man.* New York: Devin-Adair, 1973.

CHAPTER 7

Galton, L. *The Truth About Fiber in Your Food.* New York: Crown Publishers, 1976.

Burkitt, D. P., Walker, A. R. P., Painter, N. S. "Dietary Fiber and Disease." *Journal of the American Medical Association* 229:1068.

Cleave, T. L. *The Saccharine Disease.* Bristol: Wright, 1974.

CHAPTER 8

Yudkin, J. *Pure White and Deadly.* London: Davis-Poynter, 1972.

"Diabetes and Sugar Mania: A Sour Story." *Science News* 108:167.

Froelicher, V. F., Jr. "Dietary Prevention of Atherosclerosis." *American Family Physician* 7(3):79.

Nichols, A. B., and Ostrander, L. D. "Diet and Heart Disease." American College of Physicians, annual (1975) meeting.

Altschule, M. D. "On the Much Maligned Egg." *Executive Health* X (1974):8.

————."How Much Do You 'Know' that Isn't So about Saturated versus Polyunsaturated Fats." *Executive Health* X (1974):10.

————."What Causes Your Arteries to Harden If Cholesterol Is Not Guilty?" *Executive Health* X (1974):9.

Oster, K. A. "Atherosclerosis and Homogenized Milk." *Medical Counterpoint,* November 1973.

Galton, L. *The Silent Disease: Hypertension.* New York: Crown Publishers, 1973.

"A Break for the Coffee Break." Editorial, *Journal of the American Medical Association* 231:965.

Johnson, R. D. et al. "Coffee: Treat or Trick?" *American Family Physician* 11(6):101.

"Caffeine Toxicity Mimics Neurosis." Medical News Section, *Journal of the American Medical Association* 229:1563.

CHAPTER 9

The New York Times, August 11, 1975, p. 18.

Consumer Reports, August 1975, p. 467.

Feingold, B. F. *Why Your Child Is Hyperactive*. New York: Random House, 1974.

Whelan, E. M., and Stare, F. J. *Panic in the Pantry: Food Facts and Fallacies*. New York: Atheneum, 1975.

Reding, G. R. "The Chemicals We Eat." Letter to the editor, *The New York Times*, August 11, 1975.

Jukes, T. H. "Mercury in Fish." *Journal of the American Medical Association* 233:1001.

_____."The Organic Food Myth." *Journal of the American Medical Association* 230:276.

Coons, J. M., and Ayres, J. C. *Safety of Foods in U.S. Nutrition Policies in the Seventies*. Edited by Jean Mayer. San Francisco, California: W. H. Freeman, 1973.

"The Health Food Industry." The Farm Index, U.S. Dept. of Agriculture, January 1975.

White, P. L. "Sickness from Food Handling." *Today's Health*, July-August 1975.

"Dealing with Food Poisoning." "In Consultation," *Medical World News*, August 25, 1975, p. 74.

"Watch Out for Food Poisoning." *Changing Times*, August 1975, p. 36.

CHAPTER 10

"Dietary Prudence." Editorial, *Journal of the American Medical Association* 229:691.

Eastwood, M. A., and Terry, S. I. "Diet and Gastroenterology." *British Journal of Hospital Medicine*, November 1974, p. 713.

White, P. L. "Ulcer Diets and Low Fiber Diets." *Today's Health*, July 1974, p. 8.

Buchman, E. et al. "Ulcers and Regular Diet." *Gastroenterology* 66:1016.

Galton, L. *The Truth About Fiber in Your Food*, New York: Crown Publishers, 1976.

CHAPTER 11

Mayer, J. "Calories Still Count." *Family Health*, October 1974, p. 56.

Solomon, N., and Lindauer, L. L. "The Groaning Board Groans On." *The New York Times*, Op/Ed page, August 28, 1975.

Chlouverakis, C. S. "Controversies in Medicine: Human Obesity." Editorial, *Obesity/Bariatric Medicine* 3:132.

_____. "Facts and Fancies in Weight Control." *Obesity/Bariatric Medicine* 5:208.

Morowitz, H. J. "Obesity: The Erg to Dyne." *Hospital Practice*, October 1974, p. 33.

Yudkin, J. "This Slimming Business." *Executive Health* XI (1975): No. 4.

Howard, L. "Obesity: A Feasible Approach." *American Family Physician* 12 (1975):153.

Galton, L. *The Truth About Fiber in Your Food.* New York: Crown Publishers, 1976.

CHAPTER 12

Stahlgren, L. H. "Interpreting Peristaltic Sounds in Gastrointestinal Obstruction." Monograph and Audio Cassette, 1974, Reed & Carnrick, Kenilworth, New Jersey.

Grosberg, S. J. "The Diagnostic Significance of Intestinal Gas." *Journal of American Geriatrics Society* 17:400.

"More on Flatulence." Editorial, *Modern Medicine*, July 1, 1968, p. 65.

Palmer, E. D. "To Air Is Human, to Comprehend, Divine." *American Family Physician* 8:236.

Lasser, R. B., Bond, J. H., and Levitt, M. D. "The Role of Intestinal Gas in Functional Abdominal Pain." *New England Journal of Medicine* 293:524.

Blackwell, A. K. and W. "Relieving Gas Pains." *American Journal of Nursing* 75:66.

"The Clinical Importance of Intestinal Gas: A Special Report to the Medical Profession." *Medical Tribune*, Section II, February 29, 1968.

PART TWO

Burkitt, D. P. "The Aetiology of Appendicitis." *British Journal of Surgery* 58:695.

_____. "Epidemiology of Cancer of the Colon and Rectum." *Cancer* 28:3

_____. "Varicose Veins, Deep Vein Thrombosis, and Haemorrhoids: Epidemiology and Suggested Aetiology." *British Medical Journal* 2 (1972):556.

————. "Diseases of the Alimentary Tract and Western Diets." Proceedings 11th Conference International Society. *Geographic Pathology* 39:177.

Cleave, T. L. "The Neglect of Natural Principles in Current Medical Practice." *Journal of the Royal Naval Medical Service* 42:55.

————. *Peptic Ulcer.* Bristol: Wright, 1966.

————. *The Saccharine Disease.* Bristol: Wright, 1974.

————. and Campbell, G. D. *Diabetes, Coronary Thrombosis, and the Saccharine Disease.* Bristol: Wright, 1966.

Painter, N. S. *Diverticular Disease of the Colon—A Disease of Western Civilization.* Chicago: Year Book Medical Publishers, June 1970.

————. "The High Fiber Diet in the Treatment of Diverticular Disease of the Colon." *Postgraduate Medical Journal* 1 (1972):137.

Walker, A. R. P. "Bowel Motility and Colonic Cancer." *British Medical Journal* 3 (1969):238.

————. "Bowel Transit Times in Bantu Populations." *British Medical Journal* 3 (1970):48.

————. Request editorial: "Dietary Fiber and the Pattern of Diseases." *Annals of Internal Medicine* 80:663.

Yudkin, J. *Pure White and Deadly.* London: Davis-Poynter, 1972.

Galton, L. *The Truth About Fiber in Your Food.* New York: Crown Publishers, 1976.

————. *The Disguised Disease: Anemia.* New York: Crown Publishers, 1975.

————. *A Patient's Guide to Surgery.* New York: Hearst/Avon, 1976.

Miller, B. F., and Galton, L. *The Family Book of Preventive Medicine.* New York: Simon & Schuster, 1971.

Merck Manual. 12th Edition, Merck, Sharp & Dohme/Research Laboratories, 1972.

Rubin, P. "Cancer of Gastrointestinal Tract." *Journal of the American Medical Association* 229:1183.

"Abdominal Crises in the Adult." "In Consultation," *Medical World News,* July 13, 1973, p. 21.

"Treating Acute Abdomen in Children." "In Consultation," *Medical World News,* July 20, 1973, p. 19.

PART THREE

Badley, B. W. D. "Some Aspects of Medical Management of Gastrointestinal Disease." *Canadian Medical Association Journal* 112:331.

Texter, E. C. et al. "Antacids." *American Family Physician* 11:111.

Derezin, M. "Laxatives and Fecal Modifiers." *American Family Physician*
10:126.

Merck Manual. 12th Edition, Merck, Sharp & Dohme/Research Laboratories, 1972.

Merck Index, Merck & Co.

Modell, W. *Drugs of Choice.* Saint Louis, Missouri: C. V. Mosby Co.,
1976-1977.

Physicians Desk Reference, Medical Economics Co., 1976.

Miller, B. F., and Galton, L. *The Family Book of Preventive Medicine.*
New York: Simon & Schuster, 1971.

Griffenhagen, G. B., and Hawkins, L. L. *Handbook of Non-Prescription
Drugs.* Chicago: American Pharmaceutical Association, 1973.

Index